William Epps

Land Systems of Australasia

William Epps

Land Systems of Australasia

ISBN/EAN: 9783744760829

Printed in Europe, USA, Canada, Australia, Japan

Cover: Foto ©ninafisch / pixelio.de

More available books at **www.hansebooks.com**

LAND SYSTEMS

OF

AUSTRALASIA

BY

WILLIAM EPPS

AUTHOR OF "THE PEOPLE AND THE LAND"

LONDON
SWAN SONNENSCHEIN AND CO.
NEW-YORK: CHARLES SCRIBNER'S SONS.
1894.

PREFACE.

The aim of these pages is to place before political thinkers an outline of the methods which govern the use and alienation of the public lands of the Australasian colonies. In these days of land tenure reform, land nationalisation, single tax, progressive land tax, and other theories for the amelioration of existing social conditions, any information tending to throw light on these and cognate subjects should be of value especially where it is in the direction of experience gained. The intention from the outset, has been rather to state facts than to express opinions, in the belief that a concise statement of the various systems, with a short disinterested analysis as far as it is possible of the results attained, would be of far greater value than a whole sheaf of individual ideas.

It is specially hoped by the writer that his work may be of some value to his fellow colonists. A journalistic experience in three of the provinces has shown that the people generally know very little of their own laws and less about those of their neighbours; which statement applies even to many of the most prominent politicians. This want of knowledge may be due in part perhaps to the absence of literature bearing on the question. Yet the subject of the disposal of the public lands is of the most vital importance to the people of a new country. It is in their power thoughtlessly to raise up barriers to the happiness and progress of millions who may follow them, and a study of the land legislation here outlined of one at least of the colonies will show that, even at this early period, the baneful affects of past unwise action are manifesting themselves in a marked degree. How much more then will this be apparent in another half century, when our children and our children's children will be reaping the harvest of the heedlessness of our fathers and ourselves?

It is a difficult task to compress into the small space comprised within these pages a comprehensive statement of the intricate land systems of seven distinct provinces. Much of interest and importance has consequently been unavoidably omitted. But it is hoped that all the main points with respect to present conditions have been put forward in a sufficiently clear manner. It has been the desire to bring the information wherever possible right up to date. The historica *résumés* of the changes which have been made in the systems of the various provinces are necessarily cursory. This part of the work has been unexpectedly laborious, as it has involved the examination of many old records, etc.; but it was deemed to be essential to a complete appreciation of existing methods that those of the past should be first described. In this connection the author freely acknowledges assistance gained from the works of historical and other writers, some of which have been quoted; and he desires also to express his thanks for the receipt of much valuable data from the heads of departments in the various colonies, and for help cheerfully rendered by both personal friends and strangers.

SYDNEY, N.S.W.,

CONTENTS.

Chapter
I. INTRODUCTION . . . . . Page 1.
Australia an ideal land for colonisation.—Lord Sydney failed to appreciate the occasion.—Convict element a great drawback to settlement.—The order of colonisation.—Two groups of colonies.—Geographical situation—Physical features—Climate.—Small rainfall—Quality of soil.—Lack of rivers.—Area.—Population.—Industries.—Systems of Government.—Transfer of property.—Some points worthy of adoption elsewhere.

II. NEW SOUTH WALES.—Early systems . . Page 8.
The first settlers.—Governor Phillip's "First Fleet".—Sydney and Norfolk Island.—Free immigrants encouraged.—First grants of land.—Assignment of convicts—expansion of settlement.—Introduction of wool-growing.—Captain Mac Arthur.—Native grasses, valuable herbage.—First leases.—Commons.—The settled districts—Limitation of boundaries.—First sales of land.—Land Boards.—First Land Act.—Rapid alienation.—Introduction of immigrants.—System of transportation ceased.—"Squatting" system.—The "Wakefield Theory"—Governor Bourke.—Crown Lands Act 1833.—Governor Gipps.—Crown Lands Act 1839—Endeavours to restrain the squatters—Trafficking in lands—Absentee Pastoralists.—Lord Stanley's Act.—Regulations of 1843.—Popular Opposition.—"The three Fs".—Pre-emptive rights.—The squatters successful.—Governor Fitzroy.—Earl Gray's Act.—The Orders in Council.—Objectionable practices.—No thought for posterity.

III. NEW SOUTH WALES.—Under Responsible Government . . . . Page 25.
The Gold discoveries—Influx of population.—Aggregation of holdings into large estates.—"Free selection".—Sir John Robertson's Acts.—The "squatters" and the

Chapter

"selectors".—Dummying.— Black-mailing.—Peacocking.
—Public immorality.—An amending Act.—Conditions not improved.—Public indignation.—A commission appointed.—Denounces free selection.—The Act of 1884.—A fresh patch on an old garment.—System of land settlement at present.—Conditional purchases and conditional leases. — Unsatisfactory results. — Congestion of population in towns.—Areas of holdings.—Large estates. —Small cultivation—Analysis of the causes.

IV. TASMANIA . . . . Page 51.
Its geographical position and natural advantages but minor status.—Life more English than on the mainland.—Early conditions similar to those of New South Wales.—Changes from 1848 to 1855.—Responsible Government. – Experimental legislation.—Free grants in return for the possession of capital.—Roads and bridges.—Mineral lands.—Further changes.—The Act of 1870 still practically in force.—Purchase on credit.—Classification.—Selection before survey—Compulsory improvements. — Settlement and cultivation not progressing proportionately with alienation.—More stringent fulfilment of conditions to be enforced.

V. VICTORIA . . . . Page 61.
Originally part of New South Wales. — Port Phillip District.— Early settlements abandoned.—John Henty first settler.—Batman's scheme for colonisation.—Purchases from Natives disallowed.—District formally declared open for settlement (1836).—First sales of land.—Proceeds to be partly devoted to immigration.—Lord Stanley's Act.—Gipps's regulations.—A popular outcry.—Separation from New South Wales.—The squatters and the Government. — Constitutional Government.—Land Bill of 1858 thrown out.—Land Act of 1860.—The "Duffy Act".—A scramble for the soil.—Agricultural leases.—Restrictive conditions.—Land Acts of 1869, 1878 and 1884.—Present condition of settlement.—"Grazing rights", and "agricultural allotments".—Victoria an agricultural Colony. — Cultivation.—Centralisation of population.—Land tax.—General results.

VI. QUEENSLAND . . . . Page 86.
The last colony founded.—Originally a convict settlement, and part of New South Wales.—Separation and responsible government.—Immediate land legislation.—Stringent

Chapter

conditions.—Afterwards modified. —Pastoral lands.— Changes in legislation.—The Act of 1868.—Alienation of large areas.—Homestead areas.—The present system —Liberal conditions.—Land grant railways—Essentially a pastoral country.—Grazing farms.— Small holdings on the increase.—Improved condition of both agricultural and pastoral industries.—The position of the colony.— Its prospects for the future.

VII. WESTERN AUSTRALIA . . . . . . Page 103.
Unique position of the Colony.—The largest territory and the smallest population.—Natural conditions unfavourable.—Early struggles.—Colonisation a failure.—The Western Australian Company.—Changes in the system.— Tillage leases.—Introduction of convicts the only remedy against destitution.—Classification.—Exploration licenses —Conditional sales.— Poison leases.—The "Kimberley District."—Tropical products.—Present conditions.—Agricultural areas.—Unconditional selections.— Mineral lands.—Land grant railways.—Improved position during ten years.—Cultivation on the increase.—Constitutional government. — Proposed changes. — Free grants to immigrants—Homestead leases.

VIII. SOUTH AUSTRALIA . . . . . Page 116.
Essentially identified with the land question.—Its great area.—Lack of natural advantages.—The Wakefield system—"Concentrated colonisation"—A sufficient price. —The first settlers.—Land boom.—The bubble bursts and colonisation really begins.— The Orders in Council evaded.—Early methods.—Representative Government. —Deferred payments.—Strangway'sAct.— Classification. —Effects of the credit system.—Frequent changes.— New principles.—Leases with the right to purchase and perpetual leases.— Optional tenure.—Conditional pastoral leases.— Working Men's Blocks.—State-aid to "Blockers".—The Northern Territory.—Decadence in cultivation.—Aggregation of large estates.—Areas of holdings.—The colony standing still.—The pastoral system full of anomalies.—A Pastoral Commission.—A Land Tax.—The Torrens Act.

IX. NEW ZEALAND . . . . . . Page 137.
The Britain of the South.—Its geographical features and natural advantages.—Early settlement.—The New Zealand Co.—Troubles with the Natives.—The Wairan

Massacre.—Made a separate colony.—The Canterbury and Otago Settlements.—The Wakefield system gets a fair trial.—The pioneers a superior class.—The New Zealand Co dissolved.—Representative Government.—The provincial system.—Land alienation methods become a hopeless tangle.—Changes in Legislation.—The Land Boards.—Classification. — Deferred payments. — Pastoral lands.—Provisions for roads and bridges.—The Act of 1885.—A new era in land legislation.—Perpetual leases and village settlements.—Amending Acts of 1887, 1888, and 1892.—Important changes. — The optional system.—Cash sales only after fulfilment of conditions.—Limits to the holding of land.—Occupation with right of purchase after 10 years residence.—Leases-in-perpetuity (999 years).—Special settlements Associations.—Small grazing runs.—Limitation to the number of pastoral leases to be held.—Land and Income tax.—Improved settlements with State aid.—State farms.—A graduated land tax and an increased land tax on absentees. — Resumption of land for settlement.—Drastic Legislation.—Results yet to be ascertained.

X. CONCLUSION . . . . . . Page 165.
The Suzerainty of the Crown assumed over all Australasia.—Steps taken to assert the King's Sovereignty.—Attempted French annexation.—Early methods.— Free grants with quit-rents, a form of free socage.—Occupation in return for determinate services.— The allodial period.—Leases-in-perpetuity, a return to the old free grant system.—Results of existing systems to date.—Stupendous alienation.—1250 holdings total 35 million acres.—105,000 others only 19 million acres.—Perpetual Leasing, or Leases-in-perpetuity suggested.—"Eternal" leases.—Congestion of population in towns, on the increase. —Primary producers decreasing in proportion to total Population.—Cultivation not keeping pace with alienation or increase of population.—The time has come for a change. — Will the people of Australasia rise to the occasion?

CHAPTER I.

INTRODUCTION.

To the political student or experimenter few finer fields of investigation are open than that afforded by an examination of the governing systems of the colonies comprising British Australasia. Some remarkable examples are there offered of the effect of adapting old rules to new conditions, and of the result of attempts to formulate new methods or practically apply theories which elsewhere are still in the hypothetical stage. It is a land of boundless possibilities, and one which under different auspices in its earlier years might occupy a much larger place in the world of to-day. For no more fitting place than this sea-girt great south land could have been reserved by an all-wise Providence for the realisation of ideals of purer thought and more wholesome methods, free from the demoralising influences of a past. It is as though Nature in the fulness of her heart had here raised from the ocean bed a new earth to which man might transplant himself, and live a new and truer life; or as though the Provider of All Things had said, to use the words of one long since gone—"I called this new world into existence to redress the balance of the old."

Never was such a golden opportunity offered for the carrying out of great regenerative schemes as that afforded by the opening up of this Terra Australis to the overcrowded nations of the North. Separated as it was from the chief haunts of civilised man by thousands of miles of sea and land; possessing within itself vast territory, a climate covering all the gradations from ever tropical heat to perpetual ice and snow, and a soil capable of producing all that man could need; yet having no powerful aboriginal races to be displanted; surely this was a land in regard to which no brighter ideal could have been devised than that of peopling it with men able to toss off the traditions of centuries of priest-ridden, superstitious misrule, and build up a new nation, which should in truth be that dreamt-of Utopia.

The opportunity for a glorious experiment was not wanting. It was pointed out to the Government of Great Britain that the least they could do for those loyal American citizens who had adhered to their side in the troubles across the Atlantic, during the latter part of the eighteenth century was to transplant them to some such a land, to which they could bear their Lares and Penates, and there form homes to replace those which they had lost in America. But Lord Sydney failed to appreciate the consequence of the occasion, and preferred to adopt a suggestion for the utilisation of these virgin shores as a means of escape from a difficulty which had been created by the increase of criminals in British gaols. So that Ausrtalia, instead of becoming the home of tried pioneers, who, by their fealty to a losing cause, had shown themselves to be possessed of the noble characteristics of loyalty and determination and other good qualities, was made a dung heap on which to cast the dregs and refuse, the human filth of the British nation.

In approaching the study of almost any public question in Australia, and particularly that of the people and the land, it is imperative to hark back to the early days of the Colonies' existence. In five, at least, of the seven provinces this is essential. It has to be borne in mind that the first colonists were not free—that the earliest efforts to promote settlement were hampered by the fact that the bulk of the people were transported felons. It was essential that they should be kept under severe restraint, and this necessity militated against the introduction of a proper class of pioneers, possessed of the necessary experience, mental and physical capacity, and financial means to lay the foundations of a new nation on a well-grounded basis. Even those free settlers who comprised the earliest colonists in the true sense of the term, were impeded by restrictions in consequence of this fact, and as a result the ultimate opening up of the vast interior of the continent was carried out under unnatural conditions, and in defiance of the law. Indeed, in those early days, it was difficult to secure men of good moral calibre as immigrants, and it was not until after the convict element had become very strong that a right class began to arrive. These facts must be specially borne in mind in considering the question of the settlement of the lands of the continental colonies and Tasmania, which (with the exception of South Australia) were all greatly affected by the transportee system.

To properly appreciate the circumstances of each colony it is necessary to glance briefly at the method and sequence of their early settlement. The first Europeans to make Australia their home landed in New South Wales in 1788, when the "first fleet" arrived under Governor Phillip. They were comprised entirely of transportees, and their military guards, and it was many years before the free population exceeded that of the convict, and those who had been released from servitude. In 1803 a branch penal settlement was formed in Van Diemens Land, and for 22 years that island, (the name of which was subsequently altered to "Tasmania"), remained under the jurisdiction of the Governor of New South Wales. In 1825, however, it became a separate colony, and from this date entered upon a new life. About the year 1803, also, an attempt was made to form a convict settlement at port Phillip, similar to that at Sydney, but, fortunately perhaps, it was a failure, and the country in this portion of the continent remained a *terra incognita* for a number of years. In 1835 a party of colonists from Tasmania took possession of the country in the vicinity of the site of the present city of Melbourne, and in the following year the settlement, which prospered, was formally incorporated as an outlying portion of New South Wales, being made a separate colony under the name of Victoria in 1851. A convict settlement was established near to the present city of Brisbane in 1825, and the introduction of a free population was prohibited until 1842. It was then opened to settlement, and in 1859 the district was formally separated from New South Wales, and incorporated as a new colony, under the name of Queensland. These four provinces, therefore, at one time comprised the original colony of New South Wales, and as their earlier systems of land settlement were one and the same, and were directed from one common centre, they have been grouped in that order for the purpose of our more effective consideration.

Western Australia was temporarily occupied in 1826, by a small gang of prisoners and a detachment of soldiery from Sydney, who were soon withdrawn, when the fears of French annexation subsided. Nothing was done in the way of the colonisation of this part of Australia until 1829, when about 1000 settlers from England, who had received grants of land from the Imperial Government, arrived at Freemantle, and the colony proper was established. This was the first attempt to form a colony without Government aid and apart from the convict element. The second resulted in the foundation of South Australia, which was first established in 1836 by settlers brought direct from England under the auspices of the South Australian Colonisation Company. The central point of the new colony, was the present city of Adelaide, its capital. The only other province of the group is New Zealand. Between the period of the first formation of New South Wales and the year 1840 many Europeans (principally whalers) visited, and some settled in the Northern island, and in 1835 a British resident was appointed by the Governor-General of New South Wales, under whose jurisdiction the island nominally remained. It was not formally taken over as a British possession, however, until 1840, when a Lieut-Governor was appointed, under the Governor-General; but in the following year it was freed from the control of the mother colony, and made a separate province. The circumstances surrounding the establishment of these three colonies were entirely different from those of the others, and they may therefore be regarded in the discussion of the subject as a separate group.

Passing from the early conditions of colonisation, which of course have had a marked effect upon the land legislation of the various provinces, it may be of interest to consider briefly some other aspects of the subject. The physical features of British Australasia, though differing widely from those of Europe in the main, possess some of their most diverse characteristics. The continental mainland, on which are situated New South Wales, Victoria, Queensland, South Australia, and Western Australia,—lying as it does between 10° 39′ and 39° 11¼′ south latitude, and the meridians of 113° 5′ and 153° 16′ east longitude—is partly within the tropic of Capricorn. Consequently its mean temperature is hotter than that of South Europe, and it has less varied climatic conditions. Certainly, on the high lands near to the eastern coast a cool bracing atmosphere is to be met with, but generally speaking, and especially in the interior, the characteristics of the climate are a perpetual dry heat, with comparatively small rainfall. These conditions are adverse to cultivation as it is known to northern nations, and as a result the great bulk of the lands of the continent are only adapted to sheep and cattle rearing and grazing. On the eastern and south eastern coastal districts, over a region extending inland perhaps 200 miles, agriculture may be safely and profitably carried on, and so fertile is the soil in parts that almost any article of food may be produced. In the colonies of Tasmania and New Zealand, a cooler temperature prevails with a more humid atmosphere, and these islands are more largely devoted to agriculture than the mainland. Consequent also upon the more regular rainfall, the average agricultural yields of crops are higher. In their climatic conditions they more nearly resemble the southern portions of Great Britain and France.

The configuration of Australia renders it difficult of comparison with any other country of similar dimensions. Indeed it may be said to possess characteristics peculiarly its own. Unlike any other of the great continents of the world, it has comparatively few mountain ranges, and consequently but few large rivers. Practically there is only one great mountain range, which follows the eastern, north-eastern, and south-eastern coastline, and develops inland into a vast plain, situated generally at a height of from 1000 to 2000 feet above sea-level. In the form of a large shallow basin, or saucer, dipping towards the south, this immense plateau occupies about two-thirds of the whole superficial area of Australia, the balance being the margin adjoining the coast. On its outer eastern edges are to be found chiefly the varied natural riches of the continent, both as to soil and mineral wealth, and here consequently the present population is most dense.

The nearer one approaches to the centre of the continent, the more sterile becomes the land, until it resolves itself into what is practically a huge desert, ill-watered waste, capable under present conditions of carrying but a small population. As might be supposed, the great majority in number of the rivers are to be found on the outer eastern margin, running towards the ocean from the main dividing range. These possess as a rule, however, but short courses, and are not generally adapted for purposes of navigation. The river systems of the interior are confined to two—that of the River Murray, which empties itself into the ocean near to the city of Adelaide, and the Lake Eyre system, consisting of a number of small rivers, which flow into the Lake, and are absorbed in its saline swamps. The Murray River, though small in volume compared with the great rivers of other continents, has an immense watershed: it has for its chief affluents the Darling, the Lachlan, the Murrumbidgee, and other minor streams, which together drain a stretch of country nearly 1000 miles in diameter.

The chief defect in the interior is thus the want of water, and the inland population is consequently small. Up to the present little has been effected in the way of water conservation or the utilisation of the supplies of the Murray system, which are allowed to run very largely to waste. But attention is now being directed to this subject and in the future more will probably be done by means of canalisation and irrigation to utilise for purposes of cultivation the vast arid wastes of the far west, which have been proved by experiment to require water only to make them render fabulous yields. Something has been done, already, by artesian wells, to tap the immense subterranean aqueous supplies known to exist, and as some splendid results have been achieved, this method will probably be more extensively adopted in the near future.

The area and population of the seven Colonies, are as follows—

Colony.	Area in square miles.	Population in 1891.
New South Wales. .	310,700	1,165,300
Victoria . . .	87,884	1,157,804
Queensland	668,497	410,345
South Australia . .	903,690	325,766
Western Australia. . . .	1,060,000	53,285
Tasmania	26,215	152,619
New Zealand . . .	104,471	634,058
Totals. . .	3,161,457	3,899,177

These figures show a density of population to the square mile of 1.21 as compared with 106.9 in Europe, the population of which is 380,200,000,—the area, being approximately 3,555,000 square miles.

The staple of Australia is undoubtedly its wool, the fruit of its pastoral industry. Next in point of value comes agricultural produce; then gold and silver; and for the purposes of comparison it may be of interest to state the estimated value for 1890 of the total products in these departments for all the colonies. They are officially stated as follows— †

Colony.	Pastoral.	Agricultural.	Gold.	Silver.
New South Wales .	11,973,050	4,131,422	460,285	2,762,554
Victoria	3,625,655	7,520,298	2,354,244	4,869
Queensland . . .	4,871,810	2,233,151	2,137,054	56,639
South Australia .	1,602,199	3,569,686	101,577	12,819
Western Australia.	292,540	366,936	86,664	—
Tasmania. . . .	568,242	962,751	87,114	26,487
New Zealand . .	5,928,517	4,829,456	773,438	6,162
Australasia . . .	28,862,013	23,613,700	6,000,376	2,869,530

† These figures are collated from Mr. T. A. Coghlan's "Seven Colonies of Australasia," 1892—Government printer Sydney, N.S.W.

These figures, taken together with those in the previous table, will be of interest, in considering the question of the land systems of the various colonies, as showing roughly the importance and general characteristics of each province. It will be seen that the chief industry of New South Wales is wool-growing, while in Victoria, South Australia, and New Zealand, agriculture and wool-growing are both very largely represented. The same in a modified degree applies to Queensland, where, however, more cattle are raised than in all the rest of Australasia.

Each of the colonies now enjoys local autonomy, and an analysis of the conditions of land settlement in each is significant as showing in what different ways different sets of people may approach the same question under similar auspices. It is not here necessary to refer to these conditions further than to say that in two respects at least the land systems of the Australasian colonies afford an example deserving of consideration by the powers that be in older countries—viz, with respect to the rights of succession and land transfer. The law of primogeniture has for many years been removed from the Australian codes. Each colony has its own statutes dealing with intestate real estates, and the general characteristics of the legislation are in the direction of a partition of real property between representatives of the deceased, in the same manner as in the case of personal property. Likewise there is no such bugbear as the question of entail, which to most colonists would now be a subject almost beyond comprehension.

In the matter of the transfer of real estate, what is known as the Torrens system is practically in force in each of the colonies. This is a method under which title by regisrration is substituted for title by deed, (just in the same manner as the transfer of shipping property may be effected) while giving at the same time absolute indefeasibility of title. Further reference will be made to this subject later on. It is sufficient at this stage to say that it is a method universally adopted in Australia, and one which has been an incalculable boon to the general public.

Sufficient has been put forward to show that the people of Australasia, despite adverse conditions in the past, have at times proved themselves capable of successfully solving difficulties, and, while casting aside old world notions, of striking out a path for themselves. That the various colonies have all succeeded in evolving satisfactory land systems is more than can be honestly stated, but a consideration of their different methods will show that there are at least some points in each worthy of adaptation or adoption elsewhere.

CHAPTER II.

NEW SOUTH WALES.—EARLY SYSTEMS.

LITTLE more than a century has passed since Australia received its first colonists. They were not, it is true, as a rule such pioneers as might now be selected for the purpose of founding a new nation. Convicts can scarcely be expected to possess those qualities which develop the highest type of citizen. But the first occupants of the soil of this great southern land did this much for their successors, they, proved its capacity to provide homes for a vast population in the years to come. In their train rapidly followed others, free men, with the necessary attributes to enable them to conquer difficulties to which men of less indomitable courage must have inevitably succumbed. Upon these we may and do proudly look back as our pioneer settlers. They, showed us how to wring such treasures from the thirsty earth as have justly won for Australia the name of the "Land of the Golden Fleece," and made it one of the brightest gems in the British Crown.

New South Wales claims the distinction of having seen the first act of colonisation in these seas. It was Sydney cove where Governor Phillip landed in 1788 with his sad freight of depraved humanity,—the first to people the vast continent which is now the home of millions—and there was set in motion by him the machinery which has wrought such a change in the appearance of the country. The land system in its conception was essentially simple, and compared with the intricate methods now in force, perhaps crude. But it was framed to meet simple conditions. New South Wales, at the period when its history begins, comprised merely the land now covered by the City of Sydney and its immediate neighborhood, and Norfolk Island. At each of these points were centred a considerable number of convicts, with their military guards, and these communities were dependent, during the earlier years of their existence, at any rate for a means of subsistence, upon intermittent supplies from England. When these supplies did not come to hand in time, which happened more than once, the isolated unfortunates had either to starve or obtain sustenance from the land about them. There were no indigenous foods, though the soil in certain localities was speedily found to be marvellously fertile.

Settlement upon the land thus became a pressing necessity to obviate periodic decimation of the people for want of food. Governor Phillip, with much sagacity, appreciated this fact from the outset, and in his earliest despatches to the Imperial Government, urged the introduction of free settlers, possessed of the necessary capital and experience to enable them to profitably cultivate the soil. By this means he hoped to make his little colony gradually independent of the mother country for its supplies. These immigrants, he proposed, should be supported by the authorities for the first year or two, and have the services of a number of convicts for a specified time, during which they should cultivate and clear a certain portion of the land. His representations were not at the outset seriously regarded, but in August, 1789, a dispatch from Whitehall authorised the Governor to make grants to non-commissioned officers and marines, and to grant to immigrants "lands to such amounts as you shall judge proper." In return the new settlers were to maintain and feed a certain number of convicts, and pay quit-rents on the lands after five years' occupation. These instructions were subsequently so enlarged as to enable the Governor to make grants to superior officers in the forces.

At the outset, while these negotiations were still in progress, Phillip gave grants of 30 or 40 acres to the prisoners as they became free. In 1791 there were no less than 34 of such grantees and one free settler, holding 1640 acres in the neighborhood of Parramatta; and there were 52 grantees at Norfolk Island, holding 2620 acres. Of the latter ten were marines or sailors, who received 60 acres each, the remainder being convicts. The first free settlers, five in number, arrived in January, 1793, just a century ago. They were each guaranteed two years' provisions, and had assigned to them convict labour free of expense, with one year's clothing and two years' rations for each convict. The married men were granted 80 acres of land, and the single men 60 acres. In May of the same year, the number of grantees had increased to 22, who held 452 acres. From these small beginnings the future Commonwealth of Australia sprang.

As previously mentioned, Phillip's aim was to make his colony selfsupporting, and as a means to this end, his policy was that any one might obtain free acres who would employ the convicts and provide them with food and clothing. Naturally these conditions soon tempted military officers and others to possess the soil, and the bounds of the settlement expanded rapidly as the pioneers went further afield in their search for arable and pasture lands. This colonisation was encouraged in every possible way, and before many years the need had arisen of a new outlet for the energies and increasing flocks and herds of the settlers. The country comprised in the then known districts, which were hemmed in by the Blue Mountains—a natural obstacle to further progress—became congested.

The discovery of the native grasses of the country, and the introduction of wool-growing on a large scale by Captain MacArthur—Australia's Abraham—together with the natural increase in the flocks, had thus early demonstrated the need of larger areas for pasturage, and in 1804 Governor King, who succeeded Phillip, found it necessary to issue the following proclamation, to enable the settlers to obtain the use of the land adjoining their grants:—

"Whereas it is necessary for the preservation and increase of the breeding stock, that portions of land should be reserved adjoining those districts where a number of settlements have been fixed in small allotments, bounded by others, and it being impracticable to locate larger allotments to all who possess or may hereafter possess stock, in order to secure to their use pasturage for rearing and maintaining cattle and sheep, His Excellency has deemed it advisable to allot by grants under His Majesty certain portions of grazing land hereunto stated. The *leases* will be made out in the names of those persons resident in each district who are named by the rest and approved by the Government."

This was the first introduction of the method of leasing the public lands of the Crown in Australia, which policy was later on to figure so largely in the land legislation of all the colonies. In effect, however, the new system was really an extension of the principle of setting aside commons for the general use of certain communities, which had prevailed for so many years in England. The Governor, writing on the matter, a year or two later, said— "To give all two or three hundred acres would soon alienate all the disposable land adjacent to the settlers, and to give particular people three or four hundred acres, in places of their own selection, would soon reduce the small farmer to sell his farm and stock, (because he cannot feed them,) to the person who can command money or its worth." And in a Gazette notice he intimated that these common lands "were to be held and used by the inhabitants of the respective districts, as common lands are held and used in that part of Great Britain called England."

But even these common lands could not for ever maintain the steadily increasing population and flocks of sheep, and the finding of a way across the Blue Mountains, to the vast areas believed to exist beyond, became a pressing necessity. This having been accomplished, the settlers rapidly spread over the new country, and gradually the boundaries of the settled district were increased so as to comprise a tract about 200 miles square. These "Old Settled Districts," as they were afterwards called, were defined by a surveyed line known as "The Limit of Settlement," beyond which the colonists might not pass. Outside of this boundary no land was allotted, and no pursuits were permitted; in fact, in consequence of the condition of colonial society for some years after first settlement, a necessary check was kept upon the habits and movements of the people. It was indeed a misdemeanour to pass the limit, which was guarded by a cordon of police. But the settlers nevertheless cast longing eyes at the far beyond. They could see fortune in the immense grassy plains of the interior, and they hungered for them.

Meanwhile the landholders, who at this period were agriculturists and pastoralists combined, were subject to many inconveniences, especially from the shifting quit-rents. "These were raised to 3*s* for every 20 acres, and then fixed at five per cent upon the supposed value of the land. Each grantee, also, was obliged to keep and clothe one prisoner-servant for every 100 acres; this was to relieve the Treasury, and the order was not cancelled until March 15th, 1826. Worst of all, the order of December 24th, 1824, required the holder of 100 acres to maintain five convicts, and he who held a grant for 2000 acres, though pasturage, had to keep 30 convicts and cultivate 120 acres. Then the grass lease was only secure for six months, and the run was limited to two miles any way from his stockyard." *

Gradually, in consequence, the necessity for granting an absolute freehold of the land had been urged upon the Government by the settlers, and in 1824 Governor Brisbane agreed to sell at 5*s* an acre; but to retain the hold of the State upon the land, he still subjected the purchasers to the payment of a quit-rent of 2*s* per 100 acres. The demand for land on these terms was nevertheless so great, that the affrighted Governor withdrew the concession after six months. Then, in 1829, a Land Board was appointed, with power to inspect areas and submit them to tender by the public. But owing to the unpopularity of the tendering pro-

---

* Bonwick's "Romance of the Wool Trade," 1887, p. 106. London, Griffith, Farren, Okeden and Welsh.

visions, the scheme had to be abandoned; and in 1828 the land approved by the Board was put up to auction for persons who had previously obtained the permission of the Governor to bid. In 1829, this privilege was also withdrawn. About this time, indeed, the system was constantly undergoing change, and the settlers were necessarily much harassed.

The system of grants, dedications, and orders, which had now been in force since the inauguration of the colony for a period of about 40 years, had resulted in very large areas of land being alienated. Up to August, 1831, no less than 3,422,538 acres had been disposed of in the choicest parts of the colony then known. In this month, the first Land Act was passed. This measure permitted sales by auction at an upset price of 5s per acre, subject to a peppercorn quit-rent, and all mines of coal and precious metals were reserved. The Act also provided that "any purchaser who within ten years of his purchase shall, by the employment and maintenance of convicts, have relieved the public from a charge equal to ten times the amount of purchase, will have the purchase money returned, but without interest. It is computed that for each convict employed and wholly maintained by the purchaser for 12 months, £12 will have been saved by the public." By the accompanying regulations, the upset price of the land fixed for the towns ranged from £2 an acre in the small outlying centres to £20 in such towns as Liverpool and Parramatta, while at Double Bay, now a fashionable suburb of Sydney, it was fixed at £40, and in Sydney itself at £1000 an acre.

These regulations effected an even more rapid expropriation of the public estate than had been previously going on. The first year under the new conditions saw the sale of 20,861 acres; in the following year, 29,001 acres were parted with; and during the years ending August 31st, 1834 and 1835, the areas disposed of jumped to 91,339 and 271,945 acres respectively, while the next six months alone witnessed the sale of 170,014 acres. The total receipts by the State from sales during these 4½ years amounted to £202,638; and this rapid accession to the public revenue largely helped to more than double it in the same period.

A considerable proportion of the revenue from land was devoted to bringing to the colony immigrants, principally females. There was thus contemporaneously with the increased sales of land a marked increase in the population, which on the 5th July, 1836, numbered 77,000 persons. Of these about 27,000 were convicts, and 50,000 free settlers and their children. By this time public sentiment in New South Wales had become strongly averse to the continuance of the importation of convicts. Indeed the assignment to free settlers ceased soon afterwards, (1838), and the whole transportation system was brought to an end in 1840.

An interesting report, bearing upon the method of appropriating the land revenue to immigration, was presented by the Legislative Council of the colony in 1835, from which the following may be quoted. — "Your Committee ..... trust it will not be deemed irrelevant to state their opinion of the justice as well as the policy of applying the proceeds of the Crown Lands exclusively to the introduction of a moral and industrious class of inhabitants. The first emigrants were induced to embark their fortunes in this distant colony under the promise of receiving free grants of land, and in the confidence that the same policy would be continued as the best means of settling the country. If it has since been deemed expedient to sell the lands in lieu of granting as before, it is considered by the inhabitants merely as the conversion of capital into another form, and that the proceeds of the sale of land should still be applied to the same purposes as the land itself..... That the colonists have derived many advantages from the transportation of convicts cannot be denied; but the system has brought with it a long train of moral evils which can only be counteracted by an extensive introduction of free and virtuous inhabitants, and the only means upon which the inhabitants can safely rely for accomplishing this vital object, is the revenue arising from the sale of land. It is for these reasons that your Committee are anxious to record their opinion, as well as that of the whole community of the colony, that the funds arising from the sale of lands should be appropriated exclusively to the purpose of introducing a moral and industrious population; and that they consider this appropriation alike indispensable to the present interests and the future prosperity and character of the colony."

It is needless to say that the principle advocated by the Committee has long since passed out of sight, and that the revenue from land is now expended upon purposes which can frequently be said to effect no improvement in settlement, or in any way benefit the occupiers of the land.

The year 1831, which permanently introduced the system, previously described, of sales by auction for cash, was, however, equally memorable as inaugurating what may be termed the first "squatting" period in the history of the colony. Hitherto grazing had been carried on upon lands leased, purchased, or occupied under authority of the Government. But now a change took place. The settlers, unwilling longer to submit to the restraints imposed by the

Government, took matters into their own hands, and boldly launched out on the vast territory beyond the "limits of settlement," in defiance of all constituted authority, and without being given any right or title even to utilise the grass upon the soil which they occupied. In fact they took possession of the new land, and "squatted" on it.

Mr George Ranken, one of the best authorities on the land question in New South Wales, thus describes this remarkable movement.* "A state of things arose which was unprecedented, unrecognised by authority, and was totally unintelligible according to all official and business authority. Some hundreds of young fellows founded a Bedouin commonwealth in the inland grass country. There was no scheme or intent to do anything of the kind. It arose instinctively and spontaneously, and there was never a grander instance of the working of the Viking's spirit. Neither 'Westward Ho!' nor the story of eastern adventure can show anything more characteristic." And there can be no doubt that, however illegal or immoral this exodus may have been, it hastened the day of Australia's supremacy as a wool-growing country.

It may be well here, to trace the causes and extent of this movement, which really introduced a new era in the system of land settlement. With the commencement of sales by auction, the old and simple method of free grants, with the payment of quit-rents, had ceased. Then followed, almost contemporaneously with the new method, an attempt to give practical effect to what has since been known throughout Australia as the Wakefield system. A school of economists, of whom Mr Gibbon Wakefield was the head and front, had become prominent in London through their advocacy of a scheme for selling the public lands of Australia in small contiguous areas, at a high fixed price,—termed by Mr Wakefield the "sufficient price,"—and so bringing about a comparatively closely populated community, with all the conditions which prevailed in the Mother Land. The money to be derived from these sales was to be devoted to bringing out from Great Britain agricultural laborers who should be able to obtain small areas of land and engage in working the farms of the larger proprietors, as at home. Thus there would be gradually reproduced in the new land the old class distinctions and class interests, with their accompanying benefits—and evils—from which in reality many of the colonists had already fled.

This new party possessed sufficient influence with the Imperial Government to induce Ministers to attempt to give

* "Our Wasted Heritage," 1893, Chapter VII.

effect to their scheme. The colonial executive officers were directed to cut up portions of the available land within the old settled districts in small conterminous parallelograms, to be sold for cash. The upset price, which was originally 5*s* per acre, was raised to 12*s* in 1839. This as might be expected, acted as a deterrent upon the wholesale and speculative alienation which had previously prevailed. It did not have entirely the desired effect, however, and the upset price was again raised to 20*s* per acre in 1843. This has since become the standard upset price for land in all the colonies, and the main portions of the large areas alienated throughout Australia have been parted with at that figure.

At the very time of the introduction of the new policy, the pastoralists were longing for the use of the grassy lands known to exist in the far back country. But, instead of gaining their wishes, they were confronted with this counter movement for decreasing the available land, which was to be obtained only at an increased cost. They asked for bread and got a stone. It was inevitable that there must be some collision. As Mr Ranken remarks—"This proceeding acted like the silent closing of a flood-gate.The population was expanding, and the sheep and cattle were increasing still faster..... Impelled by a common impulse, the pioneers headed for the boundary..... Shortly they were pouring across the frontier in scores, north, south, and west..... In the course of a couple of years, hundreds of adventurous young pioneers had crossed the boundary. The Governor could not have prevented this, because all the police and military in Australia could not have guarded an open frontier 500 miles in length..... The trespassers had now found a name for themselves; they had developed a strong *esprit de corps*, and their confidence and courage were unbounded. The inland frontiers of the United States were then infested by outlaws and vagrants who called themselves "squatters," * and this name was also adopted by the Australian adventurers who had flut-

---

* The term "squatter," now a household word as applied to pastoralists generally, but really a misnomer at the present day, conveyed at the outset rather a stigma. Many of the men who joined in the migration across the borders, were ex-convicts, who perpetrated "cattle-duffing," (i. e., stealing and altering brands, etc.) and even more felonious acts on a large scale. The first official use of the word appears in a report from a select Committee of the Legislative Council on police matters, issued in 1835:—"The nefarious practices of these men are greatly facilitated by the system of taking unauthorised occupation of Crown Lands, or *squatting* which now prevails. It appears that many convicts who become free by servitude, or who hold the indulgence of ticket-of-leave take possession of Crown Lands, in remote districts, and thus screened from general observation, erect huts for their temporary purposes, and become what is generally termed "squatters."

tered the dovecotes of the Colonial Office about the year 1835."

Sir Richard Bourke held the reins of Government at the commencement of this migration, but he had sufficient sagacity to see that his instructions from the Colonial Office were impossible in view of the circumstances. Consequently he remained practically quiescent until the matter was in other ways brought under the notice of the Home authorities. Then, in 1835, he received a despatch from Lord Glenelg, the Colonial Minister of the day, requiring an explanation of these proceedings, which were so much at variance with the policy laid down. In his reply, Bourke pointed out that the effect of the Wakefield system had been to force the settlers out into the back country; and he explained:—"It is only by a free range over the wide expanse of native herbage which the colony affords that the production of this article (wool) can be upheld. The colonist must otherwise restrain the increase (in the flocks) or endeavour to raise artificial food."

Recognising very early, however, that a new tenure was in effect being created by the squatting system, Bourke had already in 1833 passed trough the Legislative Council an Act to "prevent the unauthorised occupation thereof (Crown Lands) being considered as giving a legal title thereto." This Act appointed Commissioners of Crown Lands to warn off trespassers from the outlying country. But their efforts were hopeless. The squatters steadily continued to cross the boundary, and in 1837 a new Act was carried, admitting their right to graze, after payment of a license fee. This measure also provided for a border police, to be paid out of the fees which were to be imposed upon the squatters.

Sir George Gipps, who succeeded Bourke, made a strong effort to carry out the instructions of the Colonial Minister; but his attempt was quite unavailing, and so continuous was the stream of settlers across the borders that in 1839 the new territory is reported to have held 4380 persons (mostly males), 3300 horses, 233,000 head of cattle, and nearly a million sheep. This was almost as much stock as could be found in the whole of the Old Settled Districts, and we are told that in the country fed over,— ranging from the Darling Downs in the north to Port Phillip in the south, there were 1200 miles of defined roads, over which wool was brought from the stations to Sydney. By the Act of March, 1839, which was carried at the instigation of the Governor, every step was taken to restrain the new movement within bounds, and returns of stock were made compulsory, while an annual assessment (payable half-yearly) of one penny per sheep, threepence per head of cattle, and sixpence for each horse depastured on Crown Lands, was charged. In May of the same year, the annual license to graze was fixed at £10; at which figure it remained for some time.

This squatting movement forms one of the most interesting incidents in the history of Australian colonisation. It certainly developed to a marked degree the faculties of courage, self-reliance, energy, and perseverance, which distinguished the earlier pioneers, and in a few years brought the country prominently to the front as a wool-growing community. Men and money were speedily attracted to the new venturous, but profitable enterprise and, as we have seen, the population outside the line of settlement increased rapidly. Although in the first instance prohibited from taking up the new land, the squatters, as Gipps found by personal inspection, established a community or commonwealth of their own outside the pale of Government interference. They made homes for themselves in a rough and ready way, and conducted all the business of life without any departmental control or even cognisance.

The increase of population caused by immigration together with various other influences exerted about this period, induced an unexpected trafficking in land, and in a few years the whole conditions of the colony were changed. The auction sales for cash enabled speculators to purchase land cheaply for purposes of re-sale at a profit, and the squatters' licenses, which could be obtained by any approved person, also soon became the object of attention for speculative or even more objectionable purposes. Trafficking in every direction became rampant, and all classes of persons, whether possessed of land or not, entered into the unhealthy competition with avidity. Then, for the first time, absentee pastoralists, with persons to manage their runs, came into existence. Prices rose, and there was a rapid and unwarranted inflation in values, which resulted in subsequent inevitable collapse, producing a terrible state of depression throughout the colony. An examination into the causes of this state of affairs, which was held before a Committee of the Legislative Council in 1844, showed that in the opinion of most of the competent witnesses the system of land settlement was at the bottom of the trouble, and that the new Wakefield scheme had not resulted in legitimate cultivation in proportion to the areas of land alienated.

The remedy was proposed in a Crown Lands Sales Act, introduced and passed through the Imperial Parliament in 1842 by Lord Stanley. This measure was made to apply to all the colonies them existing. Under its provision there were to be no more gratuitous grants, and land was to be sold by auction, the minimum upset price being one pound per acre. Subject to a primary charge for survey (unless provision should otherwise be made in any colony), half the proceeds from these sales were to go to defray the cost of immigration of persons to the colonies in which the revenue accrued. The Governor was empowered to raise the upset price, and the price when so raised could only be reduced by the Queen. The principle of opening up lands prior to sale, by means of roads and bridges, was now also introduced, as in transmitting this Act to Governor Gipps, Lord Stanley desired him to retain money with which to make bridges and main roads to lands contemplated for sale. It would appear, however, that so far as New South Wales was concerned, the Act only became operative to a limited extent; at any rate sales as provided were not largely effected.

Meanwhile Gipps within the colony was preparing a 'rod in pickle' for the backs of the outlying squatters. He had, according to instruction, endeavored to restrain them as far as possible, and in 1843 he directed the Commissioners of Crown Lands to "consider maturely and report as to assimilating licenses to leases, the quantity of land which would suffice for 500 head of cattle or 5000 sheep, and the limitation of runs for each of which a separate license was to be taken, the encouragement of cultivation by giving an occupier a kind of right to purchase a portion of his run or otherwise to obtain secure possession for a term of years after occupation as tenant at will for a fixed term,—say for five or seven years—and the prevention of irregular transfers or sales which were occurring frequently at the time without the sanction or even the knowledge of the Government." Upon these reports, Gipps, without placing the matter before the Legislative Council, issued regulations requiring the tenants, *inter alia*, to purchase half a square mile of their land, 320 acres, at £1 per acre.

The principle thus enunciated, of the Governor imposing regulations upon the squatters without the concurrence or even consideration of the Legislative Council, raised a perfect storm of opposition, not only from the squatters themselves but also from the citizens resident in the towns, who resisted this attempt of the Governor to over-ride what was considered to be the popular will. Throughout the whole of the colonies the matter was taken up most warmly, and an organisation calling itself the Pastoral Association, which received support from merchants and other influential men in England and all classes in the colony, was formed to combat the Governor. Amongst those who took an active part in protesting against the regulations was the afterwards famous Robert Lowe, and so effective was the agitation that the Governor intimated to the Legislative Council, through a member of that body, that he proposed to make the concession that persons purchasing homesteads in accordance with his regulations should retain undisturbed possession of their runs for eight years. A second purchase of a similar area was to extend the period of occupation, "so that each successive purchase of 320 acres will act virtually as a renewal of an eight years' lease. The right of the Crown is to remain absolute, it being well understood that the Crown will not act capriciously or unequally, and will not depart from established practice, except for the attainment of some public benefit."

The public feeling was calmed somewhat by this explanation, but not satisfied; and the squatters kept the agitation aflame. Indeed, the matter affected them seriously. As the licensees of the land, they had come to look upon themselves as possessing a prior right to their runs over other persons, and they fought determinedly for the "three Fs" as they were termed—Fixed tenure, Fixed rents, and Free sales of rights. A protest was drawn up against the action of the Governor, and was forwarded through him to the Secretary of State. It denounced the upset price as being unreasonable, and complained of the absence of a pre-emptive right as unjust and ruinous to the squatter (who had to compete at auction for his land), the absence of fixity of tenure, and other matters. Gipps, in commenting on the protest, pointed out that under the existing methods the squatters did not even pay a quit-rent for their lands, and that "if, therefore, the present system of squatting remains unaltered, it is evident that the Government will have gained nothing by the abolition of free grants, which, if applied to the areas then in occupation, would have brought to the Treasury a large revenue in quit-rents."

Lord Stanley stoutly upheld Gipps's views on this matter, and stated that it was his intention to resist the action of the squatters to the utmost. At the same time he recommended that fixity of tenure be conceded by giving eight years' leases of the runs. But this proposition met with little favour, and popular excitement continued. When the Legislative Council met in 1844, a Committee, which was at once appointed, unanimously recommended that the upset price of £1 had been injurious, that the regulations should be recalled, that the license fee should be abolished or reduced to a nominal sum, that quit-rents due for more than six years should be waived and others reduced, that the Land

Sales Act should be repealed, and that in future the Governor and Legislative Council should control the land legislation.

For a time this was the all-absorbing topic in New South Wales, and the fight between the Governor, (who stood firm to his policy) and the public and squatters, with whom were allied the Legislative Council, continued to be bitterly waged. As one act of retaliation, Gipps called for returns, showing how the land was held on squatting tenure, which indicated that the four largest holders occupied no less than 7,750,640 acres. The effect, as intended, was to draw attention to the difference between the amounts of the license fees paid for these immense areas, and the quit-rents and license fees of the Crown grantees.

It will thus be seen that in effect Gipps's policy was to retain the absolute possession of the lands for the Crown, except such portions as formed the homesteads of the squatters, which they should purchase. In return he would have granted them the privilege of grazing over the surrounding country until it was required for sale in the ordinary way. This policy is now conceded by most historians and writers on the subject to have been at least a reasonable one, and one which under other conditions might have been accepted by the people generally. But Gipps had, in a high-handed manner, issued his regulations without even consulting the then only deliberative body, the Legislative Council, which was at this period beginning to agitate for responsible Government. His opponents, who were many and powerful, both in the Legislative Council and the country generally, therefore made his action from a constitutional point of view a strong object of attack. The squatters, who had by this time become very influential, made this public feeling a cover for agitating for the concessions they desired, but particularly for the right of pre-emption and fixed tenure. In effect they claimed that, having first opened up and settled on the new lands, they had a prior claim over any other person to lease or purchase them, and that, until they were required to purchase, for which there was then no immediate need, they should have long leases at a fixed rental of the lands they occupied.

The jurisdiction of the Governor of New South Wales still extended over the Port Phillip district (now Victoria), and the immense territories of what has since become the colony of Queensland, and the new country in the occupation of the squatters comprised some of the finest land in the whole continent. The demands of the squatters, if conceded, practically meant that they should be allowed to take present possession of this vast area, to the exclusion of any other settlers, with the first claim to purchase it if they desired. Gipps discerned this underlying fact, which appears to have escaped the attention of the general public in the hurley-burley of the struggle over his alleged unconstitutional action with respect to the regulations. Unfortunately, by his action he had placed himself in such a position that the influence upon the public mind was small, but being a man of strong moral fibre, he would not recede from the stand he had taken. The only point he was finally willing to concede was that the squatters, instead of being compelled to purchase their homesteads, should be allowed to lease them without competition. The remainder of the runs, he maintained, should be leased by auction, but "for the present at least no run should be disposed of by lease at auction, except on the application of the occupier."

But, though Gipps successfully opposed the proposals of the squatters, during his term of office, they eventually gained their end, and what is now acknowledged to have been a grievous wrong was inflicted upon the future colonists. Lord Stanley retired from the Colonial Office, and was succeeded by Earl Grey, upon whom sufficient influence was brought to bear from different quarters to induce him to grant the demands of the pastoralists. Unwittingly, in all probability, but "whether compelled to obtain ideas from others, or prone to seek them in wrong places, Earl Grey succeeded in putting the Government into a position from which it could not extricate itself without damage to its own honour or to some large interests which relied upon its good faith,—in conferring boons which he had been warned were unjust—in encouraging an unjust withdrawal of them, and in creating class hatreds which were to poison men's minds for long years to come."*

Governor Gipps was succeeded by Sir Charles Fitzroy, but before the return of the former to England, Earl Grey had (1846) passed through the Imperial Parliament a new Crown Lands Sales Act. This measure did not abrogate the provisions of Lord Stanley's Bill, but it made it lawful to regulate the pre-emption of the runs held under either lease or license, by granting leases for terms not exceeding 14 years, under regulations to be afterwards drafted.

Fitzroy, to whom fell the administration of the new Act, though more diplomatic, was more pliable than his predecessor. One of his first acts was to promulgate an order in

* Rusden's "History of Australia," 1883, pp. 341—2. London, Chapman and Hall, Ltd.

reference to quit-rents, (which had become at this period a subject of discontent with many), allowing persons in arrear, to commute their indebtedness on favourable terms; freeing from rent all lands on which 20 years' payments had been made; refunding all payments in excess of 20 years' rents, which had already been made. Thus for the future all lands were either to be held under lease or upon an absolute freehold tenure.

Orders-in-Council, giving effect to Earl Grey's Act were received in the colony in 1847. These now famous regulations provided that all lands were to be classed as settled, intermediate, or unsettled, and the provisions of the Act were made to apply to the two latter. The settled districts were to comprise the old settled districts situated around Sydney, and lands within an area of ten miles surrounding Bathurst, Brisbane (now the capital of Queensland), and a few small towns on the Clarence and Richmond Rivers. In the Port Phillip district (Victoria) the settled districts comprised the land within 25 miles of Melbourne, fifteen of Geelong, and ten of Portland, Alberton, Belfast, and Warrnambool. The intermediate districts in Port Phillip covered a comparatively small area, and the great bulk of the colony, including some of its richest country, was as will be shown, thus brought within the possession of the squatters or their prototypes.

The lands in the intermediate districts were to be leased in areas of 16,000 acres, (five miles square) for periods of fourteen years, and the lease of each block of 16,000 acres carried with it the right to purchase 640 acres at a fixed price of £1 per acre. The conditions as to the unsettled division were similar, except that the areas leased were twice the size of the leaseholds in the intermediate districts, and the leases carried with them a right of renewal for a further period of five years. One most important principle of the Orders was expressed thus—"During the continuance of any lease of lands occupied as a run, the same shall not be open to purchase by any other person or persons except the lessee thereof." *

The leases for these lands were to be tendered for, but the tenderers were neither required to be the original squatters only nor stock-owners. Any person, provided he knew the country, might although he had not a hoof of stock to put on it, thus tender for any land already occupied by another man, under license. There was no provision, either, limiting the number of tenders which might be put

---

* Cap. 2, sec 6.

in. "A scramble followed the initiation of the tendering system, in which most of the prizes fell to business men and officials. Commissioners were appointed to examine the country applied for and report upon the tenders. These functionaries varied much in their morals and methods. Some filled their positions honorably—but such were by no means in the majority. Some commissioners sold runs like stock and station agents, while others became partners in squatting firms. A laxity as to public duty was prevalent, and a secresy and mystery in official dealings were maintained that provided a screen for every kind of fraud. A very common trick practised by functionaries was to make a copy of a tender received, ante-date it, insert the name of an accomplice or friend, recommend it to the Minister for official acceptance, and then intimate to the true claimant that the country applied for had been already allotted under a prior application. Some real squatters, with stocked country, had tenders put in over their heads, and lost their runs; but most of them, by taking time by the forelock, and pressing their claims personally, saved themselves. However, the portions of grazing land which they secured, were mere scraps compared with the enormous principalities acquired by Government officials, commission agents, wine merchants, and jobbers. Tenders were also cooked up from explorers' journals. An accepted tender became at once marketable: it supplied the means to satisfy a pressing demand, or to smooth one's way through the asperities of the public departments." *

Thus were established evils which have since left their impress upon our life as a nation. Huge areas of land were secured by men at an absurdly low rental, with the right to purchase practically as they might please. As was only to be expected, the latter provision was well taken advantage of. Choice blocks with river frontages, and positions, the possession of which would prevent other persons in the future from using the surrounding land, were speedily alienated. And thus was placed in the hands of a comparatively few men a power fraught with incalculable danger to the generations then unborn. Amongst the evils brought to birth at this time, and which have since grown to the full development of maturity, was an absentee landlordism; the locking up of land in the hands of a few which might have carried a population a hundredfold larger than its existing occupiers, and which would have doubled its productive power; an unnecessary antagonism between agriculturists and pas-

* Ranken's "Our Wasted Heritage," chapter VIII.

toralists; and grossest of all, a highly immoral tendency, which has since had a most pernicious effect both on the private and public life of the people.

A former Surveyor-General (Sir Thomas Mitchell) had years before put forward a suggestion for a system which would have remedied the evils then only prospective. But he spoke to men who cared not for the future, and who—like the legislator, when asked to think of posterity—would probably have replied "Posterity! What has posterity done for me?" He had in 1843 recommended a maximum water frontage free grant of 2560 acres, carrying with it a proportion of back country as pasturage, which, when properly watered by the tenant might have been purchased by him at a low price. His main idea was to promote colonisation and settlement, as compared with which he considered the price per acre a matter of little moment. It is indeed to be regretted that the advice of a man with such ability and lifelong experience was not adopted. The position of New South Wales, Victoria and Queensland would have been different this day.

CHAPTER III.

NEW SOUTH WALES.—UNDER RESPONSIBLE GOVERNMENT.

THE land legislation of New South Wales entered upon a new era with the institution of the Orders-in-Council of 1847. A few years later (1855) responsible government was conceded to the colony, and under the new *régime* many changes were effected in the land system. Shortly after the main portions of New South Wales, Victoria, and Queensland had, as previously shown, been practically handed over to the squatters and speculators, Australia was convulsed by the discovery of gold in New South Wales and Victoria, and a marvellous influx of population followed. Both colonies soon contained hundreds of thousands of people. As might have been expected, the supplies of gold gradually decreased after the first few years, and the diggers, who comprised men from all walks of life, began to look round for new avenues of employment and investment. Naturally they first turned at once to the land, and as the pastoral industry had about this time begun to show signs of proving a very lucrative one, many invested their mining gains in new squatting ventures. Money was plentiful, speculation became rife, and runs—or to speak more correctly, sheep and cattle, with the right to graze over certain areas of Crown Lands—changed hands frequently, at rapidly increasing prices. Many men thus made immense fortunes, in too many cases, however, to be followed by their departure from the colonies with their easily-earned gains.

During this period numerous banks and mortgage institutions sprang into existence, and in most of the colonies acquired a hold on the land by advancing money for the purpose of enabling the squatters to extend their operations. Under this influence, as time went on, holdings were merged one into another, with the result that, immense areas came to be under the control of absentee proprietors, and with the exception of a manager and a few boundary riders or shed hands, the country was occupied by an extremely small population. Consequently, instead of the country being cut up into moderate-sized runs, capable of carrying a few thousand sheep each, and finding profitable employment for leaseholders and their families, the real holders or lessees of the soil are the depositors or shareholders in monetary institutions.

It speedily became manifest that the new conditions were not popular. The whole of the inhabitants could not be squatters, and many of the new arrivals desired to become farmers and make a living by cultivating the soil. Then it began to dawn on the people that they had made a grievous mistake in having so fatuously supported the agitation which led to the Orders-in-Council of 1847 and the consequent locking up of the land for pastoral purposes. A counter movement was the result, and before many years the antagonism of the general public to the squatters was as strong and unreasonable as previously the feeling had been in their favour. But they had now obtained the leases and portions of the freehold of the land held by them, and in their own way they made the best use of it. At the same time much valuable agricultural country was known to be in their possession, and they became the object of attack on all sides. Politicians desirous of working up popular feeling denounced them, and in a few years there was within the new Legislative Assembly a strong party pledged to secure for the people once more the "birthright" which had been but recently so thoughtlessly parted with. Henceforth there was no moderation on either side. The squatters held on with tenacity to what they legally possessed, and the other side, in a perfect political frenzy, cried out for their total spoliation.

The political watchword in these years was "Free selection over the public lands of the colony." A genuine, but, as it has proved, mistaken attempt to give effect to this principle and settle an agricultural population in place of the squatters, and thus gradually cover the vast uninhabited sheep walks of the interior with smiling homesteads and waving cornfields, was made by Mr (afterwards Sir John) Robertson, who became Minister for Lands in 1858, and was the apostle of the new creed. Immediately upon his accession to office, he issued a regulation to the effect that all pastoral leases should be subject to such conditions as Parliament might impose, but shortly afterwards his party went out of power. His successor prepared a Bill giving a limited right of selection over proclaimed agricultural areas, but unfortunately for the colony this measure never received Parliamentary sanction, and in 1860 Mr Robertson was placed at the head of a new administration. His first business was the introduction of a Bill permitting "Free selection over the public lands, surveyed and unsurveyed," but the main feature of this measure having been rejected by the Assembly, he appealed to the country. He came back in 1861 with a powerful majority, with flying colours carried his measures—The Crown Lands Alienation Act, and the Crown Lands Occupation Act. For a period of 23 years afterwards, these enactments for all intents and purposes, formed the land law of the country. It was without doubt a praiseworthy effort on his part to induce legitimate settlement of the lands of the colony, but it was in reality the cause of more heart-burning, public immorality and private chicanery, and class antagonism than any measure ever passed in Australasia.

It may be of interest here to give a brief outline of these enactments. The Crown Lands Alienation Act provided that any person might select from 40 to 320 acres of any Crown Lands, (excepting town, suburban, and reserved lands) at a fixed price of £1 per acre, of which 25 per cent was to be paid as a deposit on application, three years being allowed in which to pay the balance without interest. After three years, interest was charged at the rate of five per cent. A condition of residence for three years was imposed, and improvements to the value of £1 per acre had to be effected. There were a few reserves for townships, and religious and other purposes, but practically the whole of the unalienated surface of the colony, irrespective of its value or situation, was thrown open for selection. That is to say, any man might go upon any portion of the Crown Lands, and take possession of an area covering half a square mile, for which he had to pay 5s an acre cash, the balance being allowed to remain at interest at five per cent. Mineral lands might be taken up under similar conditions, but at a price of £2 per acre, and upon the expenditure of £2 per acre in improvements.

The Crown Lands Occupation Act, which was to regulate the use of land for pastoral purposes, divided the colony into first-class settled districts, second-class settled districts, and unsettled districts. The runs in the first-class settled districts were only available on annual leases, at £2 per square mile, or three farthings per acre, while in the second class and unsettled districts runs ranged in area from 25 to 100 square miles, according to the quality of the country, and the leases, which were for five years, were opened to competition by public tender, the rents being fixed by appraisement in open court, at a time previously proclaimed. Owners of purchased land were allowed to lease adjoining land to the extent of three times their freehold, at a rental of £2 per square mile per annum.

The baneful effect of this new legislation speedily made itself apparent. Within a very few years a class war of a most determined character arose between the pastoralists and a body who henceforth occupy a prominent position in consideration of this subject—the "selectors". There were of course amongst these many men who had a genuine desire to obtain land for purposes of cultivation. They were not for the most part, however, farmers in the ordinary sense, but made a business of buying land on the easy terms offered by the Government, and selling at a profit for cash to the pastoral lessees, who completed the purchase. The latter, where the land was of sufficient value,—and large areas were of much greater value than 20*s* per acre—also commenced to select through representatives or "dummies," to use the colloquialism in use to describe those who practised this form of illegal vicarious selection.

"Selecting" in either form became a profitable means of gaining a livelihood, and many thousands made a snug income out of the system. The facilities offered by the Act for the blackmailing of the squatters by the selection of such portions of their runs as would cause them inconvenience in the working of their stock, were at once utilised. A species of civil war followed which was generally carried out in the bitterest spirit; and in the form of a regular campaign. The selectors frequently attacked a run almost in a body. They would pounce upon the choice portions, and commence active aggression by impounding the squatters' stock, when it came upon the selected land, a course which was permissible by law. Sometimes they were bought off by the payment of a fixed sum to induce them to forfeit their selections, which could then be purchased at auction for cash. In other cases they waited for an offer of purchase from the lessee at the end of the term of residence required by the Act, and if this did not come readily there were plenty of means of putting on the screw to induce such an overture.

On the other side the squatters "dummied" extensively, purely for the purpose of obtaining the possession of cheap freehold land, and by this means large areas of the best country passed into their hands. But the aggressiveness of the selectors also brought about vicarious selection by the squatters in self-defence. When the immediate advent of selectors to a run became probable, the lessees endeavored to circumvent them by dummying all the positions which offered the best means of blocking the selectors from getting to water. This system, commonly known as "peacocking," was assisted by the use of Volunteer Land Orders. Each member of the Defence Force was entitled, after five years' service, to an order enabling him to take up fifty acres of Crown Lands, in any position he chose, without conditions or regulations as to improvement or residence, and he could sell or assign

these orders at any time. They proved most valuable to
the lessees in harassing or hemming in the selectors, and
were a marketable commodity, no well-regulated pastoral
lessee being without a supply for offensive or defensive
purposes. Auction sales of land under special survey were
likewise the means of securing to the lessee many points
of vantage, and these were assisted by purchases ostensibly
for mineral purposes. Armed with these various means of
obtaining the best positions on his run, the lessee was enabled
to beat the selector, and it is almost needless to say that
under such a state of affairs fraud and roguery flourished
to a marvellous degree. Indeed such was the debased condition of morality in the colony amongst the great bulk of
people interested in land matters, that it was considered to
be a "smart thing" rather than otherwise to evade the law
and "work a point."

To quote once more from a writer already pretty freely
drawn upon, but upon whose statements the utmost reliance
may be placed: *

"False declarations were made daily alike by squatters
and selectors. Fraud, perjury, subornation, and bribery were
universal. Any man who refused to do as his neighbours
did, or to lend a hand when wanted, incurred the certainty
of social enmity. Truth and honor ceased to be considered
virtues in dealings connected with the public lands. Those
who practised those antiquated rules of life were ignored
and tacitly condemned by all men possessing sound practical
opinions concerning pounds, shillings, and pence..... The
reckless waste of the territory was not less pronounced
than the moral deterioration. In place of the orderly survey
kept ahead of settlement as of old, a wolfish mangling of
the country is displayed everywhere. This disgraceful spoliation went on with the full approval of the department and
of Parliament. Official records state that there are fifty
millions of Crown Lands open to "settlement," but no published maps can show where these lands are. If such a
map were compiled, the fifty millions of acres would appear
in the form of countless shreds, remnants, and strips of soil,
here, there, and everywhere; a chaos of waste, and a record
of pilfering that must pile disgrace upon every Parliament
between 1861 and 1882."

Need it be stated that these proceedings at length caused
a general outcry amongst the disinterested portion of the
community, and that numerous efforts were made to remedy
the evils referred to. The law was constantly tinkered, but

---

* Ranken's "Our Wasted Heritage", chapter XI.

there never appears to have been a fair grip by Parliament of the wants of the country at any time. Mr Robertson, being again in office in 1875, brought in an amending Act, the chief features of which were that personal selection should be enforced, dummying and illegal contracts were made misdemeanours, while no person was to be allowed to select who was below the age of 16 years. Previously, any "person" could select, and the names of the veriest infants were used for this purpose. The Act also increased the maximum area which could be selected from 320 to 640 acres, and after certain conditions as to residence and improvements had been carried out, further areas of 640 acres might be selected, while for every 640 acres so purchased, a pre-emptive lease of the adjoining land might be obtained to the extent of three times the area of the free selection, at a rental of £2 for every 640 acres. It was also provided that annual payments after the third year should in future be 1s instead of 9d per acre. The latter provision was made with the intention of causing the selector to pay interest and at the same time partly extinguish his indebtedness.

Under this enactment, it will be seen, any person might select 640 acres, for an annual payment of £32, to cover principal and interest, and obtain the use of 1920 acres of adjoining country for a sum of £6 per annum. The free selector might thus still further harass the pastoral lessee. A family of five persons above the age of 16 years could take up 12,000 acres, and this privilege, properly utilised, enabled them to confront the lessee with still more powerful weapons of offence. The old troubles were at any rate not removed by the new measure, and the conflict between selector and squatter continued, with the result that the public estate was parted with at an alarming rate. At length the land question became a burning one; the general public were now thoroughly alarmed at the state of affairs; and several ministers tried, but unavailingly, to give effect to the manifest desire for a change.

Eventually, so nauseous had the whole thing become to the public taste, that a commission was in 1883 † appointed to inquire into the "state of the public lands and the land laws." The Commissioners took voluminous evidence from all sorts and conditions of people capable of giving infor-

---

† The commission comprised Messrs Augustus Morris and George Ranken. The latter is the author of "Our Wasted Heritage" and other publications on this subject and also of the "Federal Geography of Australasia", a most valuable topographical work, published by Messrs Turner and Henderson of Sydney.

mation or expressing an opinion, and they presented to Parliament a very able report. Even at the present day much of the information elicited and the deductions drawn are remarkably applicable. The ability and integrity of the Commissioners have never been questioned, and it is matter for regret that their recommendations have not received greater attention.

They reported that they had found the system of free selection to have worked well in the old settled districts, notwithstanding the fact that the land was somewhat poor as compared with that in the intermediate districts. The reason for this was that the original system of free grants, with the right of occupation of surrounding country had been a sound one; and, generally speaking, "selection had shaken down alongside the old grants without bringing monopoly or debt in its train." The most important portion of the report, however, was undoubtedly that referring to the intermediate territory, which had been most largely affected by the Act of 1861. Of the 86,000,000 acres in these districts, including some of the finest lands in the colony, it was found that no less than 25,000,000 acres had been alienated. Referring to the effects of free selection before survey in this division, the Commissioners reported—

"That policy offered for sale to one class of occupants the same land which was simultaneously assigned under lease to another class. There was no partition of the soil to provide for both classes. There was abundant space and to spare to satisfy all reasonable wants then, as there is yet; but this self-evident method of meeting the requirement was not adopted. Thus two separate forms of tenure were instituted by law, both authorising the occupation of the same ground. . . . A policy such as this would be intelligible and expedient, perhaps, if some stringent necessity arose to supplant a condition of lawless commonage, or nomadic barbarism by a system of civilised industry and social security; but one may search in vain for a reason justifying its application to lands used in a legal and orderly manner, in harmony with the recognised industry of the community. . The men whose enterprise was thus telling daily in reclaiming a wilderness could not be expected to receive with favour a law which authorised any stranger to seize upon each spot as soon as it became of any value. But there was a peculiarity in the tenure originally acquired under the Orders-in-Council which gave the squattage a different character from a merely permissive occupancy of the pasture, and told greatly in the squatters' defence against selection. The pre-emptive right enabled the lessee of a run to buy one square mile in every 25, and through the exercise of this privilege the water frontages and choice spots—the oases on which the value of every station depends—often became private freeholds. In this way, from the possession of these advantageous positions, a station acquired a certain permanence of title, altogether apart from the leasehold, and these positions formed the centres from which schemes of systematic defence against selection were afterwards organised."

"It has no doubt been often pointed out that the "Orders-in-Council," with all belonging to them, were abrogated by the legislation of 1861; but this same abrogation could not void what had been done under the prior tenure. . . . . Neither could the Act of 1861 obliterate the financial and business interests concerned in these stations. Squatting as a productive enterprise had been as it were cemented into the commerce and banking of the colony. . . . . It is no wonder, then, that the standard interests of the country have been arrayed in opposition to the spread of colonisation —at least of such colonisation as was proposed for the pastoral districts under the present law. The way out of the difficulty for all interests is still plain. The squatting industry would be much better carried on, more cheaply, more securely, and with much greater proportionate results, on a reduced area under a safe tenure; while real honest settlement would thrive most where a settler could get a sufficient extent of ground without the risks attached to contending with an antagonistic tenure. There was then, as now, plenty of land to provide for the two interests apart."

To the report was appended most valuable information, showing how the contest between the pastoral lessees and selectors had been carried out, and after a perusal of the summarised evidence collated, one might well agree with the commissioners, who said—

"It would be a wonder if a law so framed showed any fixed principle and consistency in its administration. The history of its whole operation for years has been an unintelligible chaos, in which the rights and interests of all mainly concerned have been the sport of accident, political interest, and departmental disorder. As the law became more intricate and involved, Ministerial patronage and Parliamentary interest became more and more in request, and the chief fruits of the policy now apparent are the huge pastoral freehold estates accumulating in the best of our grazing country, and much spurious prosperity in Sydney, engendered by a vicious system of administrative centralisation, which forces all dealings and litigation to the metropolis."

The aspect of the question from the point of view of private and public morality was necessarily forced upon the attention of the commissioners, whose conclusions were shown thus—

"A long training to use the law in any way to their own advantage has rendered lessees and selectors alike adepts in evading its provisions, irrespective of moral obligations. This may appear a terrible indictment to prefer on parole evidence, abundant and concurrent as that is; but the sketch maps, produced by photo-lithography, with which this report abounds, are incontrovertible witnesses to a moral obliquity, which the present land laws can never make straight."

And again, speaking of the provisions of the Act,—

"It has barred the advance of honest enterprise in all directions, and has at the same time opened a door for the entrance of every phase of abuse and fraud, to be shared in by all classes and conditions. It would be well if the moral and social evils which have grown from the law could be depicted as vividly as the waste of the national estate has been displayed; but it needs little argument to prove the vice of a policy which of its very essence divides the rural population into two hostile camps; and it would be superfluous to state that the personal virtues of veracity and honorable dealing have been tarnished by the daily habit of intrigue, the practice of evading the law, and by declarations in defiance of fact universally made. It is in evidence that self-interest has created a laxity of conscience in all matters connected with the land law, and that the stain attaches to men of all classes and all degrees."

As the basis of amending legislation, the commissioners recommended the abolition of survey before selection, except as applied to lands in the old settled districts; the adoption for all lands (except town, suburban, and special lands) of a system of leasing; that pastoral leases be granted to former lessees of one half their runs with compensation for certain improvements; conditional leases for a period of 15 years, with the right of renewal, of a maximum area of 2560 acres in the intermediate, and 5760 in the unsettled districts, to be obtainable after survey, (upon conditions as to residence and improvements) by persons other than pastoral lessees; and the administration of the lands by non-political commissioners and local boards. These broad principles, if adopted with a provision for classification, would undoubtedly have changed the whole aspect of the land legislation of the colony, and proved generally acceptable to those who desired pure administration and genuine settlement. But, alas! for the colony, twenty years of class hatred and internecine struggles had left behind them such a poisonous rankling in the minds of those who were directly interested in the question of land legislation, that it was impossible for the members of Parliament—who in many cases were returned as the direct representatives of the opposing factions—to bring to the subject that calm unbiassed consideration necessary to produce a wise, national measure of reform.

Truly the colony then needed a Hercules to cleanse its Augean stable.

A new Land Bill was passed in 1884, but alterations became speedily necessary, and an amending Bill was carried in 1889. The main principles laid down in the measure of 1884 were adhered to however, in the latter enactment, and as the joint legislation of these two years provides the machinery for our present system, it may be as well to consider them together. The new Acts retained the old method of selection before survey, but upon a new basis, and thus, although there has since been some improvement in the conditions of settlement, many of the evils formerly rife are still existing, and the old feud between pastoralists and selectors goes on, though, in a modified degree. After all, the amending legislation was but a fresh patch on an old garment. Consequently there has since been constant jarring between conflicting interests, while new troubles have arisen to make it necessary for Parliament to pass a further amending Act. A Bill for this purpose was indeed placed before Parliament during the session just closed, but it was not proceeded with, and a Bill to permit persons to mine on private property, which was also introduced, was not carried.

The Act of 1884 invited the squatters to divide their leaseholds into two portions, to be known as the leasehold and the resumed areas respectively. The former they were to be allowed to re-lease for fixed periods, on conditions to be hereafter stated, and the balance they were to be permitted to occupy under annual licenses, on the condition that it was to be open for selection as formerly, but under new methods. No attempt was made in the direction of separating the arable land from that which was suitable only for pastoral purposes; but to meet the conditions of the colony, it was cut up into three new divisions, known as the Eastern, Central, and Western. These to some extent took the place of the former Old Settled, Intermediate, and Unsettled districts, but the boundaries were more arbitrarily fixed. Practically they divided the colony into three strips of country running north and south, and approximately parallel with the sea-coast.

The Eastern Division, comprising about 60,000,000 acres, or 94,000 square miles, includes the country abutting on the ocean, and extending inland about 150 to 200 miles. It contains all the original centres of population, and some of the best agricultural land in the colony. The principal geographical feature of this division is the Great Dividing Range, which runs through it from north to south. Rising up almost perpendicularly from some parts of the coastal districts, the Range spreads out into upland plains, situated from 2000 to nearly 4000 feet above sea-level. This Division has a distinctive character of its own. In parts there are mountains and forests, but generally speaking the land is cultivable more or less, and having a fine invigorating climate, and good rainfall, it is capable of growing almost any article of food. From the western side of the Range, the country slopes away gently towards the inland plains, which form the main natural features of the continent. The land on these slopes is of very superior quality, but is mostly devoted to pastoral uses.

The Central Division, which is contiguous to the Eastern, contains some 55,000,000 acres, or about 86,000 square miles, and runs from north to south, varying in width from about 100 to 250 miles. Here the mountains and forests disappear, and are succeeded by gentle undulations, covered with scrub, which in itself is becoming a great drawback from its propensity to spread rapidly. Owing to the scarcer rainfall the land in this division is not generally so valuable for agricultural purposes as that in the Eastern Division, nor will it carry as large a proportion of sheep to the acre,; but it includes nevertheless some stretches of magnificent country, declared by experts to be equal to any wheat-growing land in the world. It is here that any great increase of the rural population may be anticipated in the immediate future.

The Western Division, comprising about 80,000,000 acres, or 125,000 square miles, reaches away for hundreds of miles from the boundary of the Central Division to the Western frontier. Here the land assumes the character more of semi-desert,—vast arid plains, watered but by one or two large rivers, and depending principally for moisture upon heavy but infrequent rains. At times there is no rainfall for months, or almost years together, and the sheep then depend but little upon the grass, which, however, springs up in a perfectly miraculous manner. After heavy rains where there is a lack of grass, the stock feed chiefly upon low saltbush, and other indigenous shrubs, which are, however, of a stimulating tonic character, The land is as a rule of less value than in either of the two other divisions. It is here that the droughts are felt in their intensity, and the mortality of stock in the very dry seasons is terrible. In both the Central and Western Divisions rabbits are now very plentiful.

A knowledge of the geographical features and characteristics of these divisions is necessary to a comprehension of the existing land laws. In consequence of the comparatively small areas now available for settlement in the Eastern Division, the conditions under which land may be obtained are more restricted there than elsewhere. Any person above the age of 16 years, (not a married female dependent upon her husband) may, upon any part of the Crown Lands not specially exempted, select an area of from 40 to 640 acres in extent, for conditional purchase as a freehold. A conditional lease of ground may also be obtained, but the area must not, together with that of the original purchase, exceed 1280 acres. An uniform price of 20*s* per acre is charged for all purchased land, of which 2*s* per acre has to be deposited when the application for the land is made, the balance being paid in instalments of 1*s* per acre per annum, together with 4 per cent interest upon the unpaid balance. The payment of the instalment does not commence till the end of the third year. A term of residence for five years continuously from the date of taking possession is necessary, and within two years of occupation, the selector must fence his land and maintain the same in good order and condition; but with the consent of the local land board, he may substitute for fencing other permanent improvements. At the completion of his term of residence, and provided he has fulfilled his conditions as to improvements, he may pay up the balance of purchase money, and acquire a title to the land. He is then also privileged to again select and conditionally purchase additional areas, contiguous to his original purchase, of not less than 40 nor more than 640 acres, and if he has a conditional leasehold, he may also purchase this outright, or upon the same terms as for his original purchase. The condition as to residence is then removed, but the fencing of the land, is still made compulsory. In the case of a conditional leasehold, the lease may be for a period of 15 years, at a rental fixed by the local land board, the only condition attached being the fencing of the land within two years from date of occupation, though one fence may be placed around both the conditional purchase and leasehold. Land may also be taken up on a non-residential basis, but the other conditions are very stringent. The area selected may not exceed 320 acres, while no conditional lease is permitted. The land must be fenced within twelve months from the date of survey, and other permanent improvements to the value of £1 an acre must be effected within five years. The most important feature of these non-residential purchases, lies in the fact that the price per acre is £2, and the amounts of deposit money and instalments are double those of the conditional purchases. Non-residential conditional purchasers must be 21 years of age, and they are debarred from taking up any other conditional purchases. When land of particular value is required for settlement, it may be declared a "special area," and removed from the operations of the ordinary selector, but may be selected, in areas not exceeding 320 acres, at a price to be fixed by the Minister, of not less than 30s per acre. In this case, also, non-resident selectors must pay twice the amount charged to resident selectors. In this Division pastoral leases for five years were granted to former lessees under the Act of 1861 of half their runs, and at the conclusion of that term they were permitted to hold them on a yearly tenancy similar to that formerly existing. The unalienated Crown Lands in this division are now mostly held under this tenure, or on conditional lease, as described above.

In the Central Division, the conditions as to the purchase of land are similar to but more extended than in the Eastern Division. Land may be bought conditionally, to the extent of 640 acres, as in the Eastern Division, and upon the same terms as to residence, fencing, price, mode of payment, etc. But the area which may be obtained upon conditional lease may equal three times the area of the original purchase, and absolute possession may be in the same manner as in the Eastern Division, making a total area which may be puchased of 2560 acres. The acreage which may be purchased without residence, and the conditions regulating the sale are the same as for the Eastern Division. In the case of "special areas" which may be declared within this division, the maximum extent of a selection is fixed at 640 acres. In this division, the leases of the halves of their runs held by the pastoralists are for ten years, without any right of renewal, though an extension for five years may be granted by the Minister. The rents are appraised by local land boards, every five years, and no minimum is fixed. All improvements on the land at the expiry of the lease become the property of the Crown, without compensation, and the land may then be dealt with as desired. These leases fall in in 1895, and the method of dealing with the land so released is likely to form the subject of legislation in the near future.

In the Western Division, no land may be purchased conditionally, unless it has been declared a "special area," in which case the conditions of selection are the same as those applying to the Central Division. The land has so far been retained almost entirely for pastoral purposes, on lease, or occupation license, and this position will be maintained for probably another decade at least. In lieu of the system of conditional purchase, the portions of their runs held by squatters under annual occupation license, are open to selection in areas of not less than 2560 acres nor more than 10,240 acres, under a system of homestead leases. These leases, which are intended to permit comparatively small graziers to obtain the use of the natural herbage, have a currency of 15 years, and are granted upon application and the payment of a deposit of $1d$ per acre of the area applied for. The applicant must reside for a period of at least six consecutive months during each of the first five years of his lease, and during the first two years he must fence the whole leasehold, in accordance with a prescribed design, though the Land Board may exempt him from the fencing conditions, provided other substantial improvements are made. At the end of the 15 years an extension of the lease for another seven years may be granted, if it is considered by the Land Board that the land has been benefited by its occupation. At the end of his term, the land reverts to the Crown, without compensation to the outgoing tenant for improvements, although he must pay the occupation licensee for such improvements as he finds on the land when it is taken up by him. No person can hold more than one of these leases, and no such lease may be held by a pastoral lessee. The pastoral leases of the portions of their runs held by the original squatters, have a currency of 21 years, with the possibility of an extension for another seven years if the land has been improved in a satisfactory manner. As in the Central Division, the land absolutely reverts to the Crown at the end of the lease, without compensation to the outgoing tenants for improvements.

These, briefly, are the main conditions under which land may be obtained in new South Wales. In addition, scrub leases, of land covered with noxious shrubs, may be granted in areas of from 640 to 10,240 acres, at an appraised rental and on the condition of commencing to destroy scrub within three months of the beginning of the lease. Lands covered with snow during part of the year may be leased for 7 years on special terms, and the leases of lands of inferior character may be put up for competition by auction. Residential leases for periods not exceeding 15 years, and for areas not exceeding 10 acres, may be obtained within mineral fields by holders of miners' rights, and licenses, and on gold fields any person in duly authorised occupation under the Mining Act may purchase the land occupied under residential lease, without competition, in virtue of the improvements made on the land, at a price to be fixed by the Land Board, being not less than at the rate of £2 per quarter acre for town lands, and £2.10/- for suburban or other lands, or £2.10/- for any less area than one acre; but the maximum which may be so purchased is one quarter of an acre for town lands, and one acre for other lands. The only other method of alienation of Crown Lands is by auction. An area not exceeding 200,000 acres in the aggregate for the whole Colony may be disposed of in any one year in this manner, at an upset price to be fixed by the Minister, but in no case less than £8 per acre for town lands, £2.10/- for suburban lands, and £1 for other lands,

One of the most valuable innovations of the legislation of 1884 and 1889 was the appointment of local administrative bodies. To some extent at least the means of decentralisation were thus secured, together with greater purity of administration and a greater confidence generally in the methods of the department. The land Boards are bodies having control of one or more land districts, each district, again, being under the jurisdiction of a land agent, who is the local executive officer. A still more important body, however, is the Land Court, instituted by the Act of 1889, with the object of freeing the administration of the land law from political influences. Hitherto one of the greatest curses of the system had been the fact that some members of Parliament had acted as land agents, and used their position as representatives for the benefit of their clients. This was to a great extent rendered impossible under the new *régime*. In effect the Land Court is a permanent Appeal Court on all land matters, and it consists of President and two other members, who sit all the year round to adjudicate. The President is by common usage a lawyer, and the other members are men of special knowledge and experience in land matters Their work has undoubtedly so far been highly beneficial. Their decisions in matters of administration have the force of judgments of the Supreme Court, but when law points arise they may be submitted to the Supreme Court by the Land Court, either of its own motion or at the request of parties interested. The judgments given on this appeal are final.

The severe depression in the Colony during the past year or two, and the consequent lack of employment for a great number of people, has caused more than usual attention to be devoted to the question of placing a greater proportion of the people on the soil. As a result, a movement was instituted having for its object the formation of village settlements, in which persons of small means might be enabled to take up land in suitable areas, with State assistance at the outset. The matter was so strongly urged upon the Government that in the last days of the session just concluded (June, 1893) a measure known as the "Labour Settlements Act" was passed to give effect to the proposal. This somewhat experimental enactment provides that the Governor-in-Council may declare that certain areas of land not now under lease shall be set apart for the purposes of labour settlements and the same authority may nominate a Board of Control, comprising not more than 16 nor less than 8 persons (of whom one fourth may be females), to be a corporate body for the direction of the same. The lands may be leased to the Boards for periods not exceeding 28 years, with a right of renewal for a further similar term, at rentals to be appraised by the local Land Boards, the payment of such rents to commence after the expiration of the fourth year of the lease. The Board of Control may enrol as "members" single persons above the age of 21 years, or the heads of families, and when such a number of members has been enrolled as the Minister may approve, "it may apply to the Minister for Lands for monetary assistance, naming the persons for whom such assistance is asked, and furnishing such other information as the Minister may require." On the recommendation of the Minister, the Colonial Treasurer may pay to the Board of Control a sum "not exceeding £25 for each enrolled member who is the head of a family, dependent upon him; or £20 for each married person without a family dependent upon him; and £12 for each unmarried person." The Boards shall expend this money for the purposes of the settlements, and at the expiration of four years from the commencement of the lease, and each following year, 8 per cent of the total sum received from the Colonial Treasurer "shall be a charge on the revenues of the Board payable to the Treasury, until the said sum, with interest at the rate of 4 per cent per annum has been repaid." The Board may establish or manage any trade or industry, and apportion the profits therefrom amongst the "members," and they are empowered, for sufficient cause, to remove any member from the settlement and include any other person in his place. It may also sublease the land, (on conditions approved by the Minister) to any member. Regulations are hereafter to be prepared by the Governor-in-Council, prescribing the class of persons to be enrolled, the method of enrolment, etc., and the Board may make further regulations to deal with "the work to be done in the settlement, and the apportionment of the work among the members, and the equitable distribution of wages, profits, and emoluments among the members, after providing for their maintenance; the collection, spending and application of moneys; the cleanliness, good order and government of the settlement; and may impose a penalty not exceeding £2 for a breach of any of these regulations, to be recovered in a summary way before a Court of Petty Sessions." These regulations are to have all the force of law.

We have now traced the conditions governing settlement as they have existed in the past, and outlined briefly the legislation which provides the machinery for our present system. It may now be of interest to see what progress has been made under these conditions, and how far they have been successful in promoting settlement. From the latter point of view, it must be candidly admitted, the results are not satisfactory. While the population of the Colony has been rapidly increasing, centralisation in the towns has been the rule instead of a gradual filling up of the vast open spaces of the interior. An examination of the official statistics for the period between 1861 and 1891,— the period covered by the legislation dealing with Crown Lands since the introduction of responsible government embracing four census epochs,—unfortunately goes to show that there has been a marked tendency for the population to congregate in the towns, and especially in Sydney. In the report of the Statistician of New South Wales (Mr T. A. Coghlan) upon the census taken in 1891, some startling figures bearing upon this subject are given. The following table shows the results arrived at with respect to urban and rural population during three decades—

	1861	1871	1881	1891
Sydney and suburbs	95,789	137,776	224,939	383,283
Other towns	64,045	97,037	201,999	346,736
Total urban	159,834	234,813	426,938	730,019
Total rural	189,116	266,766	321,303	388,231
	348,950	501,579	748,241	1,118,250

The figures for the last decade show that the increase of population in the towns amounted to 303,490, while the increase in rural population was only 66,928. At the same rate of progress the urban population will double itself in 12.92 years, but a period of 36.63 years will be required to permit the rural population to achieve a like result.

Mr Coghlan, in his "Wealth and Progress of New South Wales" for 1892 * also gives the percentage of population of Sydney and suburbs, as compared with the population of the Colony as a whole as follows:—

Year	Metropolitan	Country.
1861	26.70 per cent	73.30 per cent.
1871	26.73 ,, ,,	73.27 ,, ,,
1881	30.73 ,, ,,	69.66 ,, ,,
1891	34.26 ,, ,,	65.74 ,, ,,

The increase of population during the 20 years which closed with 1891 was 181 per cent for the metropolis, while that of the country districts amounted to 104 per cent. As previously indicated, the population of the whole Colony more than doubled itself during this period, the total for 1891 showing an increase of 125 per cent as compared with 1871. These are astonishing facts, which prove that the people are neglecting the occupation and cultivation of the soil as a means of living, for a town life. They show also that if the same state of things continues, the population of the whole Colony will, at the end of another 40 years, be some five millions, of whom 2½ millions will be in the metropolis. There is outside of Australasia no instance in the history of new countries to compare with this tadpole growth which, if permitted to continue for another hundred years, would result in the total population of the Colony being over 60 millions of souls, with a population in the metropolis alone of some 45 millions. Such a prospect is appalling. It possibly is a *reductio ad absurdum;* but it is the logical sequence to the present progress of settlement.

How far then may this extraordinary state of affairs be attributed to the land legislation? Let us again revert to figures. At the close of 1891, the total area of land held in fee simple, and under the deferred payment systems, for which deeds were issued, was 23,367,000 acres; the area granted for religious, scholastic, and other public purposes, was 3,123,000 acres; and there was in process of alienation, under deferred payments, 19,241,000 acres. Altogether, therefore, an area of 45,731,000 acres out of the total of 198,848,000 acres comprising the superficial area of the Colony,—or nearly one-fourth—has passed or is in process of passing from the Crown. The manner in which that land excluding

* Page 741, "Settlement."

the small amount occupied in urban holdings, is now held, and has been held during the last 14 years, may be ascertained from the following table—

Year	Under 200 acres	In Estates comprising.			Total area of holdings
		From 200 to 1000 acres	From 1000 to 10,000 acres.	Upwards of 10,000 acres	
1879	1,890,293	4,950,938	5,692,576	10,187,796	22,721,603
1883	1,811,483	5,586,273	8,131,955	17,823,287	33,352,998
1887	1,984,940	6,181,374	9,480,412	19,170,765	36,817,491
1891	2,095,857	6,731,209	11,370,329	21,884,299	42,081,694

It will thus be seen that, while during fifteen years the total area of different holdings has nearly doubled, those under 200 acres show scarcely any perceptible increase, and those between 200 and 1000 acres have increased by less than 50 per cent. On the other hand, the area of holdings between 1000 and 10,000 acres has more than doubled, and the same applies to holdings of over 10,000 acres. These facts are very significant, and read together with the authentic statement that the average size per holding has increased from 315 acres in 1876 to 816 acres in 1892, can leave no manner of doubt that the alienated land is not being taken up for the purposes of cultivation by small holders, but is passing into the hands of a few large landed proprietors. Any doubt on this point may be removed by a perusal of the following table, which shows the numbers of persons by whom rural land has been held since 1879—

Acreage	1879	1881	1886	1891
Under 16 acres	4,974	5,186	6,512	9,201
16 to 200 ,,	21,302	20,361	21,288	22,815
201 to 400 ,,	6,199	5,753	6,382	7,392
401 to 1000 ,,	4,964	4,959	6,792	7,158
1001 to 2000 ,,	1,212	1,470	1,948	2,402
2001 to 10,000 ,,	940	1,176	1,458	1,905
10,000 acres and up	327	449	552	677
Total	39,918	39,354	44,932	51,550

Taken in conjunction with the previous table, these figures show that while during the period from 1879 the total area of land alienated has nearly doubled, the increase of holders is only about one fourth. It is again most significant that the number of holders of from 16 to 1000 acres shows scarcely any increase, while the number of persons possessing areas of 1000 acres and upwards has doubled.

Mr Coghlan also gives the following information on this subject—"From the returns of the Department of Lands it would appear that from 1862 to the close of 1891 the total number of individual selections applied for was 233,943, covering a total area of 31,185,521 acres, of which to the close of 1891 there were 161,017 still in existence, covering an area of 21,325,477 acres. (It will be remembered in this connection that the total number of holdings, including all lands alienated prior to 1861, only reached 55,550 at the end of 1891) Of the total number of selections applied for, 19,804, or 8.5 per cent have become absolute freeholds, 141,213, or 60.3 per cent are still in process of alienation, and 72,926, or 31.2 per cent, have been either declared void, forfeited, or disallowed, or withdrawn under the provisions of the various Land Acts . A comparison of the area dealt with in the following table shows how fast the original conditional purchasers are dispossessing themselves of their holdings, whilst the area selected does not exhibit any tendency to increase at anything like the same rate. An examination of the table reveals the fact that in ten years only there have been 21,097,323 acres of conditional purchases transferred against 12,884,478 acres applied for, a difference of 8,212,845 acres, which have gone to increase the large estates, distinctly to the detriment of healthy settlement. Since the Act of 1889 came into force, a slight revival of conditional purchases appears to have taken place, but there is no certainty of its continuance, as the best of the rural lands have long since been alienated, though there appears to be no great tendency amongst the country youth to follow city rather than country pursuits. Among the immigrants, there is only a small proportion who are accustomed to country life, or who possess the means requisite for coping successfully with the difficulties which surround the pioneer, while the town-bred population shows no disposition to embrace a country life."

The table above referred to is as follows—

Year	No. of selections.	Area selected	No. of transfers	Area transferred.
1882	14,607	2,392,220	8,665	2,134,319
1883	10,725	1,621,948	6,213	1,508,583
1884	10,657	1,453,937	6,017	1,525,456
1885	5,372	1,114,871	9,079	2,286,730
1886	6,061	954,560	7,154	1,861,877
1887	4,478	723,151	7,440	2,159,429
1888	5,364	862,716	10,469	3,096,051
1889	4,686	740,964	10,741	2,327,562
1890	8,526	1,713,577	13,492	1,863,508
1891	6,149	1,306,534	16,727	2,333,808
Total	76,625	12,884,478	95,997	21,097,323

Little more need be written to show that the land laws of the Colony have not promoted settlement. That they have not resulted in cultivation may be readily ascertained from the following table:—

Size of holding.	Number	Aggregate area alienated in each series.	Area cultivated in each series	Proportion cultivated to aggregate area alienated.
1 to 30 acres	11,840	121,180	38,353	31.7
31 to 400 ,,	27,568	4,164,945	416,464	10.0
401 to 1000 ,,	7,158	4,540,941	188,494	4.2
1001 to 10,000 ,,	4,307	11,370,329	167,797	1.5
Upwards of 10,000 acres.	677	21,884,299	29,788	0.1
Total and proportions	51,550	42,081,694	840,896	2.0

Thus only two per cent of the total area possessed under freeholds in the Colony, is cultivated notwithstanding the fact that the alienated country comprises some of the best arable land. Yet it is stated officially that "the area absolutely unfit for occupation of any sort has been roughly estimated at less than 5,000,000 acres; it may therefore be said that the greater part of the area adapted for settlement is also in some form or another capable of being cultivated." Of this, however, "only 0.4 per cent of the total area of New South Wales is actually devoted to the growth of agricultural produce, and if the small extent of land upon which permanent artificial grasses have been sown for dairy farming purposes be added to the area under crops, this proportion only reaches 0.6 per cent of the total area of New South Wales, and does not represent much more than one acre per head of its population."

The total value of the agricultural produce of the Colony also, unfortunately does not show an increase proportionate with the increase of population, or even of the rural population. During the decade ending in 1891, the total increase of population was 370,418, and of the rural population 66,928 persons, The total value of agricultural produce on the other hand was only £3,584,590, in 1891 as against £4,194,346, in 1881, while in the interim there were four years during which the total was even less than in 1891. Consequently, there was not only a relative but also an actual decrease in the value of the total produce from tillage, despite the fact that 14½ millions of acres of land had been alienated, for the presumed purposes of agriculture.

Among the most extraordinary statistics in connection with this subject are those which show that the Colony appears to be able to produce only about one-half the wheat necessary for its own consumption. In 1891 the total apparent consumption of bread-stuffs was 6,261,027 bushels, of which 3,120,340 bushels were produced locally, the deficiency being 3,140,687 bushels, or more than one half. For a period of about 15 years the deficiency approximated 42 per cent, while for the last five years it was about 45 per cent. Yet, to show that the conditions of the Colony are favourable to grain-growing, it need only be stated that the average yield of wheat per acre for 30 years up to 1891 was 13.1 bushels, which was higher than the yields of any of the Colonies on the Australian continent including South Australia and Victoria which have long been recognised exporters of bread-stuffs. The harvests also of wheat for hay, barley, and in fact grain of all kinds, are much less than sufficient for home consumption, while in potatoes, and many other articles of produce there is a deficiency in production of at least one-half, as compared with the consumption.

Enough has now been written to demonstrate that as a means of inducing settlement the present system has been a failure. Two great errors are held by thinking men in the Colony to have been made during the past fifty years, which are mainly responsible for the present state of affairs—viz.,

    1. The locking up of the lands and the granting of pre-emptive rights to the squatters under the Orders-in-Council of 1847.

2. The institution of free selection before survey in the land legislation of 1861.

If at the outset, it is held, a system of classification, however rough, had been attempted, and certain tracts of country suitable for agriculture, or agriculture and grazing combined, set apart for lease or alienation in suitable areas, the arable land could have been appropriated to its proper use, and there would have been ample to provide a legitimate livelihood for at least ten times, probably fifty times the present agrarian population. The remainder of the vast area of the Colony could then have been leased in specified areas, with perhaps a homestead purchasing clause, for a term sufficiently long to warrant the lessee in expending his capital in improvements, and so making the most of the soil. Then, as the leases fell in, such a contraction of the leasehold area could have again been made as was necessary to provide further land for cultivation, concurrently with the increase of population, and the remainder again leased to the pastoralists. By some such system, the land would have been gradually taken for purposes of cultivation; the capital already spent in the acquisition of land at present used only for pastoral purposes, might have been devoted jointly to the improvement of agriculture, and of the leasehold areas; the public estate would have been benefited, and the rents therefrom have become a permanent and increasing source of revenue; and there would have been land enough in considerable areas for the use of a population infinitely larger than the present.

In 1847, the land was practically handed over *en bloc* to one class of settlers, who were given legal rights over it to the exclusion of the rest of the community. Then again in 1861, instead of a statesmanlike system, which would have acknowledged the then legal rights of those who had possession and given them an indefeasible tenure for a term of years, of portion of their land at least, and retained the balance for settlement, the whole unalienated surface of the Colony was thrown into a pool to be gambled and scrambled and fought for, between squatter and selector, regardless of the quality of the soil, its location, or its usefulness. An opportunity was at this time undoubtedly presented for the adoption of some system of classification, but no effectual attempt was made in this direction, and the spoliation of the public estate was carried out in a scandalous manner for 23 years, until public opinion absolutely forced a change. Even then, either patriotism or legislative capacity were wanting, and no effort was made to set apart the land suitable for agriculture. A tentative arrangement was made under which the pastoral lessees, were allowed to select one half—naturally they would take the best—of their runs, to be leased for comparatively short terms, while the balance, though still in the hands of the squatters, was thrown open to be scrambled for once more, but with an additional concession by the Crown to the scramblers that the land might be grabbed in larger areas than before.

What has been the consequence of this last phase of the legislative muddle? The pastoralists are dissatisfied, and the selectors are dissatisfied. The former complain that, as they have no fixity of tenure and no compensation for improvements, they are not warranted in spending money on their land, while at the same time they are liable to arbitrary and unaccountable increases in rent. They claim, and with much force, that if they had the use of the land even in much smaller areas, for a lower term, and could get reasonable compensation for improvements at the end of their leases, they would be warranted in spending much more money in advancing the capabilities of the soil, by conserving the water, irrigating, and other expedients, and so finding employment for many hands. The selectors, who wish to blackmail the squatters, complain on their side, that the available country for selection is now so "peacocked" as to leave them few points of advantage, and they clamor for the throwing open of the whole leasehold areas, in order that they may commence *de novo* the old game of taking up the choice spots for the purpose of being bought out.

Meanwhile a new enemy to the common weal has appeared in the shape of innumerable hordes of rabbits. Introduced comparatively few years ago, they have multiplied marvellously, and have spread over much of the best country, eating up the herbage, and practically driving the sheep off the land. Millions of acres have in this way been rendered valueless for grazing purposes, and the leases have been abandoned. The rabbits have become so great a pest that they are now a potent factor in land matters. The evil, however, is too large to be successfully coped with by the State and the pastoralists decline to go to the expense of destroying the rabbits, or making their runs proof against the vermin, when in a few years their improvements may pass into other hands, without any compensation to them. They are willing, it is averred, to clear their leaseholds of the pest, and make them proof by fencing and otherwise against any further inroads. But they naturally wish to be certain that they will have the use of the land for such a term as will enable them to make a profit from it, sufficient to cover their outlay, and that at the end of their term they may receive compensation if the land is taken from them. These would appear to be reasonable stipulations, and if in the future they are conceded in any new leases which may be granted, and the pastoralists are assured that they will be free from molestation, it may be fairly argued that their industry, which is undoubtedly the staple one of the Colony, will be placed upon a better footing, to the benefit not only of themselves but the whole community. Above all things what is desired is some finality.

The position at present, then briefly summed up, is that there is general dissatisfaction. Yet no one seems to have a scheme of reform which would meet the case. It is not the idea of the writer to sketch remedial legislation; but it may be fairly contended that the following defects in the present system have been pretty clearly shown, and to some extent at least, they suggest their own remedy.

1. That the method of selection before survey without classification is vicious in principle, and has led to unnecessary antagonism between two classes: entailing a gross spoliation of the public estate, without adequate settlement in return.

2. That it has been possible to purchase land on such easy terms and without sufficient safeguards as to its proper use, that it has been more profitable to buy on credit for the purpose of selling again for cash than to cultivate.

3. That if land suitable for agriculture had been surveyed for lease or purchase in suitable areas, upon liberal terms, of payment, *but with strict conditions as to cultivation*, much more would have been done to attract an agricultural population.

4. That under existing conditions, only persons with the use of considerable capital have been able profitably to become pastoral lessees, and that if smaller areas had been available for lease by public competition, a greater number of persons would have been in occupation of the pastoral country, with improved results to the industry, and closer settlement.

5. That if, after setting apart land for agriculture, the pastoralists had been given the use of the remainder upon an indefeasible tenure, for a term of years, and with tenant right for improvements, much more would have been done

to utilise the soil, and greater numbers of persons would have been employed by them.

The land system of New South Wales is now a monument of muddle stupendous in its dimensions, and fraught with incalculable mischief to the present and succeeding generations. Its chief value as an object lesson is with respect to its defects. These are so glaring, and their results have been so manifest, that it is hoped some good may be achieved by this extended reference to them.

CHAPTER IV.

TASMANIA.

The island Colony of Tasmania, situated to the south of Victoria, and separated from the mainland of Australia by Bass' Straits, ranks next to New South Wales in seniority. Otherwise it occupies a minor position amongst the Australias. Excepting West Australia, its population (146,667 at the last census) is the lowest of the group, while its size is far less than that of any of the other Colonies. Its superficial area is 26,215 square miles, or slightly less than that of Scotland; there being thus a density of population of about 5½ persons to the square mile. In climatic conditions, however, the Colony has an advantage over the mainland; the soil in portions is magnificent; and there is every inducement to the settlement of a large rural population on the land. In the early days of its existence it was regarded as the garden of Australia, and even now it is looked to for large supplies of potatoes, fruit, and similar produce. It has indeed ever been essentially, an agricultural country, though owing to the salubrity of its climate, the succulence of its native grasses, and its immunity from droughts, it speedily attained a reputation as the breeding ground of a very fine class of sheep, and for its staple of wool.

Life here is in every respect more English than is usually the case in Australian communities, and the idea of mixed farming as it is known in the Motherland is more nearly borne out. The Colony has had the advantage that from an early period, owing to the comparative scarcity of good land, except that which is timbered, the selections of the settlers were soon fenced in, and it was not ranged over by temporary occupants as was the case in Australia. "The home was a settled one, the so-called squatting system had no room for expansion, and the amenities of civilization with family blessings, were to be found in the little island when Victoria and Queensland, with the greatest part of New South Wales, were in the lower nomadic stage."* But notwithstanding these facts, Tasmania has not advanced

* Bonwick's "Romance of the Wool Trade," 1887, p. 210.

by leaps and bounds, though during the last decade its population and export trade have shown a marked improvement.

The early settlement of the Colony was carried out under regulations framed to meet the conditions of New South Wales, of which it was at the outset a part. Grants were made in the same manner as in the mother Colony, and to all intents and purposes the conditions were the same. It is therefore, unnecessary to refer at length to the systems in force in its infancy. A brief and interesting sketch of the earlier methods was recently given by the Minister of Lands of the Colony, from which the following is taken:— *

"The efforts of the Government were at first directed to encouraging the settlement on the land of persons with some capital to work it, free grants being made to capitalists who possessed influence at headquarters, and to retired military officers as rewards for services to the State. In 1828 [after Tasmania had been declared an independent Colony] the sale of lands was commenced at low prices—about 6s per acre—the upset price having only advanced to 12s per acre in 1841, and a large area was thus alienated. In 1843 a system of leasing the Crown Lands, which had prevailed from the earliest days was extended, and the rentals made nominal, the result being that some 78,000 acres were dealt with, in the first year, and by 1847 1,062,989 acres were thus leased, at an aggregate rental of £14,279. The year 1848 witnessed the introduction of the principle of selling the fee simple to the highest bidder at auction or by private contract. The idea of attaching some condition of residence or improvement to the fast increasing alienation of the State patrimony seems to have been overlooked. The "Pre-emptive Right" or "Quiet Enjoyment" Regulations of 1851, which remained in force for three years, though ostensibly passed to check what was considered an alarming exodus of the Tasmanian youth to the newly discovered goldfields across the Straits, in reality offered a premium to land monopoly and to speculative selection, and as no portion of the purchase money could be demanded for ten years, resulted in large areas being locked up without, except in a few instances, any settlement being effected or improvement taking place."

It was in 1855 that responsible Government was conceded to the Colony, and from this period dates the policy under which later settlement has taken place. In 1858 the first Waste Lands Act was passed. This enactment made provision for the principle of free selection before Survey, but,

---

* Public Works Statement of the Minister of Lands of Tasmania (The Hon. Wm. Hartnoll) delivered in the House of Assembly on the 16th Nov., 1892.

owing to the smallness of the area available for selection, and the fact that much of the land was heavily timbered, the practical value of the concession then made was comparatively small. To again quote the Minister:—

"An instance of experimental legislation, of which our present knowledge of that part of the country exposes the fallacy, was the Unsettled Waste Lands Act of 1858, which set aside some 5,000,000 acres, comprising the greater portion of the West Coast and a portion of the Lake District, as an area within which any person who could prove himself to be worth one pound for every acre applied for, could obtain a free grant of from 50 acres to 640 acres, on condition that within five years he fenced, cleared, and cultivated five out of every fifty acres, or erected buildings or machinery to the value of £250 in lieu thereof. Another portion of the Act authorised the issue of gratuitous leases for not more than 10,000 acres, on condition that the lessee stocked the land with 100 head of sheep or 20 head of cattle for every 1000 acres. Under this clause, up to 31st December, 1858, 228 applications were received for 2,204,520 acres, of which 188 applications, for 1,804,520 acres, were approved, the fortunate lessees being further privileged to purchase the best portions of their lands in lots not exceeding 640 acres, at 10s per acre—no other person being allowed to purchase any other portion of the lease."

"Advantage was not taken of the liberal provision by which a lessee was entitled to obtain a free grant, and but one solitary instance is on record of a claim being made to purchase a 640 acre lot at the upset price of 10s per acre."

"In 1863 another attempt was made to secure amended and comprehensive legislation, all existing Acts being repealed. The most striking features in the Act of 1863 were the appropriation of one quarter of all future receipts of the Land Fund for the construction of roads, bridges, and jetties, and the dim recognition of the importance of securing *bona fide* settlement on the land. Sections 56 to 59 contain a principle which was never brought into practical operation, but which over 20 years later has been revived as something new. These sections provided for the proclamation of "Agricultural Areas," into which roads were to be made, and the land surveyed into blocks not exceeding 160 acres each, with road frontage, to be let at a yearly rental of 1s per acre, subject to conditions of residence; a free grant to be issued after twenty years' rental and fulfilment of the conditions."

"In this Act 'Mineral Lands' for the first time find a place in the classification of the Crown, and surprise may be expressed at the late period in which the first recognition appears of the varied mineral resources of the Colony, gold deposits being first alluded to in Regulations passed in 1859, shortly after the discovery of the Mangana Gold-field. The Mineral Lands Regulations of 1863 actually gave a lessee power to purchase the fee simple of his lease, upon a valuation, after two years occupation."

The period between 1863 and 1870 was fruitful of land legislation, no less than five amending Acts having been passed, although none of the main principles were affected. In the latter year, however, a new measure, embodying and consolidating many of the salient features of the previous enactments, was carried. A new principle was then introduced, by which each adult male was permitted to select a maximum area of 320 acres, upon a condition of residence until the payment of the last instalment of the purchase money, of 1s per acre, and the issue of the grant deed. Another and perhaps the most important feature of this Act was an extension of the principle of the Act of 1893, in the direction of devoting a portion of the purchase money derived from sales to the construction of roads and bridges, etc., by increasing the proportion so allotted to one half. As soon as 500 acres, in not less than 10 lots, had been taken up in one locality, a sum equal to 10s per acre was immediately available for the purpose of opening up the land. This wise precaution against the squandering of the revenue from land upon purposes which could have no legitimate claim upon it, is still in force, and has enabled the Colony to provide its settlers with an excellent and constantly improving means of communication, and practical experience has only made the principle more acceptable than ever.

The system which was thus amended in 1870 has been but slightly altered since, and it may be of interest to state here some of its minor details. The necessary power was given to the Governor to reserve such land as he might deem necessary for public purposes, and the lands not so reserved were divided into (a) town, (b) agricultural, and (c) pastoral lands. The first class comprised all the lands within the towns and villages; the second class included the lands which might be from time to time proclaimed as agricultural areas, or as suitable for agricultural purposes; and the third class applied to land which was deemed to be better adapted for grazing than tillage. The upset price of agricultural lands was fixed at £1 per acre; that for pastoral lands being a sum equivalent to twelve years' rental, but not less than 5s per acre.

As previously stated, any adult male might select and purchase upon private contract from the commissioners appointed by the Government an area of agricultural land not exceeding 320 acres. When selected, it was to be surveyed by the Commissioners at the applicant's expense. The conditions attaching to the purchase were that the selector, his tenant, or servant, should within one year after the date of selection, reside upon the land until the full purchase money had been paid. This could either be effected by payment outright, or upon credit. If purchased for cash, a deposit of one-fifth had to be made at the time of sale and the residue within one month. If obtained upon credit, the purchaser had to pay an additional sum of 6s 8d, (or one third extra) per acre. The latter conditions applied to all purchases of land exceeding in value £15. The method of payment is illustrated by the following supposititious purchase of 100 acres, which shows the total cost to the selector.—

	£	s	d
100 acres, at 20s per acre,	100	0	0
Add one-third for credit,	33	6	8
	£133	6	8
First payment, Survey fee.	£8	15	0
Cash deposit,	3	6	8
Two yearly deposits of £5,	10	0	0
Twelve yearly deposits of £10,	120	0	0
Grant deed fee.		15	0
Fees to Recorder of Titles—			
Assurance fee, ¼d in the £ on £133 6 8 2s 10d			
Regulations 7 6		10	4
Total cost to purchaser, including cost of survey	£143	7	0

It will thus be seen that the actual payment, including interest for twelve years, and all costs of survey and issue of title, brought the cost to nearly 30s per acre. Provision was also made for the sale of lands by public auction after survey. The upset price in these cases was fixed by the Commissioners. As in the sales under other conditions, the areas of lots on agricultural lands were limited to 320 acres.

After an experience by the Colony of this policy for 20 years, during which very slight amendments were made, a further consolidating measure was carried through the legislature in 1890, which retained the main features of the system already described. One of the chief amendments then adopted classed all lands other than town lands as rural, but power was given to the Commissioners to grant leases for

14 years of unoccupied lands for pastoral purposes the rate to be fixed at auction. These leases are transferable by consent of the commissioners, on payment of a fee of 1s in the £ on the annual rental. A curious provision of the leases is that the lessee may only cultivate "so much of the runs as may be necessary for the use of his family and establishment, but not for the purpose of sale or barter." The leases are determinable if the land is required for sale or any public purpose, after six months' notice of the resumption has been given to the lessee, who becomes entitled to receive from the Crown compensation for the value of all fences, buildings, and other permanent improvements he may have made during the currency of the lease. The islands adjacent to the mainland, of which there are a great number, may be leased in the same manner.

Amongst the other provisions of the new measure, which retained the principle of selection *before* survey, was one which permitted selectors to make further selections, provided the total area taken up did not exceed 320 acres, and did not consist of more than three lots. It was also made compulsory that selectors, after one year from the date of purchasing should begin to effect improvements; and during the eight consecutive years thereafter, should expend in each year not less than 2s 6d per acre upon improvements. Failure to carry out this obligation entailed forfeiture of the selection, provided an amount had not already been spent over and above the sum required for previous years, sufficient to cover the requirements of the Act. The total amount required to be spent in improvements need not exceed £1 per acre. In the case of purchases made upon credit, the full amount of the purchase money may be paid at any time, and the title to the land obtained. No land may be transferred until paid for in full, except with the written consent of the Commissioners, and upon the payment of a transfer fee of threepence in the £ on the purchase money. Lands are conveyed to the purchasers after the whole of the purchase money has been paid, by grant deed, for which a fee of 15s is charged. Grants are issued in duplicate, and are enrolled and delivered to the Recorder of Titles, who registers and deals with them under the conditions of the Real Property Act.

The only other lands to be considered are those reserved for mining. All lands are, for a period of five years after purchase, liable to resumption for mining purposes, "upon payment to the owner of compensation for the value, other than that of gold or other minerals, of the lands and improvements so resumed." Mining areas may be declared reserved by the Governor to be sold by auction or selected, in areas of not less than one nor more than 10 acres, if situated within one mile of any town reserves, or not less than 10 nor more than 100 acres, if at a greater distance than one mile from the nearest boundary of any town reserve. Any lands within this category, whether selected or bought at auction, must be resided upon continuously by the purchaser or a member of his family for at least five years before a grant shall be issued for the land, or be liable to forfeiture. The lands selected or purchased within a Mining Area are open to any person to search or mine for gold or other mineral thereon; after written consent has been obtained from the Commissioners, and arrangements have been made for the payment of compensation. Upon cessation of the mining operations, the original selector or purchaser may resume possession, without compensation, for any buildings or other improvements.

These are in effect the terms upon which land of all classes may be obtained from the Crown. It cannot be gainsaid that they are both simple and liberal, and apparently the provisions made for obtaining the public lands are readily availed of. Yet the system has not brought about that adequate settlement of an agrarian population which might be anticipated. This is clearly indicated in the speech of the Minister of Lands already quoted. He says:—"While settlement has extended rapidly during the last quarter of a century, owing in a large measure to the opening up of the outlying districts by a liberal public works policy, it is undeniable that the increase of settlement and cultivation has not borne a satisfactory ratio to the large area of Crown Lands annually alienated. At the present time we stand in this position.—Out of a total area (exclusive of islands) of 15½ million acres, the State has parted with 4½ million acres, comprising the most fertile lands of the Colony. Of the remaining 11 million acres of the Crown estate, probably less than one fourth might be regarded as available for profitable selection. The important question now to be considered is the formulation of a scheme for conserving the agricultural Crown lands for the use of *bona fide* settlers, and disposing of the large area of inferior land upon terms that would enable the purchaser or lessee to turn it to profitable account and thereby make at present unproductive land a valuable asset of the Colony."

Available statistics do not show the number of selections made during any given period, as compared with the number of present holders of land. It is therefore impossible to say how far actual settlement on the land has progressed during recent years. But some interesting facts are deducible, which corroborate very strongly the statements of the Minister. The most significant of these is the great falling off in agricultural production during the last 30 years, as in the case of New South Wales, not only relatively but actually. Thus we find * that in 1860, with a total population of 87,775, there were 152,860 acres in crop in the Colony, while in 1891, with a population of 145,290, (or more than double), the acreage in crop had only increased to 157,376 acres. The following table, shows in what direction the yields have varied, making it evident that as an agricultural country proper, the Colony has steadily deteriorated.

Product		1860	1870	1880	1891
Wheat,	bushels	1,415,896	896,881	750,040	642,980
Oats,	,,	926,418	691,250	439,446	519,395
Barley,	,,	126,605	161,729	169,156	99,842
Potatoes,	tons	32,589	36,028	32,548	73,158
Turnips,	,,	5829	8,342	10,294	14,596
Hops,	pounds	——	785,977	644,273	432,630
Apples,	bushels	118,810	147,614	155,237	368,986
Pears,	,,	22,049	27,553	22,086	23,204

The great falling off evidenced in the growth of wheat has had the effect of placing the Colony in the position of having to import a considerable proportion of its own breadstuffs, the total so imported during the last ten years being no less than 1,624,930 wheat bushels. Indeed, while there was an excess of wheat grown in the Colony per head of the population of 1.48 in 1881-2, there was a deficiency in 1890-1 of 0.92 bushels. The immense loss to the Colony by this retrogression in its agricultural production is indicated by the fact that in 1859-60 the total value of the agricultural produce was £1,042,541, as against £962,751 in 1890-1.

Referring to this subject, the Government Statistician, Mr Johnston, remarks. — "These figures, however, only cover a portion of the farmer's industry in Tasmania; for, unlike the neighbouring Colonies, in the naturally open tracts of Australia, the Tasmanian farmer on the average, combines to a much greater extent the allied branches of stockbreeding and the dairy." At the same time, it must be pointed out, the total value of pastoral produce for the period stated, including milk, butter, and cheese, only increased from £811,654

* "Tasmanian Official Record" for 1892, by Mr. R. M. Johnston, F.L.S. Government Statistician of Tasmania.

to £1,414,505. The total production of all kinds,—agricultural and pastoral—only increased during this period from £1,854,654 to £2,377,256, which, taken together with the increase in the population, shows an actual decline per head of the population from £21.13 to £16.30. This means that roughly there has been proportionately a falling off in the production of the Colony of nearly one-fourth. The production of gold has fallen off from a value of £286,901 in 1881 to £87,114 in 1890, while the quantities of tin produced remain about the same. These are the two chief mineral products of the Colony, with the exception of silver, which during the last year or two has been found in some quantities, but not sufficient to compensate for the loss of gold.

The undoubted conclusion to be drawn from these figures is that, even allowing for a marked decrease in the value of produce, there is a smaller proportion of the population now being attracted to the soil than was the case 30 years ago. Thus we find that during 9 years prior to the end of 1889 some 14,000 selections of land were alienated. The inference to be drawn is that these 14,000 persons had become *additional* settlers upon the soil; but on reference to the census tables for 1891 it will be seen that the 4,695,000 acres of land then alienated were *cultivated* by only 21,686 males—a number very little larger than that in occupation the year previously. It is only fair to assume that a proportion of these were merely labourers working for a wage, and that others again were merely in the possession of the land as tenants. This seems to indicate that only a comparatively small proportion of the 14,000 selectors were genuine new selectors, and that a very considerable number were either representatives of or themselves already landed proprietors, desirous of increasing their estates.

It has at any rate been pretty clearly demonstrated that the land laws of the Colony have not brought about an adequate settlement of the people upon the soil. To what extent this is the fault of the system itself it is impossible to say. The terms upon which the land may be obtained are apparently very liberal, the climate is salubrious, and the soil is generally reputed to be good. Yet it is evidently being parted with in large quantities, without a commensurate return in the form of surplus produce for export, with which to increase the wealth of the country, or even sufficient to meet local necessities. It is officially stated by the Minister that the system of withdrawing mineral lands from sale,—rendered necessary by the fact that the right to all minerals is parted with after five years' alienation—"has entailed the locking up of agricultural land which, if disposed of in small lots to working men, would have given an impetus to cultivation and production. But it is hardly likely that this fact alone accounts for the decadence of the agricultural life of the Colony. It is probably due to several causes, of which one of the most important is some inherent defect in the system of land alienation in force. The weak spot may be the lack of sufficiently stringent residential rules as pointed out by the Minister. He says: "The enforcement before the issue of a grant deed, of either residence or improvement on all agricultural selections, is the only practical safeguard against a general system of land aggrandisement. . For instance, suitable areas might be withdrawn from selection, roads laid out, and a portion surveyed into agricultural lots and sold at auction; and as settlers took up their residences other portions could be laid off in a similar way."

Since these lines were written, it has been officially intimated that it is the intention of the present Government, with a view to inducing greater cultivation, to enforce more rigorously the compulsory improvement conditions as to land purchased on credit. But this action alone will hardly right matters.

CHAPTER V.

VICTORIA.

The history of the land systems of Victoria is intimately bound up with that of New South Wales. For the first fifteen years of its existence, indeed, colonisation was effected under circumstances almost identical with those of the contemporary period in the latter Colony, of which it was originally an integral part. It will be unnecessary, therefore, to repeat at length the early land regulations.

Victoria, then known as the Port Phillip district, was up to the year 1830 almost a *terra incognita*. It will be remembered,[*] that about this time the squatting movement began which resulted in large numbers of the free settlers spreading themselves beyond the "limits of settlement", over the rich inland plains, north, west, and south. Many of these crossed the Murray and Murrumbidgee Rivers, and took up stations, but as they were beyond the pale of Government cognisance there is no record as to when they first actually entered this part of the territory. Still it is certain that several occupied land within the boundaries of the province.

In 1804, an attempt had been made to form a penal settlement in Port Phillip Bay, and Colonel Collins, with a party of military and convicts, sailed from England and landed on its shores. But Collins selected an inhospitable part of the coast, and, after a half-hearted attempt at exploration of the Bay, on obtaining permission, he lost no time in shipping his party to Tasmania, which had just received its first settlers. A further effort at colonisation was made in 1826, when a small fortification was erected at Western Port by some convicts sent from Sydney, but this was abandoned two years later. About this time John Batman, a prominent Tasmanian who desired to settle at Western Port, was refused permission to do so by Governor Darling. The first actual colonist, so far as is known was Thomas Henty. In the same illegal manner as that adopted by the New South Wales squatters,—who had begun to cross the

[*] *Ante*, p. 13 *et seq.*

borders and take up land without authority—he entered the district by sea, and in 1832, in spite of the refusal of the Government to grant him recognition, he took possession of a tract of country near Portland Bay, and settled there with his sons. The success of Henty fired Batman to again prosecute his scheme, and as the representative of an Association which included a number of prominent Tasmanian settlers, he landed in Port Phillip at the mouth of the Yarra River in May, 1835. He was charmed with the country, and having with him certain Blacks from New South Wales, at once opened up communication with the natives of the locality, with the result that he obtained the signatures of a number of leading chiefs to a parchment document (prepared beforehand and executed in triplicate,) under which, in return for some blankets, knives, looking glasses, etc., and an annual tribute of similar articles, the natives agreed to "grant, enfeoff, and confirm" to him and his assigns a stretch of country embracing over half a million acres, and including the site of the present capital city, Melbourne.

This transaction the Imperial Government, refused to ratify, however, and in August of the same year, Sir Richard Bourke, Governor of New South Wales issued a proclamation stating that "Whereas it has been represented to me that divers of His Majesty's subjects have taken possession of lands of the Crown within the limits of New South Wales, under the pretence of a treaty, bargain, or contract, for the purchase thereof, with the aboriginal natives, it is notified that every such treaty, etc., is void as against the rights of the Crown, and that all persons found in possession, without proper license, will be considered as trespassers." But the Governor wrote to the Secretary of State pointing out that it was probable that the settlers would remain, and suggesting the imposition of reasonable conditions upon Batman and his associates in preference to their removal.

Bourke's counsels having prevailed, Batman's party were not immediately dispossessed, and other colonists from Tasmania followed closely on their heels. In September, 1836, Port Phillip was formally declared open for settlement under the same land regulations as those in force in New South Wales. It was made clear at the outset that prior occupation would confer no advantage, and that legal conveyance of land from the Crown was necessary, as "without such title the land (unless required for public purpose) will be subject to be put up for competition at a public sale, to be sold to the best bidder." Occupiers were cautioned against making any improvements, in the meantime, until they had obtained their title by grant or purchase from the Crown. On the first of June of the following year, town allotments in the city of Melbourne were first sold. The little community throve, and such glowing reports were received in Sydney of the quality of the soil and its capabilities, that "Australia Felix,"—as Sir Thomas Mitchell, the Surveyor-General called the district,— attracted great numbers of settlers.

Lord Glenelg, the Secretary of State for the Colonies, expressed approval of the action of the Governor of New South Wales in permitting occupation, but informed him that it was "essential that separate accounts should be kept of the sales of Crown Lands in the district of Port Phillip, and that the proceeds of such sales should be applied to the improvement of this new settlement, and especially in the introduction of free immigrants there, who would supply the demand for labour without the use of convicts." It may be mentioned, however, that in the early days of the Colony's existence, a considerable number of convicts were assigned to the free settlers in the same manner as in New South Wales.

It will be remembered that at the date of the first settlement of the Port Phillip district, the land system of Australia was directed by the first Land Act of 1831, and the regulations of Lord Ripon, issued in the same year.* In effect these laid down the principle that all lands were to be disposed of by auction at an upset price of five shillings per acre, with certain conditions as to payment of quit-rents etc. All free persons were eligible as purchasers, and there was to be no limitation as to the area they might obtain. At the outset, also, there was no distinction made between town and country lots, but subsequently the purchase of town lots was allowed only subject to security being given for the erection within two years of permanent buildings worth at last £20. It was under these conditions that the first land sales in Melbourne took place, the average price realised being £35 per lot of half an acre. In 1839, the minimum price of all lands was raised to 12s, and stood at that figure for nearly two years.

In 1840 a change was made. The "Colonial Land and Immigration Commissioners," who were appointed to consider the whole question of the upset price of land, reported in favour of the sale at a uniform price, to be fixed from time to time by the Home Government, of all lands situated outside the 19 settled districts of New South Wales. This system, which was adopted, and consequently applied to the Port Phillip

* *Ante*, p. 13.

district, was afterwards modified, to permit the continued sale by auction of town allotments. In the despatch from the Secretary of State on the subject, Governor Gipps—who combated the proposed sale at a uniform price most strenuously—was informed that the price for the Port Phillip district was to be £1 per acre; Lord John Russell, who then presided at the Colonial Office, also intimated that "all deeds of grant throughout the whole colony should henceforward convey to the purchaser everything below and above the surface." Thus was the prerogative of the Crown to minerals disposed of off-hand in a few words.

In order to give effect to these instructions, the Governor divided the Colony of New South Wales into three parts, the southern part or Port Phillip district covering an area which included the whole of Victoria, but extended further northwards than the present colony. But no sooner had the necessary regulations been framed and promulgated, than the Superintendent of the District (Mr. La Trobe) advised that no lands should be sold at the fixed price of £1 per acre within ten miles of either Melbourne or Geelong,—which by this time were thriving towns—but that within these areas the system of auction should be adhered to. Finally these representations prevailed, and Sir George Gipps, who had discretionary power as to the upset price, amended the regulations to this effect.

The population of the new settlement increased rapidly, and in 1840 there were no less than ten thousand persons within the district. In this year, consequent upon a proposal by Governor Gipps to appropriate the proceeds of the land sales within the district to the introduction of immigrants to the older parts of the colony—from which labour and capital had been drained as a result of the opening of Port Phillip—an agitation for separation from New South Wales was started, which did not cease until the desired end had been achieved a few years later.

In 1842 the system was again revised by Lord Stanley's Crown Lands Sales Act. In effect this measure provided for the sale of land by auction after survey and delineation upon public charts, at a minimum price of £1 per acre; and provision was made for one half of the gross proceeds from sales to be devoted to the immigration of persons into "any part of the entire colony, without reference to the territorial division in which the proceeds of sales" might accrue. The Governor was empowered to grant annual licenses for occupation for pastoral purposes, and in pursuance of this policy, the Port Phillip District was in 1843 divided into four squatting divisions, known as Gipps Land, the Murray, Western

Port, and Portland Bay districts. The Wimmera district was added in 1846.

Sir George Gipp's regulations, which were met by a remarkable outbreak of popular hostility, were passed in the following year. It is needless, however to say more of them here as they have already been described on a previous page.* Gipp's high-handed proceeding raised a perfect storm of opposition, which was nowhere more strongly manifested than in the Port Phillip district, the Parliamentary representatives of which were amongst the fiercest in denunciation of the Governor's action. The Land and Immigration Commissioners to whom the matter was referred, recommended that in place of annual licenses leases for eight years should be granted to the squatters. This arrangement was likely to work most injuriously in the Port Phillip district, where the rich, well-watered country, situated quite close to the towns, would have been locked up from settlement, and Mr. La Trobe, the Superintendent, combated the proposal.

Eventually, despite the antagonism of both Governor Gipps and La Trobe, the squatters gained the day, and the Waste Lands Act of 1846, with the famous Orders-in-Council of 1847, became the law of the Land.† These divided the country into settled, intermediate, and unsettled districts, and provided that the squatters might obtain annual licenses of land within the settled districts, without a right of purchase, and that they could obtain leases of land within the intermediate districts, for eight years, and within the settled districts for 14 years, with a pre-emptive right of any portion of their runs during the term of lease, the public being meanwhile debarred from purchase. So far as the Port Phillip district was concerned, lands within 20 miles of Melbourne, 15 of Geelong, and 10 of Portland, Alberton, Belfast, and Warrnambool, were declared to be settled districts; those within the sole existing counties of Bourke, Grant, and Normanby, (not included in the settled districts) were classified as intermediate; and the remainder as unsettled. The bulk of the colony was thus thrown open to the squatters.

The Superintendent appears to have at once appreciated the significance of the new legislation, in its relation to his district. He saw that, allowing for the natural influx of population, the areas reserved were far too small for the purposes of settlement, and he fought hard for authority to act for what he conceived to be the general interests of the colony as opposed to the personal interests of the squatters. To do this effectually he directed much of the attention of the

* *Ante* p. 18.
† *Ante* p. 22.

surveyors to the setting apart of reserves for the purposes of settlement instead of to laying off leaseholds, which action was the cause of great conflict between himself and the squatters. The Orders-in-Council, provided "that nothing in these regulations or in any lease to be granted under the powers hereby vested in the governor shall prevent the said governor . . . . from making grants or sales of any lands within the limits of the run or lands comprised in such lease for public purposes, or disposing of in such other manner as for the public interest may seem best such lands as may be required, for . . . any other purpose of public defence, safety, utility, convenience, or enjoyment, or for otherwise facilitating the improvement and settlement of the colony." To a layman it would appear that such powers were there given as to permit of the reservation of such lands as might be required for the public settlement; but the law advisers of the Crown held that "the Governor, when convinced of an absolute necessity, would be justified in selling or reserving for immediate sale such portions of the lands; . . . . but we are of opinion that it would not be in accordance with the correct interpretation of this section, nor within the spirit of the Orders-in-Council, were the governor, without reference to . . . . pressing public requirements, to reserve from sale portions of lands in these districts, with a view of meeting the *prospective wants* of the community." The Governor through the Superintendent continued, however, to make the reservations necessary in his opinion to provide for future settlement.

In 1851 the Port Phillip district was formally severed from New South Wales, and converted into a separate colony under the name of Victoria." From this date may be said to commence the real history of its land systems. At the time of its incorporation into a Colony, nearly 400,000 acres of its total area of $52\frac{1}{4}$ million acres had been alienated, and a sum of £776,000 had been received as payment. The population was then about 77,000, of whom 66,000 were resident within the settled districts. It was evident that the area available within the settled districts was inadequate to meet the immediate requirements of the colony, and though about 680,000 acres had been reserved, this constituted but a very small area of the country suitable for cultivation.

At this period the gold discoveries caused a great convulsion of previous conditions. The influx of population was tremendous, and the Executive received strong support from the mass of the people in its endeavour to set apart lands for settlement. Such was the rush of work in other ways for the surveyors that they still made but little advance in the direction of laying out leasehold areas for the squatters. The latter strenuously demanded the fulfilment of the conditions contained in the Orders-in-Council, but a strong popular party opposed them, and when the new Legislative Council met, the question became a burning one. After a warm controversy, the Lieut-Governor, at the request of a majority, agreed to refrain from action in the matter of the leases, pending reference to the Imperial authorities; but he intimated that the lessees might in the meantime purchase under pre-emptive right their homesteads or other limited portions of their runs.

The question of the position of the squatters subsequently formed the subject of lengthy despatches between the Lieut-Governor and the Secretary of State. The latter eventually, after a delay of some two years advised that if the squatters were desirous of binding the Government to its pledges and insisted upon their full rights, these should be conceded within the strict letter of the law, which empowered the Governor to determine the length of the leases, and to exercise discretion as to whether land should be sold under pre-emptive right. The inference to be drawn from his words was that the law was to be evaded if the squatters were too importunate, and as little as possible was to be conceded. This was the last direct *action* taken by the Imperial authorities with respect to Victorian land matters.

Owing to tho non-committal policy of the Home Government, the matter still remained as before, and in November, 1854, a Royal Commission was appointed to enquire into the whole subject of the "Tenure of the Waste Lands of the Crown," their report formed a ponderous analysis of the general question of the occupation and alienation of the public estate. The Commissioners recommended the continuous survey and sale of Crown Lands with a view to the requirements of all classes, and in quantities sufficient to prevent the upset price of £1 being greatly exceeded; that renewable yearly licenses should be given to pastoral occupants, rentals to be based on the carrying capacity of the land at the rate of 6*d* for every sheep, 4*s* for every head of cattle, and 10*s* for every horse, and to be subjected to periodical revision, but with a minimum limit of 1*d* per acre; and that the existing territorial classification should be abandoned. Neither of the interested parties represented on the commission approved of these proposals, and the report was signed by seven of the eleven members under protest, while one declined to sign at all. No attempt was made at this time to give effect to the recommendations of the report, and the solution of the difficulty created by the

Orders-in-Council of 1847 was left as a baneful legacy to the legislature provided under the Constitution Act which gave the Colony responsible government.

The new Parliament was elected in 1856, at which date there were in existence over 1000 distinct runs in the colony upon which grazed upwards of five million sheep, and about 600,000 head of cattle, while the license fees totalled some £60,000 annually irrespective of the amounts received from the assessments on stock. The population as a result of the gold discoveries had increased to 319,000 persons.

Under the new constitution the legislature had power to control the waste lands of the Crown, and deal with all royalties, mines, and minerals. It had authority to repeal the Orders-in-Council of 1847, but until other legislation should be passed these were to have the force of law. There was no proviso guaranteeing vested or other rights which might have accrued under these Orders, and but little consideration was given to them. "Land was put up for sale, licensed occupants secured it for themselves at the upset price, or employed a low class of brokers to bid for them. The brokers levied blackmail by threatening to oppose the pastoral tenant if he should decline their services. They arranged with one another so that they might defraud the revenue by stifling competition. The Survey Office and the public were aware of the process, but it went rapidly on, and land was sold in blocks at £1 an acre which, judiciously placed on the market, would have sold at from £1 to £6." *

This was the state of affairs when the first Parliament was elected. In its opening session an attempt was made to deal with the question. The government proposed by resolution that the occupants of pastoral lands should receive leases on such terms as would result in the payment by them of an average rent per acre of 2d, and that no other persons should obtain leases unless after competition by auction. But the motion was not passed, an amendment being carried to the effect that leases should not be issued, and that the occupants should pay to use the lands by annual licenses at the rate proposed. In 1857 a Bill was introduced to give effect to the principles embodied in this amendment. But in the interim a great change had come over public feeling, a strong antipathy to the squatters having manifested itself. A Land League was formed to oppose the Bill, and a convention of delegates—met in Melbourne to discuss the subject while Parliament was sitting.

---

* Rusden's "History of Australia," 1883, vol III, p. 119.

The Bill was carried by the Legislative Assembly, but only to be hung up by the Legislative Council, in which the squatters were largely represented, in whose interests therefore it was supposed mainly to have been framed.

The first actual legislation of the new Parliament upon the subject was passed four years after its election, in 1890, when Mr James Service, was at the head of the Lands Department. The measure he carried, after making provision for special reserves for mineral purposes, etc., divided the Crown Lands into "country" and special classes. The former were available, after survey by the Government, for selection in allotments of from 40 to 640 acres, which were separated into equal divisions. Applications for these blocks, had to be accompanied by a deposit of £1 per acre, and in the event of simultaneous application by two or more selectors, the land was put up to auction, the bidding being limited to these persons. The successful applicant had the option of paying for one half the allotment in cash, or taking the whole upon the same conditions; but if he took only one half he might rent the other half for a term specified at the time of proclamation, at one shilling per acre per annum, with the right to purchase at any time during his term. No selector might obtain more than 640 acres in one year. The land was to be declared open for selection in districts, and when one-fourth of the lands proclaimed as being open had been selected, the purchasers could use the remainder jointly for depasturing purposes as a "farmer's common" "Special lands," situated near to towns, villages, railways, rivers. etc., were sold quarterly by auction, at a minimum price of £1 per acre, which could be raised by the Governor at discretion. This enactment was the cause of dissensions in the Cabinet of the day, and, the ministry resigned before an accompanying measure to deal with the "Occupation of Crown Lands for Pastoral Purposes" could be passed.

In 1861 the Minister in charge notified a proposal under which, in supposed conformity with the Act just referred to, it was possible to grant licenses for the "occupation of agricultural waste lands of the Crown for purposes of settlement or cultivation." These regulations were held by the Legislative Council to be *ultra vires*, and subsequently the Assembly took the same view, with the result that the Government went to the country on the subject, and were successful. It was in this year that in New South Wales Sir John Robertson's Act, providing for selection before survey, became law, and an agitation was at once initiated for the adoption of a similar scheme in Victoria. The Minister of Lands, Mr (now Sir Charles Gavan) Duffy, warmly took up the proposal, which he embodied in a Bil that passed both Houses in 1862, and was afterwards generally known as "Duffy's Act."

This measure provided for the setting apart of ten million acres of land, to be proclaimed in agricultural areas, of which four million acres should be opened within three months of the passing of the Act, while thereafter two millions of acres were always to be available for settlement. The competitive clauses of the Act of 1860 gave way to a provision under which the exclusive right of purchase was given to the first selector, and the minimum area of the allotments was reduced to 40 acres. Otherwise the methods previously adopted were adhered to, except that the term for which a lease of one moiety of an allotment might be granted, upon the purchase of the other, was fixed at 8 years, while the rent per acre was raised to 2/6. A new principle was now, however, for the first time introduced into the land legislation of the colony. Alternative conditions, at the option of the selector, were imposed, as follows, upon all purchasers—(1). The selectors had to enclose their holdings with a substantial fence, or (2) place a habitable dwelling on the land, or (3). cultivate one acre out of every ten taken up. In the event of more applications than one being received simultaneously, the successful applicant was agreed upon by lot instead of as formerly by competition. All lands not in the agricultural reserve were open for sale by public auction, at an upset price of £1 per acre.

A new method was likewise introduced by the Act for the regulation of the occupation of pastoral lands. The former system of license fees and assessments on stock was abolished, and provision was made for the payment of rent for runs according to their value, which was based on their carrying capacity computed at the rate of eightpence per annum per sheep, and two shillings per head of cattle. No license was in future to protect any run from sale, or proclamation as a common, and all runs were to be confined to areas capable of carrying not more than 5000 sheep, nor more than 1250 head of cattle. Licensees were to be debarred from cultivating more land than was sufficient to meet their own domestic requirements. The Act likewise set apart one-fourth of the total land fund for the purpose of assisting immigration from the United Kingdom.

The principle of selection before survey, thus brought into practice on lines very similar to those in force in New South Wales, effected the same inevitable results—viz., a mad scramble ofr the soil, conflict between pastoralists and selectors, public and private immorality, the taking up of land for speculation rather than cultivation, and the aggregation of large estates. In a very short time "dummying" and other obnoxious methods were in full swing, and large properties were built up with incredible rapidity. In 1885 an amending Act was passed restricting the power of the Government in the matter of throwing open lands for selection in agricultural areas which had previously been surveyed. Leases were to be granted for seven years, at a rental of 2*s* per acre, per annum, personal residence for three years being made a necessity. In addition, the lessee had within two years to effect improvements to the value of 20*s* per acre. At the end of three years he might purchase the fee simple by paying a sum of 14*s* per acre—making the total money paid 20*s*—or he might require the Government to put up his land at auction, at a reserve of £1 per acre, plus the value of his improvements, and to have the latter repaid to him out of the purchase money. A novel feature was contained in one provision of the Act relating to the occupation of unsurveyed land near to goldfields. Persons might obtain licenses to occupy such lands in blocks, of 20 acres, to an aggregate extent of 160 acres by each individual, upon conditions of residence and the cultivation, of one-fifth of the area. The provision was intended originally to apply only to land adjacent to goldfields, but it was by regulation afterwards extended in its application to land within a radius of 30 miles of goldfields.

The next legislation on the subject took place in 1869, but as the period intervening since the passing of the Act of 1860 forms a distinct epoch in the history of Victorian settlement, it may be well at this stage to review the results of preceding enactments. Up to 1860 cultivation had not proceeded at all proportionately to the rate of alienation of the land, as at that date only seven-tenths of an acre had been cultivated per head of the population. But the people had hardly settled down yet, after the gold fever, and were still in a transition stage. The Act of 1860 did not, however, tend to greatly increase the cultivation, but it resulted in the alienation of over a million acres in two years. This land comprised 65 parishes, of which 42 were classed as agricultural. Under the Act of 1862, there was still more rapid expropriation of the public estate, 1,888,000 acres being disposed of in three years, consisting of 230 parishes, of which 48 were agricultural, 64 grazing, and the balance partly grazing and partly agricultural. The Act of 1865, resulted in the foundation being laid of numbers of large estates, and in four years 3,526,000 acres passed into private hands. At the end of this period the cultivated area in the colony averaged one and one-fifth acre per head of the population, and "it might be supposed that the increased area under cultivation was owing to the alienation of more land. Such was not the case. The land taken up under these Acts did not come under cultivation to any appreciable extent. It was the land sold before 1860 that principally contributed to the increased area under cultivation . There was certainly a large amount of settlement under the occupation licenses; there was less trafficking in the land taken up under these licenses than in other selections, and a considerable number of the occupation licenses are still in occupation of their land." *

The Act of 1869, which consolidated and amended all previous legislation, retained the system of selection before survey, as applied to all unoccupied lands of the Crown. The selected area, which was limited to 320 acres, was at the outset to be held under license for a period of 3 years, during the first $2\frac{1}{2}$ of which the selector had to reside upon the land, fence it, cultivate every year one acre out of every ten, and generally effect improvements to the value of 20s per acre. During this period rent at the rate of 2s per acre per annum had to be paid half-yearly in advance. At the end of the term, if the selector could obtain a certificate from the Board of Land and Works that he had complied with these conditions, he might purchase the land right out at the rate of 20s per acre, towards which the rent of 6s per acre previously paid, was credited; or he might obtain a further lease of the land for a period of seven years, at a rent of 2s per annum. This sum was also credited to him as payment in part of the fee simple, which could be obtained at any time during the term of the lease, on the payment of the balance of the full sum of 20s per acre. No person might select who had already selected under previous Acts. The Governor-in-Council was authorised to dispose of not more than 200,000 acres per annum, by auction for cash, at an upset price to be fixed, not lower than 20s per acre. The proceeds from these sales were to be devoted to railway construction.

Under this Act pastoral lands could be occupied under two methods—either as "runs," under license or lease, or under "grazing rights." The runs were to consist of those already in occupation, when the Act came into operation, termed "existing runs," and those created since that date, which were defined as "new runs." The former class, which

---

* Speech of the Minister for Lands, Victorian "Hansard," July, 9th 1884, page 497.

comprised the great bulk of the pastoral country, and were of unlimited areas, were held under the same tenure as formerly—annual license. The "new" runs, which were few in number, were occupied under lease for periods of 14 years, at auction, and were limited to such an area as would carry 4000 sheep or 1000 head of cattle. The lessees were entitled to the pre-emption of 320 acres as a homestead, upon payment at the rate of £1 an acre, without conditions as to improvements, residence, etc. The annual rental for both classes of runs was fixed according to the estimated carrying capacity of the land, on the basis of 1s for every sheep and 5s for every head of cattle. The Governor-in-Council was also authorised to issue a license described as a grazing right, which authorised the holder to depasture live stock upon any park lands, reserves, or other Crown Lands, not forming part of any run or common. The unoccupied lands were mostly subdivided and taken up for grazing under these licenses.

This Act remained in operation without alteration till 1878, during which period between 10 and 11 millions of acres were disposed of. In 1878 the conditions of selection were greatly restricted, and the immediate effect was to cause a considerable falling off in the areas taken up. The original conditions under which land for agriculture could be secured were retained, but with the important modification that the period during which land had to be held on license before the fee simple could be obtained was increased from 3 to 6 years, residence being made compulsory for a period of five years. But to tempt people to select for purposes of actual cultivation, the annual rental was reduced from 2s to 1s per acre, per annum, and the payment of the sum of £1 per acre required to obtain the fee simple was extended over 20 years instead of 10 as formerly. Non-residential selections were also permitted by this Act, under more restricted conditions than for residential selections, but the non-residential selections were confined to an area not exceeding 200,000 acres in one year.

The Act of 1878, like that of 1869, ceased by effluxion of time in 1884, but in 1883, previous to its expiration a measure known as the "Mallee Pastoral Leases Act" was passed. This enactment, which, with amendments made in 1885 and 1890, is still in force, deals with what is known as the Mallee country, a tract of about 11½ million acres, situated in the north-western portion of the colony. This large area, which was more or less covered with Mallee scrub—an indigenous shrub or stunted tree—and great numbers of rabbits, is separated into two main divisions, known as the "Mallee country" and the "Mallee Border." The latter is parcelled out into areas not exceeding 20,000 acres, which are described as Mallee allotments. These may be leased at an annual rental of from 10*s* to 40*s* per square mile for terms expiring not later than December, 1903. The lessees have the pre-emptive right to purchase 320 acres of their leasehold, under the ordinary conditions of selection. The "Mallee country" is divided into "Mallee blocks." These blocks are each sub-divided into two parts, for either of which (at the option of the selector) a lease may be obtained at auction for any term of years, not exceeding twenty; while the lessee is bound to occupy the other sub-division for five years, under license. Rent for the leased portion of the blocks is charged at the rate of 2*d* for each sheep or 1*s* for each head of cattle depastured during the first five years of the term ; 4*d* for each sheep and 3*s* for each head of cattle during the remainder of the term. For the unleased portion of the blocks the rent is to be paid at the same rate as for the leased portion for the first five years of the term, but it must not be less than 2*s* 6*d* per square mile. No portion of the blocks can be acquired in fee simple. The main conditions for both Mallee allotments and Mallee blocks and for the licenses for the latter are that the lessee shall destroy all vermin such as native dogs, rabbits, etc., during the first three years of his term and keep in good repair all improvements on the land during the whole of his lease, at the end of which all improvements revert to the Crown. The legislation dealing with the Mallee country has had the effect of settling a considerable population in the Mallee districts, which were previously very sparsely occupied, and greatly over-run with rabbits.

The whole system of land occupation and alienation except so far as regards Mallee lands, was altered by the Act of 1884, which was rendered necessary by the desuetude, through effluxion of time, of the Acts of 1869 and 1878. This measure was amended to some extent by subsequent legislation in 1890 and 1891, and these three enactments, which mainly govern the existing system, are so interwoven, that it may be well to consider them together. The principal new features of these Acts consist of a restriction of the alienation of land by public auction and the substitution for the previous method of selection of a system of leasing lands within certain defined areas, with the right of purchase, under deferred-payment, of a portion of the leasehold area. Classification on a systematic basis was this time first attempted, and the public estate, apart from the Mallee country, was divided into the following—Pastoral lands;

lands which may be sold by public auction; auriferous lands; swamp lands; State forest reserves; timber reserves; and water reserves. The areas of the lands in the different classes were shown on maps sealed with the seal of the Board of Land and Works, and deposited with the Clerk of Parliament. No lands may be disposed of in any other manner than that described for their particular class in the Land Acts, but the Governor may by proclamation alter the boundaries of any of the areas except those which are to be sold by auction. From the first of August, 1890, all land must be sold, leased, or licensed with the proviso that it may only be used below the surface to such a depth as the Governor-in-Council may direct.

The pastoral lands of the Colony are now leased in "pastoral allotments," which it was stipulated by the Act of 1884 should be of an area capable of carrying from 1000 to 4000 sheep, or from 150 to 500 head of cattle; but which by the Act of 1891 may now be varied in size from 7500 acres to 40,000 acres. No person may hold more than one of these allotments. The lease may be for any period not exceeding 14 years, at the end of which period the land reverts to the Crown, and the incoming tenant pays to the retiring lessee a sum equal to the price paid by the latter for the improvements he has effected, which are calculated to increase the carrying capacity of the land, up to 2/6 per acre. The annual rent, which is payable half-yearly in advance, is based upon the carrying capacity of the land, at the rate of 1s per annum for every sheep, and 5s for every head of cattle, reckoning not more than 10 acres to one sheep, or 50 acres to one head of cattle. All vermin must be destroyed during the first three years of occupation, and all buildings and improvements must be kept in good repair during the currency of the lease, while no timber may be cut except under special authority. At the termination of a lease, it may be again granted to the first applicant, after it has been declared available, and if there be more applications than one lodged on any one day before the hour of one o'clock, the right to the lease is put up to auction. No lands forming part of a leasehold may be alienated during the currency of a lease, except to the lessee, who, after the fulfilment of the conditions of his lease, may select for purchase 320 acres of his allotment, as a homestead at £1 per acre. No lessee may assign or transfer his lease, without departmental consent in writing, upon pain of forfeiture.

Agricultural and grazing lands may be obtained on lease by any person above the age of 18 years, in "grazing areas,"—which may not exceed 1000 acres—for periods not longer than 14 years. The rental is fixed by valuers, but it must not be less than 2*d* nor more than 4*d* per acre per annum, plus five per cent on the capital value of the improvements on the ground at the commencement of the lease. At the end of the term, as in the case of pastoral lands, the land absolutely reverts to the Crown, but the outgoing lessee is to be paid by the incoming lessee the value of all fences, wells, reservoirs, tanks, and dams, constructed by him, up to the value of 10*s* per acre. The conditions of the lease are the same as for pastoral lands, and residence is not compulsory except the lessee select a portion of his holding as hereafter described.

If a lessee is desirous of securing a portion of his grazing area as a freehold, he may select any portion of it, not exceeding 320 acres, as an "agricultural allotment." This allotment is separated from the grazing area leasehold, and an agricultural allotment license is granted for six years, during five of which the licensee is compelled to reside upon the land. He must also fence it, generally effect improvements to the value of 20*s* per acre, and cultivate 1 acre in ten during each year, The rent during this period is 1*s* per acre, but if at the end of 6 years the licensee can obtain from the Board of Lands and Works, a certificate to the effect that he has carried out the conditions stipulated, this amount is credited to him as part payment for the fee simple. He may then pay outright a sum of 14*s* per acre, and secure the fee simple, or he may obtain a lease of the allotment for a further period of 14 years, at an annual rental of 1*s*, due payment of which for the whole of the term entitles him at its conclusion to obtain a grant in fee. The freehold may be obtained at any time, however, upon the payment of the balance of 20*s* still due after deducting the rent paid. Licenses for agricultural allotments may also be applied for direct, without the necessity for obtaining grazing area leases, where they do not exceed 320 acres in area, and non-residence allotments may be obtained upon condition that a rent of 2*s* per acre is paid, while subsequent payments of 2*s* per annum are necessary to obtain a 14 years' lease, and the total purchase money for the freehold is 40*s* per acre. Improvements to the value of 40*s* per acre have also to be made, of which one half must be effected during the first three years of the term of the license. The area for which such licenses may be granted in any one year is limited to 50,000 acres. No licenses are transferable, but to enable licensees or lessees of agricultural allotments to obtain a Crown grant of part of an allotment for the purposes of a hop garden, orchard, vineyard, etc., it is provided that they may at any time upon payment of the balance of the money due, after deducting the rent paid, obtain the fee simple of an area not exceeding 20 acres. Persons are permitted to borrow money upon the security of their holdings. At the expiration of two years from the date of a license, any licensee may give to any person from whom he receives an advance of money a "license lien" over his improvements to the extent of one-half their value. These liens are registered in the Crown Lands office, and have the force of a mortgage when the grant in fee is issued. It is stipulated that married women may obtain pastoral leases or grazing area leases, but they cannot select agricultural allotments. Two or more grazing areas may be taken up by one person, provided their total area does not exceed 1000 acres, and more than one agricultural allotment may be held, provided the total area selected does not exceed 320 acres.

Auriferous lands, not situated within a city, town, or borough, and not required for mining purposes, may be occupied under annual license for residence or cultivation, in areas not exceeding 20 acres. Blocks not exceeding 1000 acres may also be occupied for pastoral purposes only, for terms of seven years or less, under licenses renewable annually at the option of the licensee and terminating not later than December 29th, 1898. The rent is fixed by appraisement according to the quality of the land. No such lands may be alienated except those which have been declared to be "worked out," and these have first to be let by license for periods of seven years, for residence, business, or cultivation, in blocks not exceeding 5 acres each. If at the expiration of the term of the license, its conditions have been complied with, and the purchase money (less amounts paid as rent) be forthcoming, a Crown grant may be issued.

Other lands which must be specially defined, may be sold by auction at a minimum upset price of £1 per acre, to the extent of 100,000 acres per annum. The proceeds from these sales are paid into "The Railway Construction Account," "for the purpose of making provision for the construction of any railways which may be hereafter authorised by any Act of Parliament." Provision is also made for the occupation of swamp land, forest reserves, and water reserves,

Such are the conditions under which the public lands of the colony are now being occupied or disposed of. It will be observed that there is no provision for the formation of village settlements or working men's blocks, as in some other colonies, but the matter has been receiving considerable public attention during the last year or two, and in

1892 a Bill passed the Legislative Assembly with respect to the matter which was afterwards thrown out in the Legislative Council. At the time of writing (July, 1893) a second Bill has just been introduced by the present Government, which permits the establishment of village communities, homestead associations, and labour colonies. It is proposed that land for village communities shall be set apart in allotments of from 1 to 20 acres, which may be occupied for a period of three years at a nominal rents, on a condition of residence. Leases may then be granted for 20 years, at a rental of 1/- per acre, (unless the land is of special value) payable half-yearly in advance, and at the expiration of the term the fee simple may be obtained upon fulfilment of conditions similar to those now in force with respect to agricultural allotments. The clauses relating to homestead associations provide that blocks not exceeding 2000 acres may be set apart for the purposes of Associations of not less than six persons who may wish to settle on Crown Lands adjacent to each other, of whom no one is to obtain more than 50 acres in addition to a township allotment. The leases are to be for 20 years, and the rental is to be arranged between the Board of Lands and Works and the association; but it must be not less than 5 per cent on a capital value of £1 per acre. Similar conditions to those regarding village communities are imposed upon the individual purchasers. Adjoining every homestead association block there is proposed to be a township site, and every lessee of a homestead section shall be entitled to the lease of a township allotment, which shall accompany and be transferred with his main lease. No selector under previous Acts or the possessor of a freehold exceeding two acres in area may come under either of these schemes. It is also proposed that sums not exceeding £10 may be advanced during the first two or three years of their leases to leaseholders under either scheme, to be devoted to building upon and improving their holdings. Not more than £20,000 shall be so advanced in one year, and the money must be repaid in 20 equal annual instalments. The Governor is permitted under the third part of the Bill to set apart areas of 1500 acres which shall be vested in five trustees, who are to establish, maintain and manage labour colonies thereon. A subsidy will be granted by the government to the extent of £2 for every £1 contributed by public or private subscriptions towards the funds of the colonies. The trustees are to use the funds in paying allowances for work to persons employed on the colonies; for the erection of buildings and the purchase of implements, and generally carrying on the settlements.

In arriving at an estimate of the result of the various systems which have been in force in Victoria from time to time, and especially with respect to that which is still in operation, the fact must be borne in mind that the colony has been settled under conditions differing from those which have prevailed elsewhere. Its area is less by far than that of any of the other continental colonies. Its chief seaport and market is centrally situated and as a rule, within easy distance of the people on the land, and its population is generally very much more dense than is the case with any of the other provinces. These conditions have been contributed to by two factors—the gold discoveries, and the suitableness of much of the soil for cultivation. The former brought immense numbers of people to the colony, and the latter has kept them there. It is not surprising, therefore, that of late years, at any rate, Victoria has become essentially an agricultural community; but this fact is also probably due in part to the fiscal policy of the Colony, which has been (by means of heavy import duties on cereals) to protect the agricultural industry, and prevent foreign competition.

These circumstances combined have helped to attract the rural population more largely to agriculture than has been the case elsewhere, except in South Australia, and it is difficult in consequence to ascertain what influence has been exercised by the land laws alone in this direction. A glance at the statistics of the Colony * shows hat during a period of 40 years the area under cultivation has increased more than proportionately with the increase of population, and that the province, instead of as formerly, having to import large quantities of bread-stuffs, has become the greatest wheat exporter of the Australian group. As the population was settling down after the partial falling-off in the gold yields in the fifties, the most reliable statistics for the purpose of comparison are those between the years 1861 and 1891, as far as they are available. In the former year, with a population in the colony of 541,800 persons, there were about $4\frac{1}{4}$ million acres of land which had been alienated, of which only 179,983 acres were in cultivation. The produce from the soil was insufficient for the requirements of the population, and 1,867,024 bushels of bread-stuffs were imported. In 1891 the population had increased to 1,157,678 persons, and a total area of $22\frac{1}{2}$ million acres had been alienated or was then in process of alienation, of which 2,687,575 acres were under cultivation. During the same year, instead of importing bread-stuffs the colony

* Hayter's "Victorian Year Book", 1892. Government Printer, Melbourne.

exported no less than 6,906,496 bushels of wheat, flour, etc.

The following table shows the increase of population, the areas under cultivation, and the relative positions of the imports and exports of bread-stuffs together with the export of wool, during each quinquennial year between 1861 and 1891—

Year	Population	Crown Lands in cultivation	Bread-stuffs		Wool Exported
			Imports	Exports	
1861	541,800	439,895	1,867,024	344,507	23,923,195
1866	636,982	592,915	1,997,518	242,819	42,391,234
1871	747,412	937,220	1,295,015	115,432	76,334,480
1876	801,717	1,231,105	355,704	96,773	106,265,877
1881	879,886	1,821,719	157,234	4,050,308	103,449,080
1886	1,000,510	2,417,582	225,489	2,452,396	107,984,839
1891	1,157,678	2,687,575	379,769	6,906,496	164,805,907

These figures show that while the population has rather more than doubled within the period, the area of land under cultivations has increased sixfold; the production of bread-stuffs, in which there was a deficiency in 1861 showed a great surplus in 1891; and the production of wool has increased more than seven times in quantity. As previously stated the extent of land alienated or being disposed of under deferred payments was about 22¼ millions of acres in 1891, while the total area alienated in 1861 was about 4½ millions. A comparison of these figures with the table shows that proportionately to the area alienated there was also a greater area under cultivation in 1891 than in 1861. Whatever else may be said on the subject therefore, it is evident that an increased use is being made of the soil in the colony both from an agricultural and pastoral point of view.

It is curious, however, that despite the fact that the increase of production is greater than the increase of population, the latter is rapidly becoming urban rather than rural. The following table, showing how the population was located in the years 1881 and 1891 is most significant in this respect—

DISTRICTS.		Estimated area in square miles	Population in 1881		Population in 1891	
			Total	Proportn per cent	Total	Proportn per cent
Urban	metropolitan	256	291,464	32.73	491,942	42,49
	extra metropolitan (other towns)	376	198,839	22,33	194,084	16,76
		632	490,303	55,06	686,026	59,25
Extra urban or rural		87,252	400,167	44,94	471,652	40.75
Total		87,884	890,470	100,00	1157,678	100,00

Thus, while the population has increased by nearly 270,000 in 10 years, only about 70,000 persons have been added to the rural population; the remainder having all congregated in the city of Melbourne. These facts alone are positively alarming in themselves, and the figures which indicate the occupations of the people for the years 1881 and 1891 are equally calculated to arrest attention. The primary producers, as they may be termed—those engaged in winning from the soil, such as agriculturists, pastoralists, miners,—have barely increased in numbers at all, there being a total for 1891 of 119,082 only, as against 117,712 in 1881. There is certainly an increase of 9700 persons engaged in agricultural pursuits, and of about 1700 persons engaged in pastoral pursuits, but these have been either taken from the miners, or the latter have adopted other pursuits.

·Unfortunately it is not possible to show from official statistics how the land is held in the colony, in the same manner as in some of the other colonies. The number of present landholders is not available, and the only means of estimating the manner in which the land is privately possessed is by a comparison of various sets of figures. The following table shows the number of approved selections made under deferred payment during each quinquennial period since 1870, and the areas taken up—

Year ending	Number of Selectors			Areas selected.
	For purposes of cultivation	For residence and cultivation near goldfields	Total	
1874	31,630	5160	36,790	4,501,968
1879	31,670	4666	36,336	5,797,717
1884	20,189	5356	25,545	3,771,026
1889	5,889	1085	6,974	1,059,800
1890-91*	1,127	—	1,127	198,538
Total	90,505	16,267	106,772	15,329,049

From these totals have to be deducted the number of forfeited selections, which are estimated to include an area of about 4 million acres, or about one-fourth of the total. This would still leave a total area alienated, or in process of alienation, by selection, of about 11 million odd acres, and the number of selectors at about 80,000. It is needless to say that these selections are not all now held by the original selectors, nor by other small holders, as evidenced by the fact that of 79,414 males engaged in agricultural persuits in 1891, only 35,447 were farmers, the remainder being comprised of sons, labourers, etc. It is safe to assume therefore, that only one-half, or probably only one-third of the original selections remain intact, and the remainder have gone to swell the areas of larger estates.

It is worthy of notice that since the Act of 1884 came into force, the number of selections has greatly diminished. This indicates that the land is now being taken up to a greater extent for purposes of actual cultivation, and that the stringent regulations as to residence, improvements, and cultivation have tended to check the wholesale alienation of the public estate merely for the purpose of building up large freehold properties. In this respect the system of leasing before selection has materially assisted. It was officially stated before the Act was passed that the best of the arable lands had been parted with, and the people were being driven into the hilly country, with the result that the choice spots in the valleys were being rapidly selected, and the more barren hillsides left untouched. The method of leasing and license combined has since resulted in many persons taking up portions of hills and valleys together, and in the two being profitably worked under a sytsem of mixed farming.

* Two years.

Victoria claims the distinction of having first instituted a land tax in Australia. The origin of this legislation is thus stated by Mr Rusden, in his "History of Australia" *—"The Act (that of 1860) had afforded facilities for acquiring land under false pretences, and plundering the State. There were honourable exceptions. The fraudulent may have been a minority, but . . . . by rich and poor, with the aid of the Government, the State was defrauded, . . . and it was contended that the only way to mete out justice was to pass a "progressive land tax," starting at a high point, and rising by leaps and bounds, in a manner which would make lucrative tenure of large estates impossible. The adopted phrase was that it was necessary to "burst up large estates." . . . An Education Act passed in 1862 had created a deficit. It had raised the cost of education to the State from an annual average far below £200,000 to one exceeding half a million sterling, and its cry was still that of the horse leech. It was deemed popular to demand fresh taxation from a special class. If the rich should resist, or if the Council, daily taunted as the representative of property, should demur to a partial impost, popular indignation might be aroused."

The Act was passed in 1877. It provided that valuers should classify the land in such a manner that all freehold estates over 640 acres in extent, and valued at a sum greater than £2500, whether in one block or in separate blocks, not more than five miles apart, should be taxed at the rate of 1½ per cent upon their capital value, after deducting therefrom the sum of £2500. There was a proviso that in the case of a person possessing more than one estate only one such exemption should be made. The valuers classed the estates as follows, and this basis has since remained continuously in force—Class I, estates carrying 2 sheep or more to the acre, £4 per acre; Class II, those carrying 1½ sheep to the acre, £3; Class III, those carrying less than one sheep to the acre, £1 per acre.

The following table shows the results of the operation of the Act during the years 1882 and 1892.

* Vol III pp 413 and 414.

CLASS.	1882					1892				
	No. of proprietors.	No. of estates.	Total area of estates assessed.	Average area to each		No. of proprietors.	No. of estates.	Total area of assessed estates.	Average area to each	
				Proprietor.	estate.				Proprietor.	estate
I	102	113	333193	3266	2948	102	122	308756	3027	2531
II	197	215	810816	4116	3771	202	227	769909	3811	3392
III	328	381	2508740	7648	6584	319	410	2533872	7943	6180
IV	235	298	3376448	14368	11330	240	360	3351838	3966	9311
Total	862	1007	7029197	8154	6980	863	1119	6964375	8070	6224

The capital value of the estates in 1892 according to the valuation prescribed by the Statute was over 12 millions sterling, but after deducting the exemption of £2500 the net taxable value was reduced to ten millions sterling. With reference to this point, Mr. Hayter, the Government Statistician, says— "It may be pointed out that although it may, perhaps, have been necessary to fix arbitrarily a scale for valuing estates for purposes of taxation, yet there is no doubt that the taxable value so arrived at is in most cases very much below the actual value of the estates." In 1892 the tax payable varied between 9¼d in class I and 2¼d per acre in class IV, the average being nearly 4¼d per acre. The amount payable by each holder averaged £145, ranging from an average of £175 in class III to £111 in class IV; that for each estate averaged £112, the amounts ranging from £96 to £136 in the different classes. The total amount derived from the tax in 1892 was £125,066.

Some very valuable information is obtainable from the table just given, if it is read conjointly with the fact that during the period dealt with (from 1882 to 1892) there were 24,024 new selections of land approved, and nearly 4,000,000 acres of land disposed of under deferred payments. It shows that whatever may have been the accumulation of estates below £2500 in value, the very large landed proprietors have remained almost stationary. They were only advanced in numbers by one person, and the number of estates increased by but 112, while the area jointly possessed by the persons paying the tax actually decreased by about 65,000 acres. In every class except class III, there is an appreciable fall in the average areas held by each proprietor, and the areas of the various estates also show a marked decrease all round. It is difficult with the imperfect data at disposal to draw conclusions as to the causes which have led to this condition of affairs, but it is probably due to the fact that most of the choice spots suitable for homesteads for large estates were acquired prior to the adoption of the Act of 1878, and that the stringent conditions attached to selection under later Statutes have militated against "dummying" and selection for the purposes of blackmailing which previously existed. Be that as it may, there is little doubt that in Victoria a yeoman class is now being settled upon the soil, under wholesome conditions, and without the class hatreds and bitter feeling which have been engendered in some other provinces of the group.

CHAPTER VI.

QUEENSLAND.

QUEENSLAND is essentially a modern province from the point of view of the student of its land system. As a Colony proper it was the last of the Australian group to be founded, and, with the exception of Western Australia, it was the last of the group also to be entrusted with a constitution of its own. Previous to the latter event, in 1859, the Moreton Bay district, as it was then termed, formed a portion of New South Wales, and the history of its methods of land occupation is identical with that of the Mother Colony. Like Hobart Town, the capital of Tasmania, Brisbane, the chief city of Queensland, was originally the site of a penal establishment, to which were sent some of the worst criminals; but, unlike the island colony, Queensland was not at the same time the home of free settlers. Indeed, freemen were debarred from taking up land in the district until after the convicts had been withdrawn, so that this dark era in its history, which extended over a period of nearly 8 years, between 1824 and 1842, need not be dwelt upon.

It will be remembered that when the district was thrown open to free settlement, in 1842, Lord Stanley's Crown Land Sales Act * had just become law. It was under this enactment that land in the Moreton Bay district was first sold in 1842, while in the following year sections in the city of Brisbane were first disposed of, at high rates. Alienation of land was carried out subject to this legislation until 1846, when Earl Grey's Waste Lands Act came into operation. † This measure, with the Orders-in-Council of 1847, directed the land policy of the district during the next thirteen years. Under the Orders-in-Council, New South Wales was divided into settled, intermediate, and unsettled districts, under which classification the "counties or reputed counties of Macquarie and Stanley," (the latter including the country immediately surrounding the present city of Brisbane), and lands within ten miles of "the town of Ipswich in the county of Stanley,"

* *Ante* p. 18.
† *Ante* p. 21 *et seq.*

were included amongst the settled districts; the remainder of the present vast Colony being described as "unsettled." In the same year an Act was passed by the New South Wales Legislative Council, making a yearly assessment of ½d for every sheep, 1½d for every head of cattle, and 3d for every horse depastured on Crown Lands. These various measures, with slight amendment, governed the land system of the district during the early days of its development, during which progress was not as rapid as its natural wealth warranted. In 1859, when it was erected into a separate Colony, with a Legislature of its own, the population was probably not more than 25,000; but there were great numbers of live stock. Its rich pastures had for some years previously attracted squatters northwards, the famous Darling Downs being then, as at the present day, noted for the succulence of the natural grasses, and their other advantages. Prior to this date over 1300 acres of town land had been disposed of for upwards of £99,000, while over 85,000 acres of country land had been sold for a little more than £160,000.

With separation from New South Wales, and the election of a Legislative Assembly of its own, the district of Moreton Bay—or, as it was henceforth to be known, the Colony of "Queensland"—entered on a new era of progress, Population set steadily towards its shores, and in a very few years it commenced to take an important position amongst the provinces of the group. One of the very first Acts passed by the new Parliament dealt with the land question. Two Land Acts were passed in the first session, one dealing with the country destined to be used for cultivation and the other with the territory to be utilised for pastoral purposes.

The first enactment, laid down the principle that in no case should the price of land be less than £1 per acre. Lands were to be divided into town, suburban, or country lots, and put up to auction, at this upset price, and such as remained unsold might be privately disposed of. The chief feature of the Act was the setting apart of agricultural reserves for the purpose of actual settlement and cultivation. Six months after the passing of the measure, the Governor was to reserve 100,000 acres near to the ocean and in certain populated districts; and, within ten miles of towns with over 500 inhabitants, reserves of 10,000 acres were to be made. Free selection before survey, in areas of not less than 40 nor more than 320 acres, was permitted over these reserved areas, at a fixed price of £1 per acre. This sum had to be paid in advance, upon selection, but the completion of the contract was subject to the proviso that the selector, within six months of purchase, occupied and commenced to improve or cultivate the Land. Upon fulfilment of these conditions, a deed of grant was issued, but if the land was not improved, the section might be forfeited and the purchase money returned less ten per cent. Any officer of the British Army or Navy, not more than 45 years of age, and who had served 7 years, might receive orders for land to the value of £50, and it was also lawful for the Governor "to issue to any adult immigrant who shall have come direct from Europe to the Colony of Queensland, but not at the expense of the said Colony, or to the person who shall have paid for the passage of such Immigrant, a Land order for the amount of £18, and after such immigrant shall have resided not less than two years continuously within the said Colody . . . . to issue to such immigrant a further land order for the amount of £12. Provided that two children over the age of 4 and under the age of 14 respectively shall be reckoned as one adult under this Act." These land orders entitled the holders to take up land to the value stated.

The Crown Lands Occupation Act, which was passed at the same time, was intended to encourage the exploration and use of new country for pastoral purposes. Under its provisions any person who, having found an unoccupied area suitable for a run within the unsettled districts, had placed his stock upon it, could obtain a license to occupy the land at a rental of 10/- per square mile for twelve months. Within three months of the expiration of this term, he might obtain a lease of the run for a period of 14 years, provided he in the meantime had stocked in to the extent of 25 sheep, or 5 head of cattle per square mile. No run was to be less in area than 25 nor more than 100 square miles (in rectangular form); and the rent was fixed at 10/- per square mile for the first 4 years of the term, but was subject to re-appraisement every 5 years afterwards. Upon non-payment of rent the lessee was subject to the forfeiture of his leasehold. The whole of the land held under these conditions was liable to resumption for public purposes or sale; at any time, after 12 months' notice had been given, subject to payment of compensation by the State for improvements.

An amendment of the Agricultural Reserves Act was made in 1863, under which the reserves to be set apart for selection in the stated localities near to the sea were reduced from 100,000 to 50,000 acres, and it was provided that the reserves near to towns should also be reduced. An important amendment was made which greatly altered the method previously in force. In place of free selection over the reserves, it was provided that the land was to be surveyed previous to selection, into areas of from 18 to 320 acres. As under the previous Act 20s an acre cash had to be paid in advance, and within 12 months the selector had to make a declaration that he had fulfilled conditions of residence for six months, that the land had been fenced, and that one-sixth of its area had been cultivated. Non-compliance with these conditions entailed forfeiture of the selection, and in lieu of the repayment of the money paid, the selector received an order entitling him to take up land elsewhere, to the value of three-quarters the original purchase money. Not more than 320 acres might be held by any one person.

It was hardly to be expected that such stringent conditions as these would prove attractive in face of the easy terms then being offered by the Governments of other colonies. Indeed, many selectors threw up their holdings rather than carry out the contract, and in consequence, a measure was passed in 1865 called the "Selectors' Relief Act," which provided that where persons had forfeited their selections under the Act of 1863, by reason of non-compliance with its provisions, it should be lawful for the Governor to remit such forfeiture, if the selector could produce satisfactory evidence that he had complied with the residence conditions, and had cultivated not less than one-tenth of the selected area instead of one-sixth, as required by the Act. But even this concession had not much effect, as in the following year the Surveyor-General reported that the very strict conditions of selection "and the uncertainty attending the progress of legislation for the relief of selectors have greatly disturbed the operations of selectors of this class of land." He also stated that "Selections in agricultural reserves have fallen off nearly one-half, while forfeitures have increased, which is evidence of the disfavour with which practical agriculturists view the conditions imposed . . It may be remarked that as the actual increase of cultivation throughout the whole colony does not exceed 2500 acres, and the law requires that the selectors in the agricultural reserve shall cultivate one-sixth of selections within one year, it follows that all selections above 15,000 acres must be forfeited, even if the whole of the cultivation were restricted to the new selections, and there were no increase of agriculture on the other lands of the colony." Further legislation followed in the same year in which this report was presented.

In 1863 the Pastoral Leases Act, dealing principally with the pastoral lands within the settled districts of the colony was passed. This measure authorised the Governor to increase the extent of the settled districts, and to offer for lease by auction areas which had not been reserved for periods of five years, at an upset rental of £1 per annum per square mile. Power was also given to renew for further periods leases within either the settled or unsettled districts, at an appraised rental.

A further amendment was again made with respect to pastoral lands in the following year, when it was provided that lessees should pay a fee of £5 for each block of 25 square miles held by them, and 4s for each additional square mile, to be used as a fund to meet the cost of appraisement of runs. In default of this payment, a fixed rent was to be charged during the period from the fourth to the ninth year of the term of lease, of £27 10s for each block of 25 square miles, with an extra 22s for every additional square mile; and during the last five years the rental was to be £35 for each block of 25 square miles, with an additional 35s for every extra square mile. About this period, in consequence of the prospective falling in of the leases issued under the old Orders-in-Council, there was a very large alienation of leased areas under pre-emptive rights, and in the three years ending in 1867 there was disposed of in this manner no less than 257,000 acres, which included many of the choicest spots on the rich Darling Downs.

The pastoral industry was still the chief one of the colony, but the necessity was early recognised of introducing an agricultural population by offering attractions to a desirable class of immigrants. In 1864 an Immigration Act was passed, embodying in another form the principle, laid down in the Act of 1860, of granting land orders to immigrants. It was stipulated, that the Agent General for Immigration in London might issue to each immigrant proceeding direct from Europe to the colony and paying his own passage or the passage of any member of his family, a land order warrant. This warrant entitled the holder to receive, immediately upon arrival in the colony, one non-transferable land order on account of each person whose passage had been paid, of the value of £30 for each person of the age of 12 years and upwards, and of the value of £15 for each child between the age of 1 and 12 years. These land orders were available to their full nominal value as payment for the purchase of any country or suburban lands which might be offered for sale by auction or were open to selection; but deeds of grant were only to be issued for land so obtained after two years' residence in the colony by the holder. The Governor was empowered to advance to the holder a sum equal to one-fifth of the nominal value of the orders, upon repayment of which, with the addition of £1, at any time within two years, the land order would be returned.

It was also enacted that the Governor might issue to "any persons who shall have entered into an agreement with the government for the conveyance of immigrants from Europe to Queensland, a land order of the value of £9 sterling for each child between the ages of one and twelve years, who may be so conveyed."* The latter class of orders, which were available for country lands only, were transferable by delivery, and it was lawful "for the Governor to purchase such land orders after the expiration of six months from the date of their issue at a price not exceeding £15." This Act, with slight amendments, remained in force until 1872, when an amending measure was passed, which permitted the holder of each warrant after residence for 12 months in the colony, to obtain a transferable land order of the value of £20 for himself or any adult member of his family whose passage had been paid, and of half that value for each child below the age of 12 years. This system of land orders, though it effected some good in the direction desired, had an immoral tendency, and as early as 1866 the Minister for Lands stated that it had been greatly abused. In 1875, so obnoxious had the principle become, owing to the means which it afforded of evading the land laws, that it was done away with altogether.

Meanwhile the stringency of the conditions of the Act of 1863 and the consequent falling off in selection, rendered a further change of legislation necessary, and in 1866 the Crown Leases and Purchase Act was passed, as a partially remedial measure. It was therein provided that lands within two miles of a town which had remained unsold after being offered at auction, and lands within agricultural reserves which had remained unselected for one month after proclamation, should be available for selection upon lease, by the first applicant, for a term of 8 years, at an annual rental of 2s 6d per acre for land offered for selection at 20s per acre, and a proportionately higher rent for land offered at a higher rate. The continued payment of the rent during the term of lease, entitled the lessee to the fee simple of the land at its expiration. No lessee might hold more than 2560 acres, in this manner. At the period when this Act came into operation, about 687,000 acres of the public estate had been alienated, of which the area under cultivation was computed to be 17,000 acres. The population, at this time had reached a total of 101,000.

One of the most important measures passed during the early period of the land legislation of the colony, was the

* Section 15.

"Crown Lands Alienation Act" of 1868, which was to some extent an extension of the Act of 1866. With respect to pastoral lands, it provided that lessees might be permitted to surrender their leases, and obtain a renewal of the lease for one-half the leasehold area without disturbance for a term of ten years, at a rental proportionately equal to that formerly paid for the whole of the leasehold area. Lessees who did not accept these terms, were to be permitted to retain their runs as formerly, but the leaseholds were to be subject to resumption in whole or in part for free selection, or for sale by auction. It was stipulated that all Crown Lands within three miles of railways should be retained as railway reserves.

"Country land"—comprised within railway, township, or agricultural reserves,—was declared open for selection by conditional purchase. It was divided for the purposes of the Act into (1) agricultural, (2) first-class pastoral, and (3) second-class pastoral lands. Agricultural lands, in areas of from 40 to 640 acres, could be leased for ten years, at an annual rental of 1/6, payable in advance. First-class pastoral land, in areas of from 80 to 2560 acres, could be obtained in a similar manner at an annual rental of 1s per acre; and second-class pastoral land, in areas of from 80 to 7680 acres, at an annual rental of 6d per acre. At the end of ten years, on due payment of rent, a grant in fee could be obtained. The conditions attached to the leases in the case of agricultural land were that the selections should be substantially fenced and resided upon either by the lessee or his bailiff, during the term of the lease; but if within three years it could be shown that the residence conditions had been fulfilled, and improvements to the value of 10s per acre effected, the fee simple could be obtained on payment of the balance of the purchase money then due. In the case of pastoral lands the freehold could be obtained in a similar manner after two years' residence, and upon improvements being made to the value of 10s and 5s per acre respectively in the two classes.

Commons to an extent of not more than 20 square miles might be declared open upon the application of freeholders in a township, and on this land they alone might depasture cattle, at an annual assessment of 2s per head. Sheep, except under special circumstances, were excluded. Sugar and coffee leases, over areas ranging from 320 to 1280 acres, could be obtained on terms and conditions similar to those imposed in the case of agricultural land, except that before the fee simple could be granted, at the end of three years' residence, it had to be shown that one-tenth of the land had been devoted to the cultivation of coffee or sugar. The fulfilment of these conditions also relieved the lessee of the obligation of residence during the remainder of the lease. The latter system is said to have have been much abused.

The legislation with respect to pastoral lands within the unsettled districts was again amended and consolidated by the pastoral Leases Act of 1869, which repealed all previous enactments dealing with the subject. Leases of runs obtained under any of the preceding Acts, or the Orders-in-Council, could be surrendered for new leases for terms of 21 years, at a rental during the first seven years based on that paid previously. During the second and third periods of seven years, the rent was to be raised 10 per cent on that paid during the previous seven years. The conditions under which new runs could be taken up were very similar to those already in force. Licenses were to be obtained for one year, which, upon certain stock being depastured, could be converted into leases for 21 years. The rent during the first seven years of the term was to be five shillings per square mile per annum; for the second seven years, 10*s*; and for the third seven years, 15*s*. It was provided, however, that during the currency of the seventh or fourteenth years of the term, the Governor or the lessee might apply to have the rents appraised for the coming period of seven years. Lessees were granted a pre-emptive right of purchase at 10*s* per acre, of 2560 acres of their runs; and the Governor was authorised to resume, after six months' notice, an area of 2560 acres from any run subject to Parliamentary sanction. Compensation for specified improvements was paid by the Crown in the latter case.

The passing of the Act of 1868, which as previously shown, permitted free selection over large proclaimed areas, at once resulted in very great quantities of the public estate being alienated when the requisite periods of residence had been completed. On this subject, Mr Rusden in his "History of Australia," writes * —"Their enormous landed estate had intoxicated the men of Queensland . . . Injurious tendencies of the law were heightened by its abuse. Fraudulent selections enabled speculators to grasp larger blocks than the spirit of the law allowed. Combinations by members of a family gathered into one hand tens of thousands of acres in coveted districts. Those who had taken part in the lotteries of New South Wales and Victoria carried their experience to new pastures in order to overreach the autho-

* Vol III, pp. 606—7.

rities of Queensland. Some settlers incurred heavy liabilities by purchasing at auction lands which, if selected by others, would have rendered it impossible for the settlers to follow their previous pastoral pursuits." Mr Ranken, who was formerly a Commissioner of Crown Lands in Queensland, also remarks.* "The land law of 1868 originally devised at Rockhampton, included an extensive attempt at grazing farms. . . In the coast districts, the effort was in some measure successful, but in the inland districts—these being almost entirely in the hands of Melbourne proprietors and mortgagees—the use of the grass by the resident population has met with such resistance as might be expected."

To prevent selection of large areas of country for speculative blackmailing purposes, and as an encouragement to a resident population of small holders, a Homestead Areas Act was passed in 1872 under which heads of families and persons over the age of 21 years were permitted to select on lease, within specified areas, homestead blocks not exceeding 80 acres of agricultural or 160 acres of pastoral land, for periods of five years, at an annual rental of 9d per acre for the former, and 6d for the latter. Due payment of rent and continuous residence during the term of lease, entitled the lessee to the fee simple, provided the land had been fenced and one-tenth cultivated. No person might acquire more than one homestead allotment. This liberal measure without doubt induced a considerable number of persons of small means to take up land within homestead areas, but nevertheless the system was much abused, and numbers of selectors sold out at a handsome profit, at the end of their leases.

Some important amendments of the principles laid down by the Act of 1868 were made by an Act passed in 1876. The former system of classification of agricultural and pastoral lands was abolished, and power was given to the Governor-in-Council, within certain limits, to fix the price and maximum quantity of land which might be selected within different districts, in deciding which he had to be guided by the quality of the land and its propinquity to a market, railways, etc. The maximum area which might be selected was reduced from 7680 to 5120 acres, the minimum being as before, 40 acres. The maximum which might be obtained in various districts was to be proclaimed by the Governor before selection was allowed, but it could not be less than 640 acres. The lowest price which could be placed upon any land was 5s per acre, and any increase upon this

---

* "Our Wasted Heritage", Chap. XII.

amount had also to be proclaimed before areas were thrown open to selection. Payment was required in ten annual instalments, in the form of rent, due payment of which together with the fulfilment of the usual conditions as to residence, improvements, and cultivation, entitled the selector to a grant in fee, The improvements had to be equal to the price per acre paid for the land, up to 10*s* per acre. The price per acre for homestead blocks was by this enactment reduced to 6*d* per acre for all classes of lands, and the maximum area which could be obtained was fixed at 160 acres; while in addition to the condition as to residence for five years, improvements to the value of 10*s* per acre had now to be made.

In 1876, also an Act was passed to deal with pastoral leases within the settled districts which had been granted under the Act of 1868, and which fell in in 1878. This Statute enabled the Governor to offer the renewal of the leases for sale by auction, for a further period of five years, at an upset rental of 40*s* per square mile per annum, subject to resumption for sale. A further measure to deal with the same subject became law in 1882, under which the leases were extended without competition by auction for a further term of 10 years. The rents were to be appraised every five years, but were to be not less than 40*s* per annum per square mile.

The whole legislation with respect to land alienation and occupation was altered and consolidated in 1884, when a new Crown Lands Act was passed. This measure, which was a most comprehensive one, was itself amended in 1885, 1886, 1889, 1891, and 1892, but as its chief principles remain, and it is the governing legislation at the present day, the best course will be, as in other Colonies, to consider the principal Act and its amendments together. The Governor was empowered by the Act of 1884 to appoint, for its administration, a Land Board of two members, at a high salary, to sit as a Court to determine all matters referred to them by the general public or the Minister. The Board has the full powers of a judge of the Supreme Court, but an appeal may be made to the Supreme Court from its decisions. So far this arrangement has worked most advantageously. Crown Lands Commissioners and Land Agents act as local administrative officers, within specified districts.

The system of pastoral occupation was re-modelled under the new legislation. Previously-existing lessees were invited to surrender up to March 1887, their leasehold areas, which were to be divided into two parts, one of which was to be retained under lease, and the balance was to be available for settlement. In the case of leases obtained under the Acts of 1869, 1876, and 1882, the leaseholds were to be equally divided, and the same method was to apply to all leases, which had first been obtained twenty years previously; but where licenses had been granted less than twenty years and more than ten years previously, one-third only was to be resumed; while in the case of areas for which licenses were granted less than ten years previously, only one-fourth was to be so taken. In the case of leases of lands within settled districts, the new leases for the resumed parts of the runs were to be for ten years, and it was originally proposed that all other new leases should be for periods of fifteen years; but by the amending Act of 1886 the term might at the option of lessees be increased to 21 years, subject to a proviso that after 15 years one-fourth of the runs except the head stations, might be resumed without compensation for improvements. Rent was to be computed only upon portions of runs actually available for pastoral purposes, and in the case of leases granted for terms of 10 years it was to be for the first five years 40/- per square mile; but for all other leases it was to be appraised by the Land Board, at rates not to exceed 90/- per square mile nor to be less than 10/-. Rents payable subsequently are determined by the Board. Occupation of resumed areas by the lessee pending selection for sale is permitted under annual license, at a rental to be fixed. New unoccupied country may be taken up as formerly.

An entirely new method of dealing with lands for agricultural and grazing purposes (other than pastoral leaseholds) has been introduced in the new legislation on and after specified dates. Country lands may be proclaimed to be open for selection as agricultural areas, which are to be surveyed into convenient lots, with proper roads and reserves for public purposes; but power is given to the Governor to suspend the operation of this provision, and throw other areas open to free selection. The proclamation declaring areas open must state whether the land is on an agricultural area or not, and the maximum extent which may be selected. In an agricultural area this must not exceed 1280 acres, and in the case of other lands must be not less than 2560 nor more than 20,000 acres. The numbers and areas of the lots, their annual rent, and the purchase price must also be proclaimed. An application having been made for any allotment in a proclaimed area, by any person above the age of 18 years, other than a pastoral lessee, or a married woman, and confirmed, a license to occupy is granted. Within three years of obtaining this license in the case of grazing farms, and five years in the case of agricultural farms, the selector must enclose the land with a substantial fence or make other improvements equal in value to the cost of a fence, or forfeit the license. If these improvements have been completed, however, the licensee is entitled to a lease for fifty years, in the case of an agricultural farm, and for 30 years for a grazing farm. The rent, which is payable yearly in advance, is fixed at the rate specified in the proclamation for the first 10 years of the term under lease and license, but it must not be less than 3d per acre for agricultural land nor $\frac{3}{4}d$ for other lands. Subsequently it is determined by the Board, according to the unimproved value of the land. Continuous occupation is compulsory during the whole term of the lease, either "by the lessee himself or some other person who is the actual or *bona fide* manager or agent of the lessee, for the purpose of the use and occupation of the land, and who is himself not disqualified from selecting a farm of the same area and class in the district."

In the case of agricultural farms, the freehold may be obtained after residence for five years and the completion of improvements at the price originally proclaimed, which must not be less than 15/- per acre. Grazing farms are inalienable. The new legislation embodies in a complete form the liberal provisions formerly existing with respect to homestead blocks, though the name is changed. It is provided that if, in the case of agricultural farms of 160 acres or less, the lessee can show within seven years of receiving a license that he has personally resided on the land for a period of five years, and made improvements equal in value to 10/- per acre, he may, upon payment of a sum of 2/6 per acre, (towards which rent already paid is credited) obtain the freehold. In the event of the total rent previously paid exceeding 2/6 per acre, the balance is returned to the selector. Lessees of these farms may obtain grazing farms of not more than 640 acres, without conditions as to occupation. Town and suburban lands may be sold at auction for cash, at upset prices of £8 and £2 per acre respectively, and agricultural lands and other country lands to the extent of 150,000 acres annually may be similarly disposed of, in areas not exceedding 320 acres, at upset prices of £1 and 10/- respectively for each class. By the Act of 1891 a new principle was introduced into the land legislation of Queensland. Land may now be unconditionally selected for purchase at a price to be proclaimed, one third higher than in the case of conditional selections, and not less than 20/- per acre. A lease is obtainable for a term of 20 years, during which an annual rental equal to one-twentieth of the purchase money is charged, and at its conclusion or at any time during the existence of the lease, upon payment of the balance due, the fee simple is secured. There are no conditions attached except the regular payment of rent, non-fulfilment of which entails forfeiture.

What are generally termed "village settlements" were provided for in the Amending Act of 1886. This measure lays down that in those agricultural areas in which the maximum size of any surveyed farm does not exceed 160 acres, an agricultural township may be laid out in sections of one acre each; in the immediate vicinity of the township farms not exceeding 80 acres are to be surveyed. Every selector of one of these farms is entitled to a township section, on which to reside, and any improvements made thereon are considered as being made on the farm in fulfilment of the conditions of lease. An extension of the same principle was provided by the Act of 1891, which permits selectors of these farms of 80 acres, who may be *bona fide* associated together, to act jointly in the matter of occupation and effecting improvements, so that it shall not be necessary for all of the lessees to be upon the land at the same time. One person may perform the conditions of residence for every 160 acres, and any improvements of a greater value than 10/- per acre, made on one farm, may be credited to the lessee of another.

Another important provision was made by the Act of 1886, under which the system of land orders, abolished in 1876, was re-instated. The Agent-General is authorised to issue to each immigrant paying his own passage or that of a member of his family, a warrant entitling him to receive, upon landing in the Colony, a land order of the value of £20 for each adult or £10 for each child between the ages of 1 and 12 years. These land orders are transferable, and are available for 10 years after date of issue, either as payment for the purchase of freehold land to the nominal amount stated, or as rent for leased land under any of the various methods in force except the unconditional purchase of selections. One order of the value of £20 will thus purchase a homestead farm of 160 acres.

The provisions described are without doubt liberal. The great difficulty now experienced is that there is a lack of good land adjacent to markets, most of the best country near the railways and centres of population, having been picked years ago. It will not pay men to take up land for cultivation far from a railway or harbour; and the Government has experienced difficulty in settling a desirable class of persons on small areas at any distance from these central points. The policy has consequently been adopted of endeavouring to make the vast landed territory of the Colony pay for the construction of railway lines by private individuals, by granting to them as subsidy certain areas proportionate to the cost of the works.

During the session of Parliament of 1892, a Bill was passed affirming this principle, which provides that, when the construction of lines between certain termini has been decided upon by the legislature, the Ministry may enter into a contract with any company for the construction of railways or tramways, on one of three bases—viz., either (1), that the line when constructed may become the property of the Company for a period of not more than 50 years, or (2), become the property of the Crown, or (3), remain the property of the Company, with the right of purchase by the State on specified terms. Certain areas of unalienated land are to be set apart, and assessed at their fair present market value, and if the line is to become the property of the Crown, when completed, the Company will receive land from these areas equal in value to twice the cost of construction; if upon either of the other methods, land only to the value of the cost of construction will be given. The maximum cost of construction must be specified by contract in each case, and to partly secure to the Crown the increment of value attained by the construction of the line, the land through which it is to pass is to be divided into convenient blocks, as nearly as possible equal in value. From these the contracting Company and the Government may each select one block alternately, as sections of the line become available for traffic, and the whole of the lands selected by the Company will be granted in fee-simple on the completion of the contract. So far no steps have been taken to give effect to this legislation.

In arriving at any conclusion as to the results achieved by the legislation of 1884 and later years, the fact must be borne in mind that Queensland from its geographical position is situated differently to the other Australian provinces. The greater part of its immense area of 668,000 square miles lies within the tropic of Capricorn, while the remainder may be generally described as being within the sub-tropical region. The chief industry of the Colony is essentially grazing; but sheep have not up to the present occupied as much attention as cattle, though during the last decade the number of sheep has doubled, and Queensland has assumed the second place amongst the Australian group as a wool-growing country. It is noted, however, for its cattle, which thrive marvellously, and now almost equal in numbers the total of all the other Colonies combined.

As previously indicated Queensland, judged by ordinary

standards, occupies the lowest place amongst the Colonies in point of agricultural developments. Except as regards maize—in the growth of which it ranks next to New South Wales—the crops are smaller and the average tilled is less in proportion to the total area and population than in any of the others. But this fact is due more to the great heat in its Northern latitudes, than to a lack of fertile soil, for almost every article of food can be produced within its borders, and cotton, coffee, sugar, tobacco, and other tropical products have been cultivated in large quantities, though owing to the cost of labour the two former have of late years not been persevered with. Parliament, it may be understood therefore, has up to the present been called upon to legislate rather for pastoral than agricultural settlement, through every attention has been devoted to the latter, and judging from the results achieved since the institution of the system brought into force in 1884, it has proved successful.

Official statistics show that large leasehold areas, in few hands, are gradually giving place to greater numbers of comparatively small holdings. The following table, giving roughly the results of the operations of the various Land Acts during the last three years, shows very clearly the trend in this direction.

Year.	Area of pastoral holdings	Agricultural farms selected.		Grazing farms selected.	
		No.	Area	No.	Area
	Square Miles		Acres		Acres
1890	446,411	879	173,251	213	1,922,914
1891	438,165	1,145	252,728	146	997,540
1892	433,279	1,088	236,456	113	608,420

These figures show that, while in three years the big squattages have decreased in area by about 8,000,000 acres, the total area taken up in other ways has increased by four million acres. The average area of the agricultural farms selected during this period was about 212 acres, and of the grazing farms about 6170 acres.

Unfortunately there is no data in the possession of any of the public departments, to show how freehold land of the Colony is now held, or the number of present holdings. The increase of settlement can only in consequence be arrived at by a comparison of different sets of figures, and in roundabout ways. The following table, covering a period of 10 years, from 1882 to 1891 shows the relation of the total population to the alienation and cultivation of land, and the number of live stock in the Colony in each year:—

Year	Population	Alienated areas		Areas Cultivated	Live Stock	
		Number of Allotments	Area		Cattle	Sheep
	No.	No.	Acres		No.	No.
1882	248,255	1959	591,985	158,686	4,089,715	12,043,893
1883	287,475	2178	633,707	167,476	4,246,141	11,507,475
1884	302,090	1935	514,870	199,580	4,266,172	9,308,911
1885	315,489	2210	628,685	209,130	4,162,652	8,994,322
1886	338,580	2340	725,783	221,843	4,071,563	9,690,445
1887	354,510	1898	536,235	205,737	4,473,716	12,926,158
1888	367,950	1881	474,294	214,002	4,654,932	13,444,005
1889	380,530	1886	452,884	247,073	4,872,416	14,470,095
1890	399,215	2040	338,218	239,618	5,558,264	18,007,234
1891	410,330	1308	317,344	258,004	6,192,759	20,289,633

The total area alienated prior to 1882 was a little over 45¼ million acres, and a great proportion of the areas shown above as having been disposed of between 1882 and 1891 was really parted with under contracts made previous to the act of 1884. At the end of 1892, there was also in process of alienation under the Crown Lands Alienation Act of 1876 306,100 acres, and there was held under license and lease, with the right of purchase, under the Crown Lands Acts from 1884 to 1892, 1,483,275 acres. These facts, read conjointly with the two previous tables, indicate that under present legislation both agricultural and pastoral interests have progessed proportionately with the increase of population. While the population did not double itself in the period dealt with, the area under cultivation was more than doubled and the same may be said with respect to sheep. Cattle also were nearly doubled in numbers during the decade. It is likewise a noticeable fact that between 1882 and 1891 the area of country devoted to pastoral pursuits under lease or license, apart from that held as grazing farms, decreased from 306 million acres to 280 millions of acres, a considerable proportion of the resumed area having been taken up as grazing farms by small holders.

The grazing farm system indeed, appears to have been very largely availed of, the long terms of lease, having induced great competition,—and as a necessary result, some "dummying"—for the best areas. Amongst the agricultural farms the greatest demand has been for those of 160 acres and under, for the obvious reason that they can be secured at a comparatively much lower price than any of the larger areas. The village settlements have not proved the success which was anticipated, as "the popular feeling appears to be that the areas of the farms as allowed by the Act—80 acres—is not large enough, and that 160 acres should have been the maximum; and departmental experience points to the conclusion that had the areas surveyed into settlements been proclaimed open as ordinary agricultural farms of 160 acres, they would, when the land was good, have been eagerly selected, the average selector not valuing very much the gift of the town allotment." * The system of unconditional selection had not during the first year or two after it came into operation, been largely availed of, probably for the reason that the price is one-third higher than that for conditional selections. Another part of the system which has proved a failure is the method of granting land orders. Departmental experience shows that "the more seen of the land order system the more it is certain that it is an utter failure . . . . The fact is, land orders as a rule are not popular or utilised unless money can be made out of them, and the sooner their issue is stopped the better."

But, on the whole, it would appear, to judge from the expressions of opinion of both interested and disinterested persons, capable of forming sound views, that the land system of Queensland has had the effect of increasing settlement; and considering its magnificent territory, and its many natural advantages, there is every prospect of the province within a very few decades taking a leading if not the foremost position amongst the continental group.

* Annual Report of the Under-Secretary for Lands, 1892. Govt. Printer, Brisbane.

CHAPTER VII.

WESTERN AUSTRALIA.

WESTERN AUSTRALIA occupies a unique position amongst the provinces. With an area of about 1,000,000 square miles, its territory greatly exceeds that of any of the Colonies, yet its population is less than any other. The problem of settlement of the vast tract comprised within its boundaries is, therefore, full of interest. Attention naturally turns, however, rather to the legislation for the present than to that of the past, which,—judging from the fact that the Colony has been nearly 65 years in existence, and has now a population of little more than 50,000,—has not proved successful. This result is in a great measure due, perhaps, to the geographical position of the country. It is separated from the Eastern provinces by an immense barren waste of territory, and has thus had largely to depend upon its own resources and its own consumption without the stimulating influences of intercolonial markets for its produce, which have aided elsewhere.

Nature was not kind when apportioning her gifts to this western part of the continent, which, while possessing few and small rivers, consists very largely of an immense plateau, the great bulk of which comprises arid, waterless tracts, unsuitable it appears, for the habitation or use of man. The cultivable portions of the country are mostly to be found in its South-Western corner, in which the population is mostly congregated, and which includes the towns of Perth, Freemantle, and Albany, the former being the capital. This district is known as the South-Western Division, the remainder of the coastal districts being portioned off into five other divisions, which in places are suited for pasturage, but consist very largely of semi-desert country.

The story of the colonisation of Western Australia is a harrowing tale of struggles against untoward natural conditions, official misconception, and lack of population; and there have been few finer displays of indomitable British pluck than were afforded by its early settlers. It was the first Australian Colony to be founded by private enterprise certainly. In 1826, a military and penal settlement was founded at King George's sound, but subsequently this was abandoned. Captain Sterling, RM. who had previously surveyed the coast, then recommended the Imperial Government to establish a settlement at Swan River, (on which the present city of Perth stands) and the idea was taken up readily. At this time plans for colonisation were rife in the English mind, various inducements, more or less warranted, being held out to persons to emigrate.

In the case of Western Australia, the first settlers were offered large grants of land proportionate to the capital they might be able to invest, in the ratio of 40 acres for each £3 of invested money; but they had to expend 1/6 per acre in the way of making improvements, before they could obtain the fee simple. The story of how they fared is thus succinctly told:— * "Under such influences the settlement of Western Australia began. In 1829 thirty vessels were despatched, and landed one thousand settlers at Freemantle. The land had been given away in London in enormous tracts to such individuals as had undertaken to take out emigrants . .
No preparations had been made to receive or provide for a population. The large grants issued in England were marked off on paper from the boundary of the town, or rather of the proposed site of the town. The original projector of the scheme is said to have allotted to himself 500,000 acres, beginning at the landing place. The whole area granted was one million and a half acres. Settlers who got this land were so scattered by the distances that they lost the run of each other, and the immigrants brought out to work for them could not find their employers. They camped in sight of the shipping and remained there, for they could do nothing else. The farming implements lay on the beach, and the families who had come to form the society of the place, attracted by the fictions of the pamphleteers, found that they were turned adrift without the necessaries of life on the edge of a wilderness. There was neither live stock nor any other means of turning the soil to immediate use. Scenes of destitution followed. Young ladies spent their time catching fish as they saw the black 'gins' do, to save their parents and themselves from starvation."

Need it be said that the attempt at colonisation was a huge failure. As indicated by the quotation given above, numbers of people left the Colony rather than face the difficulties ahead; through in some cases they retained their land. But many remained, and against terrible odds

---

* "The Federal Geography of British Australasia," George Ranken, p. 311 Turner and Henderson, Sydney, 1891.

laid the foundation of the present Colony. The enormous free grants, however, kept the population stagnant. They could not get on the land to use it, and various experiments were tried from time to time to enable the people to get upon other suitable land. All Crown Lands were to be sold for the future, and free grants were abandoned. In 1832 a minimum price of 5/- per acre was placed on all lands, but "The immediate result was a sudden and almost total stop to emigration. From that time to the present (1888) few people have arrived here except those who have come to join their friends, or have been in some way connected with the place" * .... It may readily be understood that by the year 1838, only 20,603 acres had been sold by auction.

The great difficulty with existing holders of land was the lack of labour, to meet which Lord Glenelg, the Secretary of State, proposed to induce the emigration of a desirable class of labourers by offering grants of land to persons paying their passages; but this offered few attractions, and the Colony continued to stagnate. In 1838 a Western Australian Company was formed to render the settlement more attractive, on the lines adopted in the case of South Australia, which was then being first settled. The Company announced that they had purchased from the Government extensive blocks of land for a settlement, which they called "Australind." They were prepared to issue land orders in England, on receiving cash at the rate of £1 per acre, for lots of 100 acres, and the holders were to draw lots in London for the priority of choice of land on arrival at the settlement. But the existence of the large free grants around Perth remained a lion in the path, and as many of the original settlers were prepared to sell their land for as little as 2/6 per acre, the Company's terms were not very popular. It succeeded however, in attracting to the Colony a number of excellent settlers, though financially it proved a failure.

The people at last became quite disheartened, and almost inclined to abandon the settlement and to add to their difficulties in place of a clear-sighted policy by the Imperial Government, which would have aided them, they were met by mandates showing official misconception and ignorance of local conditions, that but added to their burdens. Up to 1839 the upset price for land in the Colony, as in New South Wales, was 5/- per acre. In that year it was raised to 12/-; and in 1840 it was by direction of the Colonial Office again increased to 20/- per acre. It is needless to say that the

* Report of a Committee appointed to "take into consideration the present state of the Colony of Western Australia," 1838.

latter edict put a stop almost entirely to all sales of land, except by private owners, who in many cases, as already indicated, disposed of their property at as low a rate as 2/6 per acre. The Colony now became in a pitiable condition.

Matters remained in this position till 1843, when new regulations were issued, under which the lands of the Colony were divided into three classes—town, suburban, and country. Suburban lands were to be sold at auction in lots of from 10 to 50 acres, and country lands in lots of from 160 to 640 acres, but special country lots of from 20 to 160 acres might also be offered. The upset price of £1 per acre was retained. In the same year an Act was passed providing that in the event of any person occupying Crown Lands for depasturing or other purposes, without proper license and authority, they were liable to money penalties ranging up to £50, and to imprisonment upon a frequent repetition of the offence.

In 1849, Earl Grey's Waste Lands Act having become law, he desired the Governor to frame regulations for its administration, applicable to the circumstances of the Colony. The Governor referred the matter to a Committee of leading men, who made recommendations which were, however, condemned by a public meeting of citizens. But all parties agreed as to the advisability of instituting a system of tillage leases. This suggestion met with the approval of the Governor, and as a result he advised that the lands of the Colony should be divided into two classes, known as A and B, the former to consist of those near to town sites or the sea coast; and the latter to comprise all other lands. It was proposed that the class-A lands should be open for lease for tillage at a yearly rental of 1/- per acre per annum, for 8 years, and for pastoral purposes under annual lease; and that lands in class-B district should be leased for pastoral purposes for eight years at a rental of £5 per 1000 acres, and 10/- for every 1000 acres after the first 1000. Earl Grey generally adopted the recommendations, but in an off-hand manner raised the proposed rental for tillage leases to 2/- per acre, and this rent proved so unreasonably high, where men were already struggling for bare existence, that it was subsequently found necessary to reduce it to the original sum of 1/-. The tillage leases were for areas of not more than 320 acres, the pastoral leases for 1000 acres, but there was no limitation, as to the total area which might be held in this manner. In both classes the lessee had the pre-emptive right of purchase at a fixed price to be specified, not less than £1 per acre. The tillage leases remained for a long deriod a notable feature in the land system of the Colony.

A condition of the first settlement of the Colony was that

no convicts were to be admitted within its borders, and for nearly 20 years the settlers held out staunchly for the maintenance of this principle. But so slow and painful was the progress, and so many the hardships endured, that finally they lost heart and came to look upon the establishment of a penal settlement and the consequent expenditure of Imperial funds, as their only remedy against absolute destitution, and an agitation was set on foot to secure this object. The subject is thus referred to in the report of the Land and Emigration Commissioners for 1858. "These changes of the land system, however, produced no improvement in the circumstances of Western Australia, and in 1847 the settlers, seeing that the Colony was year by year retrograding, and that their population was rapidly beginning to leave them,--which they erroneously attributed to the rise in the price of land—petitioned that it might be made a penal settlement. In 1849 this petition was renewed, even more earnestly, by persons in this country who were interested in the Colony. They stated that by late advices received in this country they have learned with dismay of the progressive abandonment of that Colony, which is taking place in consequence of the utter hopelessness of the task of supporting a community of settlers without the materials of such support! Eventually, in 1850, the first batch of convicts was landed on their shores, and between that day and 1856 the number sent out appears to have been 3976." The Colony remained a penal settlement until 1868, when transportation to Australia was finally abandoned. By this date the Colony had absorbed nearly 10,000 prisoners.

Meanwhile in 1864, an amendment and amplification of the land regulations was made. The chief new feature of importance was a provision, that no lands were to be sold for less than 10/- per acre, the previous minimum price being reduced by one-half. The lowest area which might be purchased in the case of country lands was reduced to 40 acres, which minimum also applied to the pre-emptive rights of tillage or pastoral lessees. The conditions for tillage leases remained the same as formerly, except that leases might be applied for on both A and B classes of land. In the case of pastoral lands, it was provided that annual licenses to occupy might be granted to the first applicant for unappropriated class-A lands, at an annual rental of 2/- per 100 acres, for sections of 1000 acres and upwards. No license was, however, to be issued for a less rental than £1 per annum. The lands so held were liable to resumption at any time for purchase or tillage leases without compensation for improvements. In class-B lands, pastoral leases were to be granted as formerly for 8 years, but for areas not exceeding 10,000 acres in one lease. Lessees retained the pre-emptive right of purchase of any portions of the leasehold area, at the reduced rate of 10/- per acre. In the North and East districts, which were considered to be outside both the A and B classes of land, and were described as class C, special inducements were offered to settlers to explore and take up new couutry. They were given the right of free pasturage of stock for 12 months over unappropriated areas, and at the end of this period they might select 100,000 acres, a license to occupy which, free of rent, was granted for a further period of 3 years. During this term they might select out of the licensed area not more than 20,000 acres, for which a pastoral lease for 8 years was granted, rental being charged at the rate of 5/- per 1000 acres for the first four years, and 10/- for the second four years. The right to cultivate was granted on these areas, with a pre-emptive right of purchase as in other leases.

Further important amendments were made in 1873. The tillage leases then gave place to conditional sales, under a system of deferred payment, sales by auction being of course also retained. It was provided that not less than 100 nor more than 500 acres might be obtained under license for three years upon payment of 1/- per annum in advance, and at the end of that term, if the land had been occupied for $2\frac{1}{2}$ years, and fenced, and one-fourth of its area cleared and cropped, the fee simple might be obtained upon payment of 7/- per acre, or a total payment of 10/- per acre. As an alternative, the licensee might, at the end of the three years, obtain a lease of the land for 7 years, with the right of purchase at the same rate of payment. A system of land grants to emigrants was now also introduced. Immigrants who occupied land within six months after arrival, and improved it as in the case of conditional purchasers, were entitled to have credited to them as rent or part of purchase money, an amount equal to the sum paid as passage money for themselves and their families, at the rate of £15 for each adult. Lands infested with a certain indigenous poison plant which was fatal to cattle, might be leased for terms of 21 years at an annual rental of 2/6 per 1000 acres, but in no case might the rental be less than £1 per annum. Pre-emptive rights for 21 years were given to persons leasing 1000 acres and upwards and paying a rental in advance of £1, under which, if, for three years before the end of the term, the poison plant had been eradicated, the lessee obtained the fee simple of the land. Lands in the North and East districts, might be selected in blocks of 40 acres or some multiple of 40, and each purchaser of 160 acres was entitled to a town lot of half an acre at the same price as rural lands.

The regulations again underwent extensive alterations in 1877. The Colony was then divided into districts—the Central, Northern, Central Eastern, and South-Eastern. Rural lands in all these districts except the Central were to be open for sale in blocks of not less than 400 acres, at 5/- per acre. Pastoral lands were divided into first and second classes. First-class lands might be rented under annual license, in blocks of not less than 3000 acres, at a rent of £1 per 1000 acres per annum. The second-class lands, were open to lease for 14 years, in blocks of not less than 20,000 acres, at a rental of 5/- per annum for each 1000 acres or part of 1000 acres. Within twelve months of the date of a lease the lessee was entitled to select from his own run blocks of not less than 1000 acres, all land which he deemed advisable to hold during the term of lease under a pre-emptive right to purchase, unconditionally, and the rental of these reserved lands was increased to £5 per 1000 acres. The prices to be paid for the freehold varied according to locality, from 2/6 to 10/- per acre. Immigrants upon arrival in the Colony, whether at their own expense, or at the cost of the Government were entitled to select, and (under certain conditions) to obtain the fee simple, if over the age of 21, of a rural block of 50 acres; if between the ages of 14 and 21, of 25 acres; if under that age, of 12½ acres. No family, however, might select more than 150 acres. Mechanics and special workmen were permitted at their option to select a town lot in preference to a rural grant. The conditions attached to the securing of the freeholds of the selections were that the occupants should reside on them for five years, and substantially fence and cultivate one-fourth of the areas. If these conditions were not complied with, the land reverted to the Crown.

In 1882 the regulations were once more amplified and amended. A new and comparatively rich stretch of country similar to the Northern Territory of South Australia, then recently discovered, and known as the "Kimberley District," was added to those previously proclaimed, and it was provided that the minimum price for the purchase of rural lands in this and the Central districts should be 10/- per acre; that for other districts being 5/-. The minimum areas which could be secured on these terms were 40 acres in the Central district; 200 acres in the Kimberley district; and 400 acres elsewhere. The terms of payment remained as formerly. Special inducements were held out for the cultivation of tropical products such as tea, coffee, sugar, etc., a free grant of 500 acres of land being offered in the Kimberley district to any person who in one year sold not less than £500 worth of any such produce. The conditions as to pastoral lands remained unaltered, except that in the Kimberley district, pastoral leases were to be for areas of not less than 50,000 acres, where there were water frontages, and 20,000 acres otherwise; and the annual rental was to be 10/- per 1000 acres. After occupying a leasehold area for four years, every lessee had to stock it with at least 20 sheep or 2 head of cattle, his own property, for every 1000 acres held, and retain this proportion of stock on the run during the term of lease. By new regulations, made in 1884, the proportion of stock to be placed on the land was fixed at 10 sheep or 1 head of cattle per 1000 acres, in default of which an increased rental of 10/- per 1000 acres was charged. Land grants to immigrants were discontinued in 1882.

The whole regulations were re-coded, and amended in 1887, and it is under these that settlement is now taking place. The Governor-in-Council was authorised under the new provisions to reserve temporarily from sale any Crown Lands within two miles of a projected railway, and to prescribe an increased price for their sale. The Colony was once more re-divided, into six districts, described as the South-West, Gascoyne, North-West, Kimberley, Eucla, and Eastern divisions. In all of these divisions, sale by auction was permitted, but otherwise the conditions of occupation differ in each, according to their geographical position.

In the South-West division, which comprises the original centres of population, and the great bulk of the settled country, pastoral land may be occupied under annual license at a rental of £1 per 1000 acres per annum. For purposes of cultivation, agricultural areas of not less than 2000 acres may be set apart, the freehold of which may be obtained by a system of conditional purchase, under deferred payments, in areas ranging from 100 to 1000 acres. The minimum price for land within these areas, which may be fixed by the Governor from time to time, is 10/- per acre—which is the present price—payable in 20 equal instalments. Upon approval of an application for a section of land, a license is granted to the applicant for a period of five years, and within six months he must reside upon the land. He must also fence it during the remainder of the term. If these conditions are complied with, a lease is granted to him for 15 years, and after the term of the lease has expired, or at any time during its currency, provided that the fence is in good order, that improvements have been made equal in value to the full purchase money, and that the balance of the purchase money has been paid either in the shape of annual rents or in a lump sum, a grant in fee may be obtained. Land outside agricultural areas is also open for free selection, upon the same conditions. Non-residential conditional purchase is permitted either within or without agricultural areas, but upon payment of double the yearly rental and the price charged per acre for residential selections. Unconditional selection of blocks of not less than 100 nor more than 1000 acres within agricultural areas, and not exceeding 5000 acres outside agricultural areas, is likewise allowed, on payment of a total sum of 10/- per acre; but the land must be fenced within three years, and within five years 5/- per acre must be spent on improvements.

In the other divisions special areas for purchase may be set apart of not less than 5000 acres, and the total quantity of land to be held by any one person in a division may be not less than 100 nor more than 5000 acres. No land can be purchased except after survey. The price per acre is 10/- payable within 10 years. A lease is granted for this term, during the first two years of which the land must be fenced, and at any subsequent date, if improvements equal in value to the amount of the purchase money have been effected, the fee simple may be obtained upon payment of the balance of the purchase money, or by the payment of the rent for the full term. Pastoral lands may be leased in each of these divisions, for periods which must all expire at the end of 1907, but generally upon different terms as to payment of rent, which ranges from 2/6 per 1000 acres to 10/- per 1000 acres, according to locality. In all the districts but the Kimberley, the leasehold areas must be not less than 20,000 acres. In the Kimberley district they must be not less than 50,000 acres with water frontage, and 20,000 acres without. Any lessee in the Kimberley and Eucla divisions may obtain a reduction of one-half the rentals stated, for the first 14 years of his lease, if in the former he has in his possession within the division 10 head of sheep or one head of large stock for every 1000 acres leased; or, if in the latter (in lieu of stock) he has expended £8 for every 1000 acres of the leasehold in procuring artificial supplies of water. If runs in any division except the South-West are not stocked within 7 years with 10 sheep or one head of cattle per 1000 acres, or a sum of £5 per 1000 is not expended in water improvements, double rent is charged. Lessees who have within five years fulfilled the stocking conditions within the Kimberley, North-West, Eucla, and Gascoyne divisions may purchase a homestead of nor less than 500 nor more than 5000 acres, at 10/- per acre, on conditions of improvement and fencing. The conditions as to poisoned land formerly in force are retained.

Mineral lands and lands on gold-fields are regulated by enactments and regulations passed in 1892. In the case of mineral lands, other than gold-mining lands, "mining licenses" for 12 months are issued, which entitle the holders to mine upon Crown Lands for minerals. Subsequently leases may be obtained for periods not exceeding 21 years, at an annual rental of 5/- per acre, for areas up to 160 acres, except for coal-mining leases, which may be 640 acres. In the case of gold-fields, miners' rights are issued, which entitle the holders during any period not exceeding 10 years, to mine on Crown Lands for gold; and subsequently mining leases are issued for terms not exceeding 21 years, which entitle the lessees to mine on areas not exceeding 25 acres for gold.

One of the most important features of Western Australian legislation is that which permits the construction of railways on the land grant principle. Several lines made upon this basis are now in existence, and others are in course of construction. Lines of railway between certain termini having been approved by the Legislature, contracts are received from persons or companies willing to construct them, on the basis of the contractors receiving a subsidy in land from the State, and retaining possession of and working the lines. Upon the completion of a contract, the State gives to the contractor grants of 12,000 acres of land for each mile of railway constructed. Such lands are to be selected within a belt of country stretching 40 miles on each side of the line; but one-half the frontage to the line is to be reserved to the State. The land received by the contractor must be selected within 12 months after the opening of the railway, and it must be taken up in areas of not less than 12,000 acres. He also has the privilege of selecting one half the lands to be so taken, at the commencement of the construction of the railway to be reserved on his behalf. So far there are but little statistical data available to show the advantages or otherwise to the Colony of this system, but on the whole it appears to have worked advantageously. The greater portion of the railway lines within the Colony are owned by private companies. On December 31st 1892, 679 miles of private railways were open for traffic, as against 197 miles of Government lines.

It is very difficult to assert, in so many words, whether the land system of Western Australia has been a success or not. The circumstances of the colony are unique, and the results achieved have to be viewed in that light. Statistics are in themselves, therefore, misleading, and they require to be careful considered in connection with other circumstances. On the face of it, for instance, the fact that at the end of 1890, when the population was almost exactly 50,000, there had been alienated within the colony a total area of 5,154,673 acres,— or something like 100 acres to each inhabitant — would seem to indicate a very lavish disposal of the public estate. But the great bulk of this country is in the hands of railway companies or syndicates, which have received grants of land, to be subsequently thrown open for settlement. The colony has a *quid pro quo* in its improved internal communication, which will assist in the opening up to settlement the immense territory still at disposal.

Unfortunately, the official statistics of the colony are very meagre, and there is nothing to show the number or area of holdings. The figures as to cultivation alone will not give a thoroughly accurate idea as to the advance made in the way of settlement. From the nature of the soil, which is patchy in quality, consisting of great barren wastes with here and there fertile tracts, Western Australia is almost essentially a pastoral country, though of late years gold-mining, has attracted much attention and the population has been considerably increased in consequence. Agriculture, of course, is carried out to some extent, but only in a minor degree, and up to the present large quantities of bread-stuffs and other produce have had to be imported, as the colony has made little progress in providing for its own necessities. The following table indicates roughly its position during the ten years ending in 1891.

Year.	Population	Land under conditional purchase.	Land under cultivation	Land under crop	Land under pastoral lease	Cattle	Sheep
	No.	acres.	acres.	acres.	millions of acres	No.	No.
1882	30,766	154,298	——	56,691	136	65,073	1,259,797
1883	31,700	178,645	——	58,111	160	64,558	1,315,155
1884	32,958	107,344	79,669	74,930	146	71,102	1,547,061
1885	35,186	297,079	77,728	60,058	142	70,408	1,702,719
1886	39,584	342,630	86,248	84,403	128	88,254	1,809,071
1887	42,488	317,238	105,582	66,162	121	93,544	1,909,940
1888	42,137	372,048	106,015	65,699	106	95,822	2,112,393
1889	43,698	445,282	117,833	73,408	105	119,571	2,366,681
1890	46,290	441,037	122,033	69,676	102	130,970	2,524,913
1891	53,285	241,763	131,900	64,209	105	133,690	1,962,212

These figures indicate pretty clearly that the colony has now made a start. It is at any rate a significant fact that, while within a period of over fifty years, up to 1882. the population had only reached 30,000 persons, during the last ten years it has nearly doubled. In the latter period, also, a large increase in the area of land held under conditions of residence, etc., is shown, though there was a remarkable falling of in 1891 from the previous year, which was probably due largely to the fact that lands previously held under conditional purchase had been made freeholds, as the revenue from land sales showed a great increase in 1890. The land under cultivation increased by about 60 per cent in 8 years, and the area under crop also showed a marked increase, the falling off in 1891 being attributed to the dry weather. The area under cultivation in 1892 was stated to have increased to 161,000 acres, and the area under crops to 79,000 acres. The figures respecting the pastoral industry are somewhat remarkable, indicating as they do that, while the area under lease has decreased very largely, better use is being made of the land, as the number of cattle has doubled, and but for the decrease of sheep in 1891, due to drought, the same remark would also apply to them.

It cannot be readily stated what share the land system, bears in these results, but that not much fault is found with it locally may be gauged from the fact that since the granting of constitutional government in 1890 no attempt has been made to change its main principles. The general feeling is that the terms under which land may be obtained are sufficiently liberal, and that the increase of railway communication to open up the country is at present more than adequate, but that a great increase of population is necessary. To effect this, the present government have resolved to revive in another form, the system formerly adopted of offering to immigrants or others not freeholders free grants of land. A Bill giving effect to this principle was read a second time in the Legislative Assembly in 1892, but it was subsequently withdrawn, and had just been again introduced at the time of writing in August, 1893, with every prospect of being carried. The original measure provided for grants of 160 acres upon the condition that the grantee should erect a house within two years; fence, clear, and cultivate one-fourth of the area within five years; and fence the whole within seven years. It was also proposed that the Government should, after the erection of a house of the value of £100, advance to the owner a sum of £50 and a further sum of £25 upon the completion of other improvements, the amounts to be repaid with interest at five per cent.

The State-aid clauses, however, proved objectionable, and for this reason the Bill was withdrawn. In the new measure the money loan clauses have been eliminated, but the system of grants with residence conditions, etc., have been retained. A new principle has also been embodied of granting homestead leases for fifty years over areas of from 1000 to 5000 acres, the leases to become freeholds when 7*s* 6*d* per acre has been paid on second-class, and 5*s* on third-class lands. With these very liberal provisions as part of its land policy, it may reasonably be supposed that Western Australia will continue to advance in a manner at least proportionate to the progress shown during the past few years. Its territory is enormous, while its position as the nearest Australasian colony to Europe offers it many advantages over the other provinces, and it now needs but population, enterprise, and capital to develop its great resources, and raise it to a more fitting position amongst the Australias.

CHAPTER VIII.

SOUTH AUSTRALIA.

The history of South Australia is essentially bound up with that of its land system. The Colony was originally formed to give effect to a new method of colonisation, based upon the settlement of the lands in a certain manner; and subsequent legislation, during recent years at any rate, has been considerably in the direction of amending or amplifying statutes previously passed to deal with the public estate. Without a doubt, special efforts have been made latterly to attract a proper class of persons to the soil, and to prevent its use or alienation in an undesirable manner, and to some extent, this end has been achieved.

The Colony ranks next to Western Australia in point of size amongst the Australasian group. It has a total estimated area of 578 millions of acres, and is thus about three times as large as New South Wales, and half as large again as Queensland. In form it is like a great belt some 500 miles in width, stretching north and south across the continent, from sea to sea. To all intents and purposes it comprises two distinct and separate portions, one known as "The Province" and the other as the "Northern Territory," which differ widely in climate and physical features, and are therefore generally treated separately in legislation. The Province includes all the country south of the 26th parallel of latitude, but this boundary line is far beyond the original settled districts, within which only cultivation is possible. This area is bounded northwards by what is generally known as "Goyders' Line of Rainfall," and a semi-desert region is entered from about the 30th parallel of latitude.

The inland features of South Australia differ from those of the Eastern Colonies. The mountain ranges do not follow the coast line, but strike across the continent, towards the centre of which they end amidst vast saline mud swamps, or salt lakes, the chief of which are Lakes Eyre, Torrens, Gaird, Prome, and Amadeus. These are fed by small streams from the ranges, which disappear in a mysterious manner in the heart of the continent. The rivers of South Australia are as a rule small in length and volume, with the exception of the Murray, which has its source in New South Wales, but enters the ocean not far from the city of Adelaide. Near to the southern coast the average rainfall is fair, and it is only here, as previously indicated that cultivation to any great extent is carried on. The pastoral lands beyond are but sparsely covered with sheep owing to the want of water. In natural advantages, therefore, South Australia cannot compare with the eastern provinces, but the enterprise of the inhabitants has done a great deal, and, had the natural conditions, been more favorable, the place now occupied by the Colony in the Australian Commonwealth, would probably have been much more important.

The Colony was established in 1836, to give effect to the principle of colonisation and land settlement known as the "Wakefield System." The fundamental basis of this scheme, as propounded by Mr. Gibbon Wakefield, was "concentrated colonisation," under which it was believed, there would be largely reproduced in these southern lands the social conditions of the mother country. To bring this state of things about it was proposed that land should be sold at a higher fixed price than that previously adopted in Australia, and that the proceeds should go chiefly towards the introduction of a suitable class of labourers to cultivate the land taken up by those who possessed the necessary capital. The price to be charged was to be a "sufficient price," — a price, that is, which would prevent people from taking up land in too large areas, and yet provide sufficient revenue for the purposes of immigration and to assist in carrying out the ordinary purposes of the settlement.

There was about this time spreading throughout Great Britain quite a wave of feeling in favour of immigration to new lands, and the scheme took such a hold that in 1831 a South Australian Company was formed to apply the principles it enunciated to a new colony. The company desired to possess absolute control of the new country, on some such basis as the grant to the East India Company, but this idea not proving acceptable to the Imperial Government, a charter was refused. Three years later a South Anstralian Association rose, Phoenix-like, from the ashes of the old company, to carry out its proposals; but its promoters wisely made no demand for the political powers previously asked for, and in the same year an Act was passed empowering the Crown to establish provinces in South Australian territory, and appoint commissioners with authority to survey and sell lands at a uniform price, being not less than 12/- per acre, the proceeds from which were to be applied to the purposes of an immigration fund, etc. It was specially provided in the Act also that no convicts were to be transported to the new province.

A South Australian Company was again formed to assist in giving practical effect to the provisions of the measure, and under its auspices nine shiploads of colonists of a superior class were despatched in 1836 to lay the foundations of the settlement. It was innocently believed that these pioneers would at once settle down into an old country groove, with distinct lines of demarcation between the various professions and occupations of the people; but the site of the capital city having been decided upon, the people instead of taking up and cultivating the available land, formed themselves into a town community in Adelaide, and speculated in town lots, which rose rapidly in value. Few seemed to think of the future, and the unwholesome gambling prevailed to such an extent that, no attempt was made to get anything from the soil. When the inevitable smash came, two years later, most of those who had arrived in the Colony with considerable means were penniless, everything having been spent in cost of living.

Then the actual colonisation of South Australia began. He price of bread-stuffs rose to a fabulous extent, those who had come out as servants secured land at absurdly low prices and commenced to cultivate. Under the original method of disposing of the land, applications for sections were made under sealed tender at a fixed price of 12/- per acre, which was raised to 20/- within a short period. These conditions were adhered to until 1843, up to which period about 323,000 acres had been disposed of. In this year a new Act was passed, providing for survey before sale, quarterly sales by auction, and a division of the lands into town, suburban, and country lands, with a fixed minimum upset price for the latter of £1 per acre, to be increased for special lots. One half of the land fund was to be devoted to purposes of immigration, and the remainder to the general cost of government of the Colony, including cost of survey. This last enactment remained in force without amendment till 1857, by which date there had been a total alienation by sales of 1,756,000 acres, at an average price for all lands of £1 5s 3d per acre.

It was in 1846 during the currency of this measure that, Earl Grey's Waste Lands Act, which proved such a curse to the neighbouring colonies, came into operation. But the Governor of South Australia, Sir Henry Young, administered the Act in a different manner to that adopted elsewhere. The Colony, in terms of the Act, was divided into settled and unsettled districts. The lands in the former were dealt with as previously described, but the lands outside of hundreds were leased for pastoral purposes for terms not exceeding 14 years, at rates varying from 10*s* to £1 per square mile, according to quality. Nothing in any such lease however, interfered with the "right of the Governor at any time to sell, reserve, or otherwise dispose of the whole or any part of the land so depastured." On becoming part of a hundred, leased land ceased to be affected by the lease, and no renewal of the lease, nor compensation for improvements could be claimed; consequently the whole of the lands of the Colony were reserved to the Crown absolutely, as any land held under lease which was applied for could be put up for competition by auction. The right of pre-emption granted to squatters elsewhere, was not accorded; but where their land was of no special value for cultivation they retained the use of it without competition.

It was thus practically laid down that squatters could become leaseholders, but their temporary possession was no bar to the sale of any land comprised in their run. No obstacle was thrown in their way if they desired to purchase any portion of their leasehold, in order to cultivate it, but they could not on their part throw any obstacle in the way of colonists desirous of purchasing.

In 1856 the present Constitution Act was passed, under which responsible government was obtained, and a Legislative Council and Assembly were elected. One of the first acts of the new Parliament was to pass an amending Land Bill. This measure, made but little alteration in the original system. Its chief novel feature was a provision that land should be offered in blocks of not more than 640 acres. These had to be surveyed and delineated upon public maps prior to sale, which was still at auction, a deposit of 20 per cent being required at the fall of the hammer.

Up to this date, it will be observed, all sales of land had been for cash, either at auction or by private purchase. But a feeling had been growing that while the system of cash sales might be beneficial from a revenue point of view, it debarred men with small means from competing for the best portions of the land. The veteran Surveyor-General, Mr. G. W. Goyder, describes the circumstances at this period as follows *—"The sales of land by public auction were satisfactory for a time, but difficulties were encountered by the farmers in obtaining suitable farms, owing to the competition from agents purchasing largely from capitalists, who let the land at second hand to them, but at high yearly

---

* "Report on the disposal of Public Lands of South Australian"—1890 Government Printer, Adelaide, p. 32.

rentals, and upon long terms if right of purchase were granted. These difficulties were augmented in the case of good lands forming portions of runs, as they then had not only to compete with capitalists, striving to secure land to let it again, on terms profitable to themselves, but also with the ordinary agents who were frequently retained in the interests of the runholders. Farmers could consequently only obtain good farms by paying the most exorbitant prices at auction, and the difficulty resulted in the suspension of ordinary auction sales—except for town and suburban lands—and in the adoption of sales by deferred payment, the purchaser being required to occupy the land."

In 1869 the measure known as Strangway's Act was passed, which, while continuing the former method of sales by auction, etc., also permitted the sale of country lands on credit, for four years, interest at the rate of 5 per cent—a total of 20 per cent—on the purchase money, being charged at the outset. A condition of the sales was that purchasers had to reside on the land, and effect improvements to the value of 12/6 per acre. The Government was empowered to proclaim certain blocks as agricultural areas, in which lands could be purchased on credit only, in areas of not more than 640 acres. In 1870, the term of credit was further extended to five years, with the option of an increase to eight years. The compulsory improvements were also made less stringent, and the purchase of the land outright was permitted after three years' *bona fide* residence, and the completion of the necessary improvements. In the next year, again, the conditions were still further modified to permit the payment of ten per cent of the interest at the time of making the application for the land, and ten per cent at the end of three years, the payment of the principal being made at the end of the fifth year as formerly.

In 1872 the Waste Lands Alienation Act was passed, which superseded previous enactments, and provided for the subdivision of lands into the following six classes—viz., town, suburban, country, reclaimed, special country lots, and improved lands. Selection was permitted on a condition of either personal or substituted residence, the personal applicant having the preference, however, where there were two or more applicants for the same land under different conditions. But where the applicants desired to select under the same conditions, the land was submitted to auction, at which these persons only could compete, the highest bidder taking the land. The system of payment was also again further amended, six years' credit being allowed, with interest at the annual rate of $3\frac{1}{2}$ per cent. Three years' interest was paid on securing the land, and the interest for the remainder of the term at the end of the first three years. At the end of the six years, one-half of the purchase money was allowed to stand over for a further period of four years, upon payment in advance of interest for the whole extended term, at the rate of four per cent per annum. Selectors were by a schedule limited in their operations to lands within a district, the boundary of which was intended to represent a line of demarcation between country over which the rainfall was fairly reliable and nearly akin to that of Adelaide and the land with a less certain rainfall. This schedule was, however, repealed in 1874, and selection after survey was permitted as far north as the 26th parallel of latitude.

With respect to the credit system, Mr. Goyder has the following in his report:—"The abolition of the usual sales of country lands for cash did two things. It put a stop for a time to large properties being obtained by monied men direct from the Crown, and it deprived farmers and others possessed of sufficient means and desirous to settle in the colony of doing so, as only inferior lands remained open to purchase after being picked over for two years by selectors under credit agreement; and those who wished to buy land and pay for it at the time, had to do so from private owners, at greatly enhanced cost, or go elsewhere, which there is but little doubt many did. The result of the sale of large areas of land by deferred payment is less easily stated. Had the selection been limited so that each individual exhausted his right under one application, and under no circumstances whatever would be permitted to select a second time, under credit agreement, (his right under the Act being exhausted;) and had the land thrown open to farmers under credit agreement comprised only localities in which the soil and rainfall were known to be suitable for agricultural purposes, much and permanent benefit to the State might have ensued. Unfortunately many of those who selected first, and obtained really good and well situated land, completed purchase at the end of the third year, sold at a profit, and again selected, but in a less favoured locality, but looking for further advantage by repeating so profitable a proceeding. Meantime the object of fixing a population on the land disposed of had to a great extent been defeated, as much of the land first selected went to swell large estates, and dropped out of cultivation, whilst the position of the selector, though he benefited in one respect by the sale at a profit of the land previously held by him, was rendered more precarious as to success by his second selection being in a less favoured situation.

He was however more fettered by the conditions imposed by his second agreement, the term of which was extended by Parliament, so as to render a second sale improbable, and he thus became more likely to settle upon the land. .... The risk of allowing lands that were situate beyond the reliable limit of a sufficient rainfall, to be open for selection under deferred payments was pointed out over and over again, but the demand for land was so urgent and so persistent that it was ultimately agreed to. ... The seasons changed at length however, failure ensued in the outside hundreds, selection all but stopped, and many thousands of acres surveyed and ready for sale were withheld. . . The seasons continued bad and failure followed failure until relief became essential, and relief was freely accorded by the legislature; but again the relief fell short of what was required, as, in addition to the money concession, the selectors should have been called upon to surrender their agreements for land in such uncertain localities, and where universal ruin prevailed. This might readily have been done, as there was abundant land then available within the line of rainfall, though perhaps of somewhat inferior character. It was not insisted on, however, and the relief granted failed to be of permanent benefit to those whom it sought to advantage, and most of them continue to occupy this outside country, and to suffer with their wives and families the wants and anxieties entailed by a succession of bad seasons, which the profits of exceptionally good ones will rarely enable them to overcome. These people appear to cling to the land with the utmost fortitude, enduring every species of privation, hope of better things being their only solace. It is now too late to offer land in exchange, as those in better and nearer hundreds have since been disposed of. The only remedy, therefore, appears to be to extend their holdings, with long leases on liberal terms, so that they may use the land during ordinary seasons, for pastoral purposes, and in good seasons cultivate available lands, and thereby earn a decent livelihood for themselves and become as far as possible useful members of the State."

From the year 1872, as indicated by these observations, changes were made almost yearly in the land laws to meet the varying conditions of the colony. The principal of these included an increase of the maximum area which might be selected to 1000 acres, irrespective of previous selections. But one-tenth of the land had to be cultivated during the first year of credit, and one-fifth during the second and subsequent year. In the event of lands which had been set apart for agricultural purposes being unselected at the end of two years, and still remaining unsold for cash at auction, they might be offered on 21 years' leases, with the right of purchase during the last eleven years of the term. The terms under which land could be obtained on credit were so amended in 1880 as to permit the payment of interest equal to 10 per cent on the purchase money upon application, four per cent in advance during the next six years, and five per cent in advance during the last seven years. Credit for twenty years was thus given, at the end of which period the purchase money had to be paid.

The last decade has been one of much unrest with respect to land matters, and nearly every government has brought in a new Bill to deal with the question. Consequently the legislation now in force is somewhat complicated. In 1886, a Crown Lands Consolidation Act was passed, and an interpretation Act in 1887, but those measures were repealed and amended by the Crown Lands Act of 1888. As this enactment, with the amending Acts of 1889 and 1890, provides the principal legislative machinery under which the present system is carried out, it may be well here to give an outline of their joint provisions. It is declared at the outset that the grant in fee simple of any land shall not be construed to convey or include any property in any metal in or upon any land, and that persons may be authorised to search for these minerals, metals, etc., upon private property.

In lieu of the previous system of sales by auction for cash or on credit, a new method was now introduced, under which land could only be obtained under a system of leases with the right to purchase, or under perpetual leases. The province was divided into land districts, to each of which a Land Board, was to be appointed to roughly classify the land within hundreds, decide upon the areas to be leased, according to the quality of the land, in blocks of not more than 1000 acres for any one leasehold; fix the price and annual rent of the same, and generally carry out the administration of the Act, under the control of a Commissioner. After notice in the Government Gazette, a lease of such lands as the Boards may decide upon can be applied for under either of the methods referred to. Accompanying the application there must be a deposit equal to 20 per cent of the first year's rent,— which is notified in the Gazette — and in the event of there being more than one application, the Board shall decide as to the successful applicant. Every lease with the right to purchase is granted for a term of 21 years, with a right of renewal for a further similar period, and carries the right of purchase under certain conditions, of the leased lands at any time after six years' occupation, at a price fixed by the Board, being not less than 5/- per acre.

The rent of land taken up on perpetual lease is fixed for the first 14 years by notification in the Gazette, and it is subsequently re-appraised by the Land Boards every 14 years. The Boards in fixing rents must take into account improvements other than those made by lessees, and should the holder of a perpetual lease fail to signify his acceptance of the rent fixed, within a specified time, he forfeits his right to a renewal, and the lease is offered to competition at the rental fixed by the Board. In the event of the lease being taken up by another person, he must pay for the improvements made by the outgoing lessee. Stringent provisions are made for the due payment in advance, of rents. A fine of five per cent is imposed if the rent is not paid on or before the date fixed, and this is increased to 10 per cent if the time in default reaches one month, while the lease may at the option of the Minister be forfeited if it is not paid up at the end of three months from the due date. Any lease may be transferred during the term of its currency, provided that the consent of the Commissioner of Crown Lands is first obtained, and that the incoming lessee does not hold the right of purchase of more than 1000 acres. It is a fact worthy of notice in connection with the payment of rents that up to the end of the present year (1893) there was outstanding as overdue rent a sum of about £150,000. The collection of rent, indeed, has proved to be one of the greatest difficulties of the system. The leases reserve to the Crown metals, ores, gems, minerals, and mineral oils, etc., as well as growing timber except such as may be required for cultivation or building purposes on the leased land. The lessees under either system of lease must fence the area within five years, destroy all vermin, and keep all improvements found on the land in good repair and insured.

Any person who has purchased land under previous Acts, on a credit agreement, may exchange his previous tenure for a lease with the right of purchase or a perpetual lease, provided the area held be not greater than 1000 acres. After the rent and price at which he may purchase have been fixed by the Board, the applicant may accept or decline to agree to the appraisements, but in the event of his accepting, he is entitled to have credited to him as rent all moneys paid by him previously as purchase money, less 10 per cent for interest paid on the original application. In the case of special blocks which are surrounded by sold lands, or lands contracted to be sold, or blocks required for special purposes in areas not exceeding 100 acres, provision is made for their sale by auction for cash, and lands may be disposed of in a similar manner which have been opened for lease for two years without application. In either case the upset price must be not less than 5s per acre.

Pastoral country is divided into three classes. Class I includes pastoral lands held under a new lease, issued under certain preceding Acts, or which, having been held under such new leases were held under other leases expiring in the year 1888, or on the first of January, 1887, and granted in lieu of such leases. Class II includes pastoral lands held on the 14th of November, 1884, and which are now held pursuant to a then existing right to a renewal of such pastoral lease. Class III include all other pastoral lands. When leases under Class I are about to expire or to be determined, the lands comprised in the leasehold area not required for other purposes may be offered for lease by public auction, in blocks most suitable for securing the stocking and development of the country and utilising the improvements, for terms not exceeding 21 years, at an appraised rental payable yearly in advance. The lessee has to pay a deposit equal to 10 per cent on the value of the improvements then existing on the lease, as security for their proper maintenance, interest at the rate of 5 per cent being allowed on the deposit, which is returned at the end of the term. This amount may be returned earlier, however, when improvements equivalent in value have been made by the lessee, but it may be forfeited if he allows existing improvements to deteriorate in value to the same extent. On the expiration of any pastoral lease, or upon the resumption of the whole or part of the lands included within a leasehold, the lessee is paid by the Crown the value of all substantial improvements on the land leased or resumed, and also for the depreciation in the value of his lease by the resumption. In Class II the leases are similar to those in Class I as to the term of years and other conditions, except that the lessee is paid for all improvements he may have effected upon the run of whatever class, during the currency of the lease. In Class III, leases may be obtained by auction for 42 years, at an upset rental, paid in advance, of 2/6 per square mile for the first 14 years, the subsequent rent being fixed by valuation every 14 years. The lessee must covenant to stock his run with sheep in the proportion of not less than five, or cattle in the proportion of not less than one head per square mile. This proportion must afterwards be retained, and before the end of seven years increased to a proportion of not less than 20 sheep or four head of cattle per square mile. But in lieu of stocking, the lessee may at his option expend money in the ratio of 30*s* per square mile before the end of the third year and £3 before the end of the seventh year. In this class no compensation for improvements is allowed at the expiration of the term.

Crown Lands may be used for mining purposes upon exceedingly liberal terms. Licenses may be obtained giving the right for twelve months to search for metals and minerals except gold upon any specific mineral lands not exceeding 80 acres in extent, and to remove therefrom one ton of the metal or mineral for analysis. The license gives to its holder during its currency a preferential right to a lease of land included in his license area, but he must keep one man at least at work on the land for nine of the twelve months, upon pain of forfeiture of the license. Leases for mining purposes for terms not exceeding 99 years may also be obtained by the first applicant over areas not exceeding 80 acres, at a fixed annual rental of 1*s* per acre, payable yearly in advance, and a further payment of 6*d* in the £ on the declared profits from the land. A sum not exceeding £6 per acre must be expended on the land every two years, but there is an optional alternative condition that the lessee may constantly employ during 9 months of the year, one man for every twenty acres of the leasehold. All improvements upon the land at the time of taking up the lease must be paid for by the applicant before the lease is prepared, and he must give to any adjoining occupier of pastoral land free access to any natural water or spring upon the land for the use of stock. Special leases for areas not exceeding 640 acres may also be granted on such terms as the Governor may approve, to discoverers of coal, guano, petroleum, or other valuable substance, other than a metal or metalliferous ore.

One of the most interesting features perhaps of the South Australian land system is that under which working men may obtain the use of Crown Lands in small areas near to centres of population. Effect was first given to this principle by the Act of 1885, which provided for the survey on town, suburban, aboriginal reserves, or other Crown Lands, of working men's blocks, in areas not exceeding 20 acres, to be leased by auction for terms of 21 years, with a right of renewal for a further similar period. Since that date, however, numerous, modifications of the system have been made. In the following year the lessee was given the right of purchase at any time during his second term, or at the end of the first term of lease. But the system of perpetual lease was still retained as an alternative. Then in 1890 it was still further provided that leases of land situated within a radius of ten miles of the Adelaide Post Office could not be taken up with the right of purchase, and the purchase of such leaseholds as had already been taken up under the previous Act was made void. Under this Act, also, the Governor was empowered to purchase private lands for subdivision into blocks. A distinctly new principle was introduced in the following year, under what is known as the "Blockers' Loan Act," which provides for a Parliamentary vote, not exceeding £10,000, to be operated upon by the Commissioner of Crown Lands, and advanced to homestead block holders, to assist them in erecting buildings and making permanent improvements. The amount advanced to any one lessee must not exceed £50 at any one time, nor be more than one-half the cost to the blockholder of the permanent buildings then existing in good repair on the block. The loans must be repaid by instalments, payable at the commencement of the fifth, sixth, seventh, eighth, and ninth years respectively, from the date of advance, which time may be extended by the Commissioner. Interest at the rate of 5 per cent is charged on the loan. The Act also permits the endorsement by the Commissioner of leases to protect the blocker's interest from encumbrance or seizure. The rents of the leases must be paid annually in advance, under penalty of forfeiture of three months in arrear, and residence for nine months out of every twelve is made compulsory on the part of the lessee or a member of his family. An essential condition of the leases is that they may only be granted to working men who gain their living by their own labour, and who have attained the full age of 18 years.

The lands of the vast Northern Territory, which is under the administration of a Resident, are dealt with by an enactment passed in 1882. This measure provides that lands may be purchased for cash, without conditions, in blocks not exceeding 1280 acres, for 12/6 per acre; they may also be obtained under the deferred payment system, to the same maximum area, and at the same price, payable in ten years, together with an annual rent of 6d per acre. Land for pastoral purposes may be leased for a term not exceeding 25 years, in blocks up to 400 square miles. The annual rental for the first seven years is 6d per square mile; 2/6 being charged for the balance of the term. Special provisions have been made to encourage the cultivation of tropical produce, such as sugar, coffee, rice, tea, indigo, cotton, etc., under which blocks of from 320 to 1280 acres may be leased for such purposes at a rental of 6d per acre per annum. If at the expiration of five years the lessee can prove that he has cultivated one-fifth of his area by the end of the second year of his term, and one-half by the end of the fifth year, he is relieved from all further payment of rent, and the amount already so paid is credited to him towards the purchase of the land in fee.

An effort has now been made to indicate the conditions under which land may be obtained from the Crown. The task is not an easy one, owing to the great number of enactments passed of late years, many of which are still partly in operation, and partly overlap each other. This difficulty may be more readily understood perhaps when it is explained that within a period of about 20 years there has been on an average something like one Act passed to deal with the land question in every year, two such in several cases having become law in one year. These facts make it evident that the question has been a burning one for a number of years past; but two great obstacles have stood in the way of a solution of the difficulties surrounding it—viz, the lack of a sufficient available area of arable land, and the fact that in the early days of the Colony's existence vested rights were created owing to the necessity which existed for the sale of large areas for cash to meet the exigencies of the public revenue. The difficulty now is not so much the absence of a proper land system, as the want of suitable lands to be dealt with under it.

It is a noteworthy fact that, though the population is essentially an agricultural one and in the past the Colony has been pre-eminent in the growth of wheat, the land has been gradually merging into large holdings, which have become in great measure devoted to pastoral pursuits. Consequent upon the dryness of the climate the average yield of wheat per acre is small, and it does not pay to expend much capital in artificial fertilising. As a result, after a few years' continuous cropping, the land has become so impoverished as to make it unprofitable to cultivate further, and the holders have been glad to part with their sections to adjacent large proprietors, by whom they have been utilised for grazing. Available statistics do not readily show how far this system of aggregation has been progressing of late, but some significant facts are disclosed by the Census Returns for 1891. The following table, based on the information there supplied, indicates how land in the Colony other than that leased for pastoral purposes was held during the years 1885 and 1891 respectively.

Size of holdings.	No. of holdings.		Freeholds.		Leaseholds.		Total area.	
acres.	1885	1891	1885 acres.	1891 acres.	1885 acres.	1891 acres.	1885 acres.	1891 acres.
1 to 5	2278	2231	3712	3061	1524	1469	5236	4530
6 to 100	3885	4573	106122	96034	60831	82879	166953	178913
101 to 250	3150	2869	309538	265008	236780	236316	546318	501324
251 to 500	4271	3882	704937	587026	881973	876569	1586910	1463595
501 to 1000	4292	3867	1154072	970897	1923214	1775244	3077286	2746141
1001 to 2000	1045	1650	685206	843537	753491	1498408	1438408	2341945
2001 to 5000	420	744	589056	594087	659869	1687905	1248925	2281992
5001 to 10,000	133	298	499537	487913	460514	1678083	960051	2165996
10,001 to 20,000	76	183	508027	609249	566112	1962008	1074139	2571257
20,001 to 40,000	41	44	663841	679803	503545	501129	1167386	1180932
40,001 and upwds	17	14	415989	373674	596934	420389	1012923	794063
	19,608	20,355	5,640,037	5,510,289	6,644,787	10,720,399	12,284,535	16,230,668

Practically the whole of the land dealt with in the table has passed into private hands, as the leases are held with the right of purchase or in perpetuity. There appears to be no difficulty in the way of their transfer, and it will be seen from the table that in the case of areas between 6 and 100 acres, there is no perceptible increase either in the number of lessees or the extent of their leases, during a period of six years. But as to estates of from 100 to 1000 acres,—in which the bulk of the land might reasonably be supposed to be held—there is an actual falling off in the area, while with respect to the country held under lease in larger areas the figures are somewhat startling. The leaseholds of from 1000 to 2000 acres in extent were almost doubled, those from 2000 to 5000 nearly trebled, and those from 5000 to 10,000 and 10,000 to 20,000 acres have increased pretty well fourfold. There is also a falling off in the area of freeholds of between 20 and 2000 acres; while in the case of those between 1000 and 5000, and 10,000 and 40,000 acres, there is an increase. Yet during the period under notice the total area held under freehold tenure slightly decreased, owing probably to the forfeiture of holdings in the dry country and the fact that many deferred payment selections were exchanged for leases; this assumption receives colour from the fact that in 1890 the total area held under credit purchase agreements was 1,258,156 acres, which was reduced to 983,359 acres in 1891 and 887,123 acres in 1892.

The official figures do not show separately the number of leaseholders or freeholders for the years given, but there are sufficient data available to prove beyond doubt that the cultivable lands of the colony are rapidly merging into fewer holdings and being less cultivated. Out of a total increase of 747 holders—both freeholders and leaseholders—between the years 1885 and 1891, about 650 possess areas ranging between 6 and 20 acres, (presumably for the most part working men's blocks), while the total area held under both tenures has increased by about 4,000,000 acres. In other words, only about 100 additional people have taken up land under the ordinary conditions of selection, but those who already hold land have increased their holdings by that immense area. In the case of holders of areas between 100 and 1000 acres, there is an actual falling off in the numbers by about 1100, with a proportionate reduction of over half a million acres of country held; while there has been a total increase in the number of holders of between 1000 and 40,000 acres of about 1200, with an increased total area taken up of 4,650,000 acres, or an average of 3800 acres each. These figures also show an increase in the average size of the whole of the holdings in the Colony from 626 to 792 acres in six years—a little over 25 per cent.

Yet despite the increased area now being taken up under what is practically a perpetual tenure, cultivation does not progress proportionately, and there is an actual falling off in the total area under cultivation from 2,753,000 acres in 1885 to 2,568,000 acres in 1891. The chief decadence is in areas between 100 and 1000 acres, and it is significant that of the increased area of 4,650,000 acres included in holdings of between 1000 and 40,000 acres, a total extent of only 80,000 acres is now cultivated. The great bulk of the remainder, therefore, is either being merged directly into pastoral holdings, or is taking the place of country formerly held by small farmers, which is undergoing the same operation. With the decreased area under cultivation the crops in all classes have necessarily fallen off. Thus in wheat there is a depreciation from 14 million bushels in 1884 and 19 millions in 1887 to nine and six millions respectively in 1890 and 1891. Oats and barley show a similar drop, and in all other classes of agricultural produce except vine-growing (which has doubled within ten years) the figures show no increase.

In almost every respect the Colony has stood still of late years, as its population has increased but nominally, the total in 1891 being only 320,000 as against 307,000 in 1884, which is less than the regular natural increase by excess of births over deaths. That many of the younger men have migrated to other colonies owing to the difficulty of obtaining suitable land on which to settle, is an admitted fact which has in great measure stimulated the Parliament of late years to endeavour to remove the difficulty. But, as shown previously, it is not one to be removed off-hand by Act of Parliament. The bulk of the available wheat-growing land is already in the hands of people who naturally prefer to work it in the manner most profitable to themselves—viz., for sheep-raising and wool-growing. The various governments of the day have attempted to meet the position by opening up new country for settlement wherever it is supposed to be adapted for agriculture or agriculture and grazing combined, and every inducement has been offered to people to go on these lands by making provision for artificial water supplies, and railway communication. But the further out the settlers have to go the less is the rainfall and the smaller the return per acre, while the greater distance from market renders cultivation less profitable than would be the case in the older settled districts.

One of the most cheering features of recent land legislation has been that with respect to working men's blocks, the results of which have been very satisfactory. In May 1891 there were 1902 of these leases current, as against 1511 for the previous year, the total area held being 29,903 acres, or an average of a little over 15 acres. An inspection of 1567 of these which took place in 1891 showed that the bulk of the leases were held as follows—By labourers, 1174; artisans, 99; men in business, 77½; farmers, 48; farmers' children, 91; and ex-farmers, 23. The different sets of blocks are divided off in the following manner—(1) Those around large towns, suitable for homes for men who have fairly constant employment. (2) Those which provide homes for the families of that class of working men whose employment is intermittent, uncertain, often distant and at no fixed place. (3) Those which will probably, without the aid of irrigation, become market-gardens, orchards, etc., and which will consequently absorb all the labour of the lessee and his family; (4) Those suitable for grazing and root crops for dairying purposes. (5) Those in agricultural districts occupied chiefly by men employed on neighbouring farms. (These are used mostly for growing wheat for the family bread, and pig and fowl feed, grazing a cow or two, etc., and are said to be a great boon). (6) Those which will probably be brought under irrigation and are suitable for special industries, such as fruit drying, etc. The amount advanced up to February, 1893, under the Blockers' Loan Act of 1891 was £3755, (or an average of £25 17 7) between 156 lessees. There were at that date extant 2375 leases with the right to purchase, at an annual rental of £2555; and 112 perpetual leases, at an annual rental of £335. These figures are taken to show that the average working man prefers to get a piece of land he can call his own, when the opportunity occurs, than to be a tenant. The system has proved so successful to date, that in all future hundreds which may be declared open for settlement, it is proposed to set apart areas to be taken up in this manner.

Without a doubt the weak spot in the South Australian land system is to be found in the provisions which deal with its pastoral country. Despite the immense area of territory available, there has been of late no increase in the area taken up on lease for pastoral purposes, and but little in the number of sheep raised, as may be gathered from the fact that the total only increased from 6,804,000 in 1881-2 to 7,646,000 in 1891-2. The reason for this state of things may be traced to three causes—defective legislation, want of water, and rabbits. To properly comprehend the present system it is necessary to understand first the position of the three classes of pastoral leases now in existence. The classification of the land does not depend upon the locality, but upon the date of the first lease. Thus the lands in

Class I are scattered up and down amongst other lands, though the bulk of them are situate near the settled districts. Such of them as have been re-let, are now occupied on lease for 21 years, the Crown having to pay for all water improvements made by the lessee during the currency of the lease or at its termination. Class II comprises leases of land issued on November 14th, 1884, or pursuant to a then existing right of renewal. These lands are falling in from year to year, and form the bulk of the pastoral lands which will be open to lease during the next ten years. They are scattered about through different pastoral regions, and as a rule are more distant from the coast than most of the land under Class I. It is on these lands that very large sums will be payable for improvements by the Crown from year to year, as the lessees have to be paid not only for improvements to conserve water, but also for other improvements, on the expiry of their leases. Such of these leases as have fallen in since 1888 have been let on 21 years' lease, similar to those under ·Class I. The lands in Class III include all lands other than those under Classes I and II. In this class no compensation is allowed for improvements, but lessees have to stock the land to a certain extent or make equivalent improvements.

The sum likely to be due to lessees in Classes I and II for improvements under the Act of 1888 is estimated at 2½ millions! This is an enormous liability, but though the legislature was informed of the position in 1890 no material steps have been taken to make any provision to meet it. Under the Act of 1890 the lessees may, if they choose, surrender their leases and their rights to the cash compensation in exchange for new leases for a longer term at a rent to be fixed by the Government; but the only persons who have availed themselves of this provision have been those who have made but few improvements and have but little money to come to them. The right to payment for improvements was determined so far as regards all leases issued after the Act passed, so that now the one encouragement to lessees to improve their holdings is gone, and if a lessee spends £20,000 or £30,000 on his leasehold he leaves it all behind him when his time is up. He will not, therefore, spend money unless his rent is so very low that after sinking his capital he can still get a profit, which would be very rarely the case.

In all probability the result of recent legislation will be that the cheapest and most temporary improvements alone will be made, and the true permanent development of the country will cease. Thus while the necessity for making the improvements is now greater than ever, less inducements than previously are offered to the lessees to make them.

In 1891 a Pastoral Commission was appointed to consider the whole subject, and it recommended that while all necessary improvements should be encouraged, and lessees guaranteed a refund of the sum expended by them on their leases; the State should not purchase improvements, but that each incoming lessee should purchase the improvements from his predecessor. The State would thus have nothing to do with any matter except the collection of the rent. The proposals of the Commission were in perfect harmony with the existing legislation as regards agricultural land, and also with an Act passed in 1891 which gave the tenants of private landlords tenant rights to improvement. It is now generally conceded that the wisest step that could have been taken in 1888 would have been to offer the lessees such terms as to induce them to accept payment for their improvements from the next lessees instead of from the Crown. This course would have given each lessee a stake in the country, which he has not at present. In opposition to the proposal to give tenant right to the lessees, it is contended that the fact of an incoming lessee having to purchase his improvements would be a hindrance to the settlement of the country by new people, and thus give a perpetual tenure to the present lessees. But the answer given by the supporters of the principle of tenant right is that there is no valid reason for the Government to be at the cost of the improvements, and that so long as the tenant is a good one, and has an interest in the land, by his improvements, there is no urgent necessity for a change. This subject was much canvassed during the recent elections in the Colony, and probably Parliament will be called upon upon at an early date to formulate some more satisfactory scheme for the occupation of the pastoral lands of the Crown.

An attempt has been made to bring about increased cultivation of occupied land by the imposition of a land tax, in conjunction with an income tax, on the assumption that increased production from the soil would be necessary to provide for the increased taxation. How far the facts have borne out the prognostications in this direction it is impossible to say, but the figures show that the largest proportion of the taxpayers is to be found amongst the smaller holders of property. By a return which was presented to Parliament in 1890 it was shown that of the 40,282 persons paying the tax, 36,335 were possessed of real property valued at £1000 and under, while only 3620 held property valued at from £1000 to £10,000. The taxation applies to all lands except the lands of the Crown not subject to any agreement for sale or right to purchase; public parks, cemeteries, etc., and lands used for charitable and religious purposes. The original Act in 1814 fixed the amount of taxation at $\frac{1}{2}d$ in the £, upon the unimproved value of all lands held under fee simple, and the return which has to be filled in by each person who should pay the tax, has to show the area and position of the property, name of occupier, name of mortgagee (if any) and the amount of mortgage, actual value of land and improvements, value of improvements alone and unimproved value alone, and the amount of the tax at the rate of $\frac{1}{2}d$ in the £ which would have to be paid on the unimproved value. The assessments on the land are made every three years. The returns for the first year's assessments showed the actual value of the landed property available for taxation to be £71,000,000, while the unimproved value was given as £49,000,000. The actual value of land in the Northern Territory was set down as £484,000 of which the unimproved value was given as £445,000. A movement has recently been started in the Colony for the imposition of a progressive land tax, with the avowed object of causing the owners of the large estates either to cultivate or dispose of their properties. At the recent general elections the subject was much discussed, as was also a proposal to impose a property tax; but no alteration in the incidence of taxation is expected to result during the present Parliament.

The Colony, which is credited with being one of the most advanced of the provinces in the matter of its legislation, claims with just pride that it originated the system of land transfer at present in force throughout Australasia. The honor of conceiving and carrying out this valuable reform belonged to Mr. (afterwards Sir R. R.) Torrens, formerly Collector of Customs at Adelaide, who endeavoured to apply to land the system of registration which regulated the transfer of shipping property. He experienced great opposition from the legal fraternity when he mooted his proposals, but in 1858 he carried a Bill through Parliament giving effect to his views, and he then resigned his seat in the Assembly,—to which he had been specially elected to afford him an opportunity of giving effect to his views—and became the official head of the new department formed to administer the Act. The system he introduced is both simple and inexpensive. The certificate of title to land is registered at the Lands Titles office, and the owner obtains a duplicate certificate, on the face of which, as also on the original, all transactions appear. By this means it may be seen at a glance whether a property is encumbered, or what charges are made upon it.

In the event of a mortgage being taken, the fact is endorsed on the certificate, and if the owner wishes to dispose of his property, he hands over the certificate to the purchaser; and, the transaction having been registered, it is complete. When the property is held under deed, it is simply necessary, to obtain a transfer, to take the deeds to the registrar, in whose office they are examined by the proper officers; then, if there is no difficulty—and full precaution is taken to prevent fraud or mistake—a certificate is issued and the former deeds are cancelled. The title thenceforth becomes indefeasible, unless it has been fraudulently obtained. Full provision is made against errors, so that no person may be damnified nor deprived of his property, and even should a wrong have been done, an innocent holder of a certificate cannot be dispossessed of his land To compensate those who through error or fraud may be deprived of their property, an assurance fund has been created by the levying of $\frac{1}{2}d$ in the £ on all property brought under the Act. This fund amounted many years back to between £30,000 and £40,000, and as at that time only £300 had been claimed from it, it is evident that the system has proved successful. At the requests of the various governments, Mr. Torrens visited the other colonies with the idea of assisting to initiate the scheme elsewhere. This was effectually done, and as a result at the present day throughout Australia "Torrens title" is synonymous with perfect security in all land transactions.

CHAPTER IX.

NEW ZEALAND.

NEW ZEALAND, the Island Eden of the Pacific, as it may justly be termed, can hardly be treated in the same manner as the Colonies of the Continent, in the discussion of its land system. It differs in climate, natural features, and soil from the provinces of the mainland, from which it is separated by some 1200 miles of the Pacific Ocean, and is only approached in its general characteristics by Tasmania, which in some points resembles the "Britain of the South", as the New Zealanders proudly describe their sea-girt home. In several ways indeed, it bears comparison with the Mother Land. Its climate, in the south at least, though more equable, approximates to that of England and Scotland, but in the North it more nearly approaches that of the South of Europe, and snow or ice are there rarely if ever seen, except upon the mountains. This difference, within an area of about 106,000 square miles,—which is slightly less in extent than that of the United Kingdom,—may be more readily appreciated when it is stated that the length of the Colony from North to South is about 11,00 miles. New Zealand is comprised of three islands, known generally as the North, South (or Middle), and Stewart Islands, which are long and narrow in conformation, averaging in width, from East to West, only about 100 miles. At no point is the settler more than from 70 to 80 miles from the sea coast, and it may, be readily understood, therefore that, the rainfall is frequent and regular, and the rivers plentiful though short. As a result there are rare periods of drought similar to those which affect Australia, and, being without the tropical latitudes, the Colony is not amenable to the cyclones and monsoon storms to which parts of the Continent are subject.

The soil of New Zealand is generally good, and in parts magnificent. This may be fairly gauged by the fact that in 1892 its wheat crop averaged 26 bushels to the acre, while its oat crop averaged 34 bushels, the former being more than double the general average for the whole continent of Australia, and considerably above that of Tasmania, while the average for oats was also much higher than in any of the others.

New Zealand is possessed, therefore, of all the essentials for an agricultural country, and in 1892 its wheat crop, was exceeded only by that of Victoria, while it raised more than double the total production of oats in all the rest of the Colonies together. But it is also pre-eminently a country suited for grazing purposes Wherever there is light and moisture, English grasses thrive marvellously, and in 1892, about 7¼ millions of acres were sown in grass, as against a total area of 775,000 acres in all the other Colonies. In each of the islands a considerable area is covered by mountains and lakes, the scenery which is very beautiful, — but fully four-fifths of its 66 millions of acres are suited for occupation in some form. In the North Island, and parts of the South, large tracts of country were originally covered with virgin forest, heavily timbered, which had to be felled, and burnt or utilised, before the land could be used. This country, when cleared, is generally very rich.

The history of settlement in New Zealand is full of dramatic and romantic incidents, and the story of the development of its land systems (for they were many), might alone well form the subject of a volume. But want of space prevents more than a very brief outline here. From the earliest days of the colonisation of New South Wales, whalers and other adventurers frequented the northern shores of the island colony, and many of them located themselves at a settlement known as Kororareka, at which in 1838 the European population was estimated at 1000 persons. Prior to this, a company comprising some influential men, amongst whom was Lord Durham, was formed in London, to colonise New Zealand, and in 1826 a vessel with 60 settlers on board arrived to take up land at the north of the Hokianga River which, with two islands in the Hauraki Gulf, had previously been bought from the Maoris on their behalf. But the colonists were welcomed on arrival by the Maoris with a war dance, which together with the alarming reports of battles between different tribes of natives, then being fought in the neighbourhood, so scared them that they went on board again and sailed for Sydney, though a few remained at Kororareka.

Meanwhile the barbarities of whalers and others, and native reprisals, and the lawlessness generally which prevailed, called for active intervention by the British Government, which, however, was slow to accord recognition to the new settlement, or accept responsibility. Matters were precipitated in 1839, when a New Zealand Company, with Lord Durham (once more), and other influential men, at its head, and Mr. Gibbon Wakefield as its guiding spirit, was formed to take up land and colonise the territory. The scheme was not favorably received by the Government, so a ship was secretly sent by the Company with Wakefield's brother (Colonel Wakefield) on board to purchase land from the Maoris, and make other necessary provisions for the foundations of a settlement. This act "forced upon Her Majesty's Government the adoption of measures for establishing some British authority in New Zealand," and Captain Hobson, R.N., was appointed Lieut-Governor, under the Governor of New South Wales. He made his capital the present city of Auckland.

In 1840, 1200 persons arrived in Port Nicholson (now the capital city, Wellington), under the auspices of the new Company. They formed the pioneers of the Colony proper, and they had a severe struggle to obtain a footing on the land, in face of the opposition of the natives, who though outwardly friendly at first, subsequently adopted a hostile attitude and actively prevented settlement for some years. Other colonies soon followed. In 1840, a new Company, formed in Plymouth, and afterwards merged into the New Zealand Company, bought from the latter 50,000 acres of land, supposed to have been purchased from the natives, at Taranaki, and in 1841 a settlement consisting largely of Devonshire people was planted there under the shadow of Mount Egmont. It was in this district that, years afterwards, many bloody fights with the natives occurred, and it is only at this day beginning to attain the position warranted by its resources. Another off-shoot of the New Zealand Co's main settlement at Port Nicholson was formed in the Valley of the Wairau, or Nelson district, the attempt to occupy which resulted in a conflict with the natives, and a massacre of Europeans.

These difficulties all arose from the fact that Colonel Wakefield purchased, on his arrival, as he believed, on behalf of the New Zealand Co, some 20 millions acres of land on the West, South, and South-East portions of the North Island, and lands in the Nelson district, whereas the chiefs who sold to him apparently had no authority for their action. Consequently, when the settlers went to take possession of property bought by them from the Company, they were met with a powerful resistance from the Maoris. The Governor declined to place the settlers on these lands by force, as previously, in 1840, a compact had been entered into between himself and the Maoris, known as the Treaty of Waitangi, under which absolute possession of their lands was secured to the natives, though sovereignty was transferred to the Queen, and the pre-emption to Maori lands was vested in the Crown. There were constant bickerings between the Governor and the Company in consequence, and between the Europeans, and Maoris, with the result that, in after years, bitter and relentless wars were waged. It would be presumptuous to refer here to these events in detail. Their chief interest, in the consideration of the subject under discussion, lies in the fact which they indicate that it was in the face of grave disabilities that the North Island was colonised. The Maori wars without doubt greatly retarded settlement there, and gave the South Island, which (but for the Wairau massacre) was never the scene of conflict, an immense advantage. This it has since largely maintained.

New Zealand was constituted a separate Colony in 1840, though the fact was not made public locally until the following year. Subsequently colonisation progressed steadily. A minor settlement under the auspices of the New Zealand Co had been formed at Wanganui, soon after the arrival of the first immigrants at Wellington, and thus there were in the North Island four separate little colonies, at Port Nicholson, Wanganui, Taranaki, and Auckland. In the South Island, the Nelson district was the only part occupied until 1848. In this year an Association, formed under the auspices of the Free Church of Scotland, founded a settlement on the site of the city now known as Dunedin, in the Province of Otago, which to this day retains a distinctive Scotch character by the preponderance of persons of northern descent amongst its settlers. Later in the same year another settlement under semi-religious auspices, was formed in the South Island at Christchurch, the chief city of the present province of Canterbury. An Association under the wing of the Church of England made arrangements with the New Zealand Co for a special tract of country at Port Cooper (now Lyttleton), and three vessels carrying some 600 persons, all adherents of the Anglican Church, arrived there in 1850, when the present city of Christchurch and province of Canterbury were founded. Other minor or branch settlements were afterwards established at various points from time to time, but these constituted and have continued to be the two main centres in the South Island.

In the province of Canterbury the Wakefield system of colonisation received its most satisfactory trial. Everything favoured the experiment, as the country was comprised for the most part of rich, open plains, and capital was available in large quantities. A high price was from the outset placed upon the land, that for rural lands being not less than £3 per acre, while the minimum for town lots was £12. By the Association's Charter, granted in 1851 one-sixth of the land fund was to be paid to the Crown (the N. Z. Co being at this time defunct) two-sixths were to be devoted to ecclesiastical and religious purposes, two-sixths to immigration, and one-sixth to surveys and other expenses. In 1852 the power of the Association to sell lands was abrogated however, and it passed into the hands of the Governor. Referring to this subject, Mr. F. J. Moss in his short History of New Zealand remarks:—"The Wakefield system, which concentrated population, and prevented many of the discomforts and drawbacks of early colonisation, was the system upon which the Canterbury settlement was formed. On the other hand it kept the labourer working for others longer than in settlements where land was to be obtained at a lower price, and where a man by hard work and privation could fight his way sooner to independence." Speaking of the colonisation of the sister province of Otago, he says:— "The Otago settlers, with less money, had greater individual capacity for work, had been generally educated in Scotch public Schools, more free from class distinctions, and came to a country, hilly broken, and totally unlike Canterbury. Their land and educational systems and their general political arrangements differed from those of Canterbury. The Wakefield system had no hold in Otago, but every facility was given for men with the smallest capital to settle upon their own land and hew out their own independence. The one settlement was regarded as aristocratic and consisted almost entirely of employers and those who worked for them; the other was more clearly democratic and contained a much larger proportion working independently for themselves."

These remarks indicate the class of men who formed the pioneers of the South Island. They were, as in the case of the New Zealand Co's settlers in the North, picked on account of their special qualifications. Each had some means, and many very considerable capital, while most of them were men of education and experience, who brought to the task of laying the foundations of the New Colony a remarkable perception of the responsibilities and grave importance of the duties which devolved upon them. Many afterwards became noted leaders of the people, and such was their high character and ability that they gave a superior tone to the provincial Councils and to Parliament, which it has since retained, and which has marked it as the premier legislative body of Australasia. At the present day, indeed, New Zealand is frequently adopted as a model by the other Colonies, with respect to its legislation and administration, and in no matter more than in its land laws has it justified this distinction.

Matters remained in a very unsettled condition as regards land alienation during the first few years of the Colony's existence. In 1846 the Colony was exempted from the Land Sales Act, which governed the sale of lands in the Australian Colonies at that period, and the Governor was empowered to alienate Crown Lands, make endowments, and to regulate their sale and management. Up to this period most of the best lands remained in the hands of the Maoris, and in 1848 steps were taken to commence the purchase from them of large tracts in the South Island and the Eastern and Southern parts of the North Island. The former gradually by this means passed into the hands of the State, the native title thus being destroyed except over such areas as were retained for the special occupation of the Maoris.

In 1851 the New Zealand Company, which had been in existence for 12 years, and had without doubt been chiefly instrumental in founding the Colony, was dissolved. In achieving its end the Corporation had expended great sums of money, and at the time of its dissolution it had liabilities to the extent of nearly half a million, against which it had assets in the shape of about a million acres of land. As a means of terminating the Company's existence it was arranged that it should relinquish all claims to Crown Land and that a previous loan of £236,000 from the Government to the Company should be wiped off, while a sum of £268,000 necessary to re-imburse the share-holders and meet other liabilties was made a charge on the Colony under its new constitution, then coming into force. The Otago and Canterbury Associations failed, in the two following years respectively, and the Crown thus secured entire control of the lands of the Colony except those in the hands of the Maoris.

Responsible Government was conceded to New Zealand in 1853, and from this date may be said to commence the real history of its land system. Under the new constitution it was divided into six provinces—Auckland, Wellington, Nelson, Canterbury, Otago, and New Plymouth,—each of which had its own elected Provincial Council, with a Superintendent, while there was a legislature for the whole Colony to deal with large questions. The Provincial Councils were very powerful bodies. They received a portion of the customs duties, and the whole of the Land Fund, together with other revenues. This was the first occasion in Australasia in which a local legislative body was given the entire control of the public estate, and almost immediately after the new constitution came into operation, the Governor, as empowered by the Constitution Act proclaimed regulations for the disposal of Crown Lands. These established sales by auction for town and suburban lands; and for rural lands outside of the imits of hundreds affixed a price of 10/- per acre, with modifications which permitted the price to be reduced to as low as 5/-, on the certificate of a commissioner. The land had to be surveyed before selection. These regulations did not apply to the land held by the Canterbury and Otago Associations, which, however, suffered greatly from the proclamation. In Canterbury the original price had been £3 an acre, and the Association could not well continue to compete with other provinces and retain that rate. But generally the reductions from the previously prevailing high prices were acceptable, and land began to pass rapidly into private hands, the foundations of some of the finest estates in the Colony being laid in these days at a cost of 5/- per acre.

In the first session of the new Parliament in 1854 the first local legislation upon the subject of the land was passed. This measure, the Waste Land Act, enabled Provincial Councils to recommend regulations to the Governor for the sale, letting, disposal and occupation of Crown Lands within their boundaries, proclamation by the Governor being sufficient to give them effect. Henceforth, therefore, there was a system of dual administration, which in a few years placed the land legislation of the Colony in a hopeless tangle. Every Province had its own system, subject of course to the controlling legislation of the General Parliament, and such vested interests on the part of the provinces gradually accrued under this system, that it became necessary for many years to leave each one to carry out its own methods, and this arrangement was not finally abrogated until 1892, when the whole provincial methods of the Colony were assimilated. It would be impossible to deal with these provincial regulations in the space at disposal, and attention will be devoted, therefore, only to the primary enactments of the Legislature. In 1856 it was provided that each province should contribute to general revenue 2/6 for each acre of land sold within its boundaries.

In 1858 an Act was passed which regulated the conditions of land settlement in the various provinces subsequently for a period of about 17 years, with very slight amendments. It provided that not more than 320 acres were to be put up to auction in one lot, and the upset price was to be in no case less than 5/- per acre. No land was to be sold for credit after the 1st August 1860, except such as might be lawfully set apart for special settlements by accepted immigrants. Priority of choice, where there were more applicants than one for the same piece of land, was in no case to be decided by lot, but the land was to be put up for auction only between the various applicants. Power was given to the Governor to make reserves and to increase the upset price of land where necessary. By the regulations framed under this measure, the upset price for land in the Canterbury province was fixed at £2 an acre, but elsewhere it generally ranged from 7/6 to £1, according to quality.

An important step was taken by Parliament in 1875, when the Provincial Councils were abolished, and a more centralised system of Government took their place. This rendered necessary a measure to make certain changes in the modes of administration of the Land laws in the following year. In 1877, a new Land Act became law, which, with a supplementary Act passed in the same session, regulated the disposal of the public Estate for a few years afterwards. The necessity for a simplification and assimilation of the land systems of the Colony had been one of the chief arguments brought forward in favour of the abolition of the provinces, and that such was needed may be judged by the fact that the new enactment repealed no less than 56 statutes, previously passed from time to time, most of them of course dealing with provincial systems. In place of the Provinces and Provincial Councils, the Colony was now divided into ten Land Districts, to each of which a Land Board was appointed. These Boards-which were the chief administrative bodies under the Minister, who occupied the position of the political head of the Department, had considerable powers conferred upon them, and amongst others that of increasing the upset price of lands of special value. Each Board had a permanent Chief Commissioner, who was a Government officer, the other members being ordinary citizens, who received a fee for their services. This system is still in force and has been found to work admirably. The Boards have the general powers of Courts of Law in matters of administration, but their decisions may be appealed against to the Supreme Court.

All lands were under the new measure classified as town, suburban, or rural. The lands in the first two classes were to be sold by auction at upset prices of £30 and £3 respectively. The rural lands which comprised all other areas, were to be disposed of in a manner specified for each land district, and which assimilated as far as possible the former conditions existing under the Provinces. Areas from 20 to 320 acres might be put up to auction at an upset price of £1 per acre, but in the case of special areas of pastoral lands, considered to be unfit for agriculture, the land could be disposed of in areas ranging between 500 and 5000 acres, at the same price. A system of purchase under deferred payment, was also introduced. Land might be obtained in proclaimed blocks, in areas of from 20 to 320 acres, to be paid for under one of two methods,—either at a price to be fixed prior to sale, or by auction, at a price equal to 50 per cent above the amount bid. Licenses to occupy suburban land were issued for five years, and to occupy rural lands for 10 years, during which the selectors had to pay annually one-fifth and one-tenth respectively of the prices arranged. Personal residence was necessary for 4 and 6 years in the two classes, though the Board might dispense with residence for 4 years in the case of rural land, if covered with bush. One-tenth of the suburban and one-twentieth of rural land had to be cultivated within one year, and one-fifth and one-tenth respectively in the second year, while in the fourth year not less than one-fifth of the rural land had to be brought into cultivation and three-quarters of the suburban land, which had to be also substantially fenced and otherwise improved to the extent of £10 per acre. The selector of rural land had likewise to effect improvements to the value of £1 per acre during the sixth year. A grant was issued in each class after the fulfilment of the conditions, and upon payment of the balance of purchase money, which might, however, be allowed to extend over the full period of the license; but the selector of rural land might also obtain a freehold at the end of three years, upon fulfilment of the conditions as to cultivation and improvements and the due payment of rent.

In the case of special blocks of pastoral land set apart for purchase, no conditions as to improvements were imposed, but residence for 6 years was necessary. Licenses to occupy were issued for 15 years, during which one-fifteenth of the purchase money had to be paid annually. These lands were disposed of by auction at an upset price of £1 per acre. In each case, non-fulfilment of the conditions entailed forfeiture of the lands. Persons owning pre-emptive rights, or the owner in fee of 640 acres of land, or married women not judicially separated, were debarred from selecting, but all other persons above the age of 18 years were eligible.

The occupation of pastoral lands under lease was also dealt with by the Act. Special provisions were made in the case of Otago and Canterbury, but all other Crown Lands then occupied might upon surrender or determination, be leased by auction as the Governor should see fit, in areas capable of carrying not more than 5000 sheep or 1000 head of cattle all the year round, at an upset rental to be fixed by local Boards, and for periods not exceeding 10 years. Such lands were subject to resumption for agricultural purposes, if required, after 12 month's notice, without compensation for improvements. The Boards might permit lessees to purchase from their leasehold areas a homestead block not exceeding 320 acres, upon conditions as to price, etc., to be fixed. Rent for runs was payable half-yearly in advance, and a penalty of £1 was imposed for each day in which rent might be in arrear.

With respect to the sale of lands under deferred payment, the following important provision was enacted:—"One-third of the price of any block of land disposed of under this part of this Act shall be handed over to the County Council or Road Board of the district within which such land is situated, to be expended in the construction of such roads within, or to open up, the block for the benefit of the selectors. And the payments made by the selectors shall from time to time, until the amount of such one-third be reached, be paid over to such County Council or Road Board as the case may be. The plans of proposed roads shall in all cases receive the sanction of the Waste Land Boards of the district." The principle embodied in this section was extended by subsequent Acts to include the payment to local bodies of one-third of the rents of lands held under leases in perpetuity, or occupied with the right to purchase, and one-fourth of the rents of small grazing runs. In the case of perpetual and grazing leases, the proportion of rent is paid for a period of 15 years. The local body has to satisfy the Land Board of the completion of the works for which this money is specially set apart.

Amendments of the Act of 1877 were made in 1879 and 1882. The Act of 1879 provided for the survey of village lands into sections of under and over one acre. In the case of the sections of under one acre, the price of the land was to be not less than £5 per section. Sections of over one acre in area, might not exceed a maximum extent of 50 acres, and were described as small farm allotments. The occupancy of these allotments, where there were more applicants than one, was determined by lot, and they might either be purchased for cash at a fixed price of not less than 20/- per acre, or they might be leased with a purchasing clause. The Act of 1882 permitted the sale of lesser areas than 20 acres in special cases, and perpetual leases of rural lands, but not more than one-third of the land open for settlement in a district at one time was to be leased, in areas not exceeding 640 acres. These leases were to be for 30 years, with the right of renewal. The term of license for deferred payment lands was extended to 14 years, and it was provided that rentals in arrear might be capitalised, until the end of the period of payments, annual interest at the rate of 5 per cent being charged, on the capitalised sum. The term of lease of pastoral lands was also extended to 21 years, valuation for improvements being allowed, but the area which might be selected as a homestead on a run under pre-emptive rights was reduced to 150 acres. An important alteration was made with respect to the areas of pastoral leaseholds, which might be increased so as to permit of the depasturing of not more than 20,000 sheep or 4000 head of cattle.

A new era in the land legislation of the Colony was opened by the Land Act of 1885, which, while retaining most of the salient features of the Act of 1877, laid down several new principles, still mostly in force. Subsequent amplifications and amendments were made in 1887 and 1888, and in 1892 the whole legislation was consolidated and again amended. The latter enactment governs the whole present system, and, though more drastic and restrictive, it so closely approximates in its general lines to the Acts of 1885, 1887 and 1888, taken jointly, that for the sake of comprehensiveness it may be wise to consider these measures together, and describe the system as it now stands. The Act of 1885 permitted a continuance of the system of separate regulations for each of the provinces, but in 1892 this cumbrous method of administration was swept away, and, except as regards special grazing regulations for hundreds in Otago and Southland, the system is the same throughout the whole of the Colony. Amongst other important matters of general interest it is provided that any person found guilty of "dummying," or aiding and abetting in such a practice shall be guilty of a misdemeanour and liable to imprisonment for a term not exceeding 12 months with or without hard labour, or to pay a fine of from £100 to £500; while to prevent conspiracy, bribery, etc., at auction sales, to keep down the prices bid for land, imprisonment for 12 months or a fine of £200 may be imposed. Another important innovation is one under which "no person who owns or who has within the previous 40 days owned 2000 acres, or upwards, of freehold land, inclusive of 640 acres of first-class land, in the Colony, whether such land was acquired by purchase, marriage, or under a settlement or will, or by virtue of an intestacy, shall be capable of acquiring or becoming the holder in any part of the Colony of any Crown Land" other than that obtained under small grazing farms or pastoral lease. But any person holding less than 2000 acres, (inclusive of 640 acres of first-class land may acquire land up to the extent of 2000 acres. First-class land is that of which the unimproved value is 20/- or over per acre, all below that value being second-class land.

The former system of Land Boards, instituted in 1877, is retained in an extended form, and very full powers are given to carry out the provisions of the Act under the Minister. It is provided that the following deposits be made with the application to purchase or lease in the case of the various classes of surveyed land:—For land to be purchased for cash, cash $2\frac{1}{2}$ per cent of the price fixed; for occupation licenses, with right to purchase, $2\frac{1}{2}$ per cent (to be applied as rent for the first half-year); for Leases in perpetuity, two per cent (to be applied as the first half-year's rent); and for small grazing runs, $1\frac{1}{4}$ per cent on the cash price of the land. In the case of unsurveyed land, a fee equal to the probable cost of survey is made, which is afterwards credited to the applicant as rent or purchase money. The deposits may be forfeited on non-fulfilment of conditions, in the case of cash lands. The age of selectors under the new conditions is reduced from 18 to 17 years, and married women are also allowed to select one-half the area obtained by males and single women. The system of classification formerly in force is retained. Lands are described as (1) Town or Village, (2) Suburban, and (3) Rural. Town, village, or suburban lands may be sold by auction, upon conditions to be fixed by the Boards, at upset prices not less than £20, £3, and £2 per acre respectively; and if not sold at auction they may be leased for periods not exceeding 14 years, at a rental equal to 5 per cent on the upset price, without compensation for improvements. Rural lands are to be classified by the Boards into first and second class, which may be disposed of under various systems, to be hereafter described, at upset prices not less than £1 and 5/- per acre respectively. The maximum area which may be obtained by selection or disposed of by auction in one lot is fixed at 640 acres, and 2000 acres respectively in each class, but any less area in private possession may be augmented by selection from contiguous unappropriated lands to those limits. Power is given to the Boards to dispose of rural land not immediately required for settlement under yearly license.

One of the most remarkable features of the present system is that which permits selection under optional conditions. This method was originally introduced by the Act of 1887, and, as amended in 1892, permits a person to take up land to the extent previously stated, either (1) For cash, with the issue of a grant after certain improvements have been made; (2) for occupation, with a right to purchase; or (3) for lease-in-perpetuity at his own option. In the case of cash purchases, one-fifth of the price is paid down at the time of application, and the balance within 30 days. A certificate of occupation is issued to the applicant at the time of making the final payment, which may be exchanged for a Crown grant as soon as the Board is satisfied that improvements of the value of £1 per acre, for first-class, and 10/- for second-class lands, have been effected. Where lands are held for occupation with the right of purchase, a license is obtained for a period of 25 years, after the expiration of 10 years, of which, provided conditions of residence and improvements have been effected, the licensee can upon payment of the upset price of the land, acquire the freehold; and if it is not purchased before the end of the 25 years, the licence may be exchanged for what is described as a "lease in perpetuity." The rent during the term of occupation is fixed at 5 per cent on the cash price of the land, and is payable half-yearly in advance. This system takes the place of a method of deferred payments and perpetual leases, provided for by the Act of 1885, under which, in the case of deferred-payment lands, payment was allowed to extend over 10 years, or be capitalised and paid at the end of that term, with annual payments of interest. The price charged was 25 per cent above that fixed for cash sales, but it was to be in no case less than 20/- per acre. In the case of perpetual leases, it was provided by the Act of 1885 that leases for 30 years might be obtained, with a right of renewal in perpetuity at reappraised rentals, the original rental for the first term being fixed at 5 per cent on the cash price of the land. These could be converted into fee simple after residence for six years and fulfilment of conditions as to improvements etc. Under the Acts of 1887 and 1889 it was possible to take up land under either the deferred-payment or perpetual-lease systems, and to change the tenure from one to the other. As already shown, the system of occupation with the right to purchase is now substituted for deferred-payments, and the perpetual leases give way under the Act of 1892 to what are known as "leases-in-perpetuity." In place of paying cash or obtaining a license for 25 years, with the right of purchase, a person may at his option, obtain a lease for 999 years (or in perpetuity), at a rental equal to 4 per cent on the cash price of the land, payable half-yearly in advance. Two or more persons may make joint application to hold rural land as "tenants in common", under either of the two systems, and any licensee or lessee may transfer his interest to a co-licensee or co-lessee. Deferred-payment selectors or holders of perpetual leases under other Acts may transfer to a lease in perpetuity under certain conditions.

The conditions under which both occupation licenses or leases-in-perpetuity may be obtained are stringent, being framed with a view to enforcing actual occupation and cultivation of the soil. Residence is compulsory (with a few exceptions stipulated by the Act) and must commence within four years from the date of selection of bush or swamp lands, and within one year in the case of open or partly open land. On lands occupied with the right of purchase, it must be continuous for six years on bush or swamp land, and for 7 years in open or partly open country; and on lease-in-perpetuity lands it must be continuous for a period of 10 years. The Board have power to dispense with residence, however, in exceptional cases, such as where a selector is resident upon adjoining lands, or is a youth living with his parents, or an unmarried woman, etc. The term "residence" includes the erection of a habitable house, to be approved of by the Board. The following improvements must be effected on all classes of land except those bought for cash or pastoral or grazing-run leases:—(1) Within one year, from the date of the license or lease, the land must be improved to an extent equal to 10 per cent on the value of the land: (2) Within two years, improvements equal to a further 10 per cent must be effected; and (3) Within six years the land must be improved to the value of another 10 per cent, and substantial improvements of a permanent character" (in addition to the above) must also be effected to the extent of £1 per acre for first-class land, and to an extent equal to the net price of the land for second-class land, up to 10/- per acre. The interest of a lessee or licensee in land may be disposed of by sale, or under lease or mortgage, after fulfilment of conditions, but only when the would-be transferee, assignee, or mortgagee has made a statutory declaration that he is not barred under the conditions of the Act from occupying the land; and no sale under a mortgage may take place until after the fulfilment of certain conditions as to publicity, etc.

Another novel feature of the present legislation is that which provides for the setting apart of rural land for special settlements, to the extent of not more than 250,000 acres a year. This land is to be taken up by persons forming themselves into Associations. The Governor may make regulations fixing the terms under which land for these settlements may be disposed of, which shall be, however, only on a system of leases-in-perpetuity, on terms generally similar to those already described for these leases; and it is stipulated that no land shall be valued lower than 10/- per acre. Existing regulations, framed in pursuance of the

Act, provide that any number of persons, exceeding twelve, may apply for a block of land of not less than 1000 acres, nor more than 11,000 acres in extent, but no member may hold more than 320 acres, except in swamp where he may hold 500 acres. Land must be selected by the Association in one block, and the cost of survey, which is not to exceed 2/6 per acre, must be borne by the Association. No person is allowed to become a member of any Association to form special settlements who has property in fee or leasehold, which, together with the land applied for, would exceed 320 acres or 500 acres in the case of swamp land. Associations of intending settlers may also be formed to take conjointly blocks of 5000 acres which may be disposed of in suitable sized lots to persons who may agree to work them under regulations which may be made from time to time by the Governor.

The Governor is also authorised to set apart certain areas to be utilised under special regulations as village settlements, which are to be surveyed either into what are termed "village allotments" in areas not exceeding one acre each, or "village-homestead allotments" of not more than 100 acres each. "Village allotments" may be disposed of either at auction at an upset price of not less than £3 per acre, or under the optional system of occupation with right of purchase, or leases-in-perpetuity; but "village homestead allotments" may only be obtained under leases-in-perpetuity, on the same terms and conditions as for rural land. No such lease may be "seized or sold by legal process for debt, or in bankruptcy." It is provided with respect to these settlements that the Governor may make regulations for their guidance, under which any sums voted by Parliament may be advanced to lessees to enable them to profitably work their allotments. The Governor may also set apart areas to be devoted to the purposes of village settlements for Maoris and half-castes only, under special regulations.

It may be mentioned here that the question of the success or otherwise up to the present of the system of village settlements, which was originally introduced by the Act of 1885, has been much canvassed. In 1886 the Minister of Lands of the day, the late Hon John Ballance, who was an enthusiast on this subject drew up regulations, advanced money, and otherwise expended considerable sums, (without first obtaining Parliamentary authority), in forming these settlements, men being chosen for them who were mostly taken from the unemployed of the towns. The method of giving advances was abrogated by his successor, who suspended the operation of the system, but it was resumed later under authority, when Mr Ballance again returned to power. Statistics published in 1891 showed that in the Auckland district, only 282 were then resident of 506 settlers who took up selections in 1886 notwithstanding that £9,270 had been expended by way of advances to enable them to improve their holdings, erect houses, etc., and that £15,397 had been spent to give them employment on road works. In other districts, on the other hand, it was shown that better results had been achieved. The facts would probably be found to be, as suggested by the independent investigations of experts from Australia, who visited New Zealand specially to report on the system* that it partly failed at the outset, because men were placed on the land indiscriminately who had no knowledge of the work, and returned to the cities when a favourable opportunity offered. Where settlers were picked men, who had previous experience, and the land was good and situated in a locality where they could work for wages on the larger holdings of others, the system appears to have been fairly successful. From the report of the Superintendent for 1893, it appears that there are now 3000 settlers with their families resident in these settlements throughout the colony. Advances have been made to the extent of £24,625, or at the rate of £ 1 1 8½d per acre of the land taken up. A considerable sum is still due as rent and interest. The total receipts by way of rental (at an average of 2/3 per acre) and interest have been £10,513. Speaking of the advances made, the Superintendent writes—"The question will naturally arise—What is there to show for this expenditure? I am pleased to be able to give a satisfactory reply, for the improvements which the settlers have placed on the land are of the value of £61,689 . . . . If the sum advanced by the Government were deducted from the value of the improvements, there remains the sum of £37,074, which represents the value of the improvements themselves, over and above the amount advanced. Both in the North Island and the South the general opinion of the officers who have charge of the settlements is that the system has had a most beneficial effect, as it has been the means of affording settled homes to a large number of the labouring classes."

To permit men of comparatively small means to take up country, suitable for grazing, the former system of deferred-payment purchase of pastoral land has been abandoned in favour of small grazing-runs; but it was provided under the

---

* Hon W. Copley, Commissioner of Crown Lands of South Australia, who reported to the South Australian Parliament in 1891 and Mr. Geo. Lewis, Local Government officer, who reported to the New South Wales Parliament in 1892.

Act of 1885, that the term over which payment should be made, for the deferred-payment selections already taken up, might be extended from 15 to 30 years, at a slightly higher total cost. Small grazing-runs are divided into two classes—First-class runs which do not exceed 5000 acres; and second-class, which do not exceed 20,000 acres. The rental, which is fixed by the Board in each case, must be not less than $2\frac{1}{2}$ per cent on the capital value per acre, which must be not less than 5/- per acre. The term of lease is 21 years, with the right of renewal for a further similar period, at a rental of $2\frac{1}{2}$ per cent on the then capital value of the land; but if the lessee does not desire to renew he may receive compensation for improvements from the incoming lessee. The runs are let, after the area and rent have been fixed, according to priority of application. It is stipulated, however, that no lessee must hold more than one such run, and he must not be a pastoral lessee, nor hold other land under freehold, lease, or license, of a greater area than 1000 acres. The lease entitles the holder both to grazing rights and to cultivate the run, but it gives no privilege to purchase, though the lessee may select 150 acres of land adjoining and includiug his homestead, and hold the same unmolested during the whole term of the lease. Residence is compulsory, if the selection be bush or swamp land, within three years, and if open land within one year, and it must be continuous to the end of the term of lease, except in special cases such as those provided for in land held under occupation with the right of purchase, or leases-in-perpetuity. Runs have to be improved during the first two years to the value of one year's rent in each year; and within six years to the value of two other years' rent. In addition, substantial improvements of a permanent character (including bush clearing if necessary), must be made within the latter period, equal to 10/- and 5/- per acre respectively for first and second-class land. After compliance for three years with the conditions as to improvements, a run may be divided amongst the family of a lessee, and new leases issued to the various members.

"Pastoral lands" proper, wich are defined as "lands suitable exclusively for pasturage, and not capable of being used with profit in areas of a carrying capacity of less than 5000 sheep," and which include country not immediately required for settlement, may be leased at auction in areas capable of carrying not more than 20,000 sheep or 4000 head of cattle, for terms of 21 years, subject to resumption for public purposes or purchase. "Pastoral-agricultural lands," which are described as lands "adapted partly for pasturage and partly for agricultural purposes, and suitable for division into areas of not more than 5000 acres," may be leased or otherwise disposed of as the Governor may direct. It is laid down that no person or company shall hold more than one run of any kind, except it be capable of carrying less than 10,000 sheep or 2000 head of cattle, when the lessee may take up other land to make an aggregate area of that carrying capacity. Each run must contain sufficient low ground to ensure the proper working of the run, and to this end high and low ground may be offered as one run, even although not contiguous. The conditions of the leases are that the lessee shall prevent the destruction of timber, and the growth of gorse, broom, and sweetbriar on the land, and destroy rabbits and prevent their increase. Pastoral-agricultural land may be resumed at any time after twelve months' notice. In the event of a renewal of any pastoral lease being determined upon, it must be offered at auction 12 months before the expiry of the term, and in the event of another person than the original lessee becoming the purchaser, an appraised value shall be paid for improvements by the incoming lessee, but not to a value greater than three times the annual rent. An exception is made in the case of rabbit-proof fencing, which is dealt with separately. If the run is not again leased, the value of the rabbit-proof fencing is paid by the Crown, but no compensation is allowed for other improvements, though the lessee may, three months before a sale, remove fences, buildings, etc.

Existing legislation also provides for other matters such as the granting of licenses for timber cutting and flax cutting on Crown Lands, and it is provided that where land is believed to contain minerals or gold it may be resumed by the Government on payment of compensation which is limited to the value of the surface soil, and improvements of a substantial character. It is laid down, likewise, that when any mineral, mineral-oil, and metal or valuable stone is known to exist on Crown Lands, the surface may only be leased-in-perpetuity, and under no other tenure, and the right of entrance to such lands is reserved to all persons lawfully engaged in seeking and working minerals. Leases to mine for gold, coal, and other minerals are specially provided for. Where curative mineral or thermal springs exist on Crown Lands, leases for 63 years may be granted, over areas not exceeding 7 acres, subject to conditions which secure the public convenience. Leases of land in the vicinity of these springs may also be granted.

Under the provisions previously referred to which permit

the Governor to make regulations to deal with village settlements, several subsidiary schemes have been formulated to permit co-operative or joint action amongst selectors by means of Associations. The most recent method, described as "Improved Settlements," is one propounded by the present Minister of Lands (Hon J. Mackenzie), which has not yet been given a trial, having scarcely passed the initial stages. The system is reported in the press to have been thus explained by the Minister in June last (1893).—"For that purpose he had set aside blocks of land in various parts of the Colony. The mode of working this new system was as follows. On a certain area of the land, say one-third or one-fourth of each block, the Government were to fell and burn the bush, and make decent roads to open up the land. When that was done the men who were employed to do the work of clearing, etc., would be allowed to select land for homesteads for themselves, on the then improved block. The cost of the improvements would be added to the original value of the land, and the selector would be asked to pay 4 per cent interest to the Government on the total cost. This would enable the industrious and careful men who are selected for the work, to acquire homes for themselves, and also to obtain employment in improving the land which they would afterwards take up. They could then be supplied with one year's work in improving the next block so as to give them a start. Provision could then be made to introduce a further number of men, who would be given the same advantages for another year, and so on until the whole block was improved."

Already blocks not exceeding 2500 acres in area have been set apart in various parts of the Colony to give effect to this proposal, and it is intended to clear 500 acres of each block per annum. The conditions provide that the work shall be carried out on a co-operative basis, and that each party taking up the land shall consist of not less than 5 nor more than 10 men, who will clear sections of about 50 acres, and be paid at a rate which will secure to them an average wage of 6/6 per day. In carrying out the work they have to provide their own tools, tents, and provisions. Another method adopted by the Government to bring about the settlement on the land of the unemployed now crowding the large towns, is the establishment of State farms, which are likewise in the initial stage at present. It is stated officially * "that the leading idea in this scheme is to provide places of refuge and instruction for those persons who, not

* Report on Bureau of Industries, 1892.

being able to succeed in getting employment in their own trades may be encouraged to undertake work in the rural districts and be prepared to engage in it. A state farm is to comprise about 1000 acres of land fit for agricultural purposes, and to this farm will be drafted the surplus workmen of the towns."

An outline has now been given of the various systems under which land may be secured in the Colony. That they are liberal in the sense that every man may get on to the land, cannot be gainsaid, but they form a daring innovation upon pre-conceived ideas as to the methods which should govern the alienation and occupation of the public estate—in Australia at least. No other Parliament in Australasia has had the temerity to say to the people: "No man holding more than 2000 acres, shall obtain any further portion of the Crown Lands;" and experience has yet to show the wisdom or otherwise of this bold edict. Another step which is a distinct advance on any existing legislation in the Colonies is that which prevents persons or companies from occupying more than one pastoral run, or which limits them to the lease of country capable only of carrying a certain quantity of stock. Other Colonies have prevented persons from taking up more than specified areas of land at one time for agricultural purposes, but nowhere else is the pastoral industry restricted in this way. It is almost needless to mention that the system of granting leases-in-perpetuity (999 years) at a fixed rental for all time of 4 per cent on the value of land at the time of selection, as opposed to the old system of periodic appraisement of rent, and sales of land for cash after the fulfilment of conditions only; are remarkable innovations on previously accepted ideas.

These experiments are likely to be watched with immense interest throughout the whole world. It is impossible at the moment of writing to hazard any accurate prognostication as to their probable effects, nor is this course necessary. The Act of 1892, which is responsible for the very marked changes just referred to, has now (August 1893) been in operation for a few months only, and statistics are not available by which to test results. During the year ended March 31st, 1893, the systems of deferred payments and perpetual leases were changed by the Act of 1892, to occupation with rights of purchase and leases in perpetuity, so that both methods were in force part of the time, and it may, therefore, be of interest to compare the figures for the previous year, as showing how the amended system had operated during the short period after it came into effect. The following table shows the area dealt with up to the 31st March of 1892 and 1893 respectively.—

	1892.		1893.	
System.	Selectors.	Areas disposed of	Selectors.	Areas disposed of
	No.	Acres.	No.	Acres.
Cash Sales............	493	40,499	552	36,326
Deferred payments....	223	40,467	169	21,084
Occupation with right of purchase...........	—	—	161	54,271
Perpetual Leases......	824	282,547	1385	122.557
Leases-in-perpetuity...	—	—	126	55,320
Village Settlements, Cash	89	428	75	528
do Deferred [Payments	23	181	29	390
do Per Lease	59	892	164	2639
Village homestead, Special Settlements.,.,.....	140	2,213	33	493
Special Settlement Associations, Perpetual Leases and leases-in-perpetuity (1893)..,.,...	13	1,922	1874	371,671
Small grazing runs...,	80	159,464	39	92,926
Pastoral Runs........	126	844,952	80	1,011,297
Totals.	2070	1373,565	3687	1,769,502

Following the above it may be of interest to contrast the general results of the various main systems of alienation during the period since the coming into operation of the Land Act of 1885.

Year.	Cash		Deferred Payments.		Perpetual Leases.	
	Selectors.	Area.	Selectors.	Area.	Selectors.	Area.
	No.	acres.	No.	acres.	No.	acres.
1885	1242	64,975	706	70,238	111	24,410
1886	848	64,677	650	59,084	296	44,986
(¹)1887	491	32,860	669	51,112	1623	122,902
1888	622	28,295	466	45,416	985	113,592
1889	756	69,162	496	55,601	1001	224,999
1890	702	47,478	426	47,181	852	238,904
1891	661	100,222	315	35,081	854	290,248
1892	581	40,930	246	40,649	1036	287,664
(²)1893	627	36,854	{198 / 161*}	{21,474 / 54,271}	{2456 / 126†}	{496,867 / 55,320}

A comparison of the results in the two years 1885 and 1893, which may fairly be said to represent the periods during which deferred payment and perpetual lease were respectively the leading systems in force, demonstrates several significant points. The total number of selections made in the latter year showed an increase by considerably more than one-half on the total for 1885, while the area taken up increased from about 170,000 acres to 660,000 acres. In 1885 the predominant system of selection was for cash, deferred-payments coming next, and perpetual leases last. In 1893, the perpetual lease selections numbered six times as many as cash and deferred-payment selections together. This reversion of popular approval was steadily but surely effected during the whole period, and the evidence seems to point to the fact that the system of perpetual lease—or as it is termed in its extended form, lease-in-perpetuity—has taken an undeniable hold on the people.

In arriving at a conclusion as to how far the systems in

(1) In this year village settlements under perpetual leases were introduced, large numbers of unemployed being placed on the land with State assistance.

(2) In 1893, the deferred payments and perpetual leases were in force till nearly the end of 1892, when licenses to occupy with right of purchase and leases-in-perpetuity came into force. The figures given are to March 31 st. 1893.

* Occupation licenses with right of purchase.

† Leases in perpetuity.

force have conduced to the actual settlement of the land, some valuable assistance may be obtained from the official statistics of the colony.* The subjoined table, showing the increase of population, alienation of the public estate, the land held under perpetual lease, the areas under cultivation, (including artificial grasses,) and exports of local produce during each alternate year between 1881 and 1891, indicates fairly well the results which have been attained.

Year.	European.	Crown Lands.		Lands under cultivation.		Exports of local produce.
	Population.	Alienated.	Held under Perpetual Lease	Holdings.	Area.	
	No.	acres.	acres.	No.	acres.	£
1881	500,910	805,959	———	26,298	5,189,104	5,762,250
1883	540,877	366,427	26,364	28,587	6,072,949	6,855,244
1885	575,226	550,330	51,367	31,763	6,668,920	6,591,911
1887	603,361	356,138	150,218	34,743	7,284,752	6,551,081
1889	616,052	128,098	544,914	38,178	8,015,426	9,042,008
1891	634,058	318,213	1,019,405	41,224	8,893,225	9,400,094

In the case of the lands alienated large areas are included which are described as "free grants," and which represent free grants of land formerly made to immigrants, naval and military settlers, and grants for public purposes, native reserves, etc. Out of the total area alienated (2,515,165 acres) during the years mentioned no less than 1,802,056 acres were disposed of in this manner,—the balance being either land sold for cash, or lands finally alienated under the deferred-payment system. The figures in the table, after making allowance for these facts, show that, while the population has increased, only about 25 per cent, the total number of holdings under cultivation has increased one-half, and the area under cultivation even more than one-half, the exports having shown a growth in like proportion. The result has been undoubtedly, therefore, a distinct advance, both relatively and actually, in the settlement of the Crown Lands and their proper utilisation.

It may be well in this connection to ascertain how the rural lands of the colony now in private hands are held. The

* New Zealand Handbook, 1892, Government printer, Wellington.

following table shows the number of holdings, and the acreage of freehold and leasehold lands (excluding Crown pastoral leases) in 1891, and the corresponding totals during 1886 and 1881, lands under one acre being excluded.*

Size of Holdings.	Number of Holdings.	Acreage.		
		Freehold.	Leasehold etc.	Total.
Acres.				
1 to 10	11,116	28,124	24,343	52,467
10 ,, 100	14,512	426,100	263,879	689,979
100 ,, 320	10,767	1,264,586	777,484	2,042,070
320 ,, 640	3,802	1,057,676	660,070	1,717,746
640 ,, 1,000	1,321	662,612	395,849	1,058,461
1,000 ,, 5,000	1,675	2,144,627	1,280,558	3,425,185
5,000 ,, 20,000	436	3,119,882	1,348,321	4,468,203
20,000 ,, 50,000	117	2,507,848	833,088	3,340,931
50,000 ,, 100,000	24	801,647	723,000	1,524,647
100,000 and upwards.	7	397,140	680,700	1,077,840
Totals 1891	43,777	12,410,242	6,987.287	19,397,529
Totals 1886	36,485	11,728,236	5,348,838	17,077,074
Totals 1881	30,832	10,309,170	4,897,727	15,206,897

It is made evident here that, as in the Australian colonies, large areas of the best lands have aggregated in the hands of a few owners, no less than 7,026,000 acres being held by 584 persons, in areas of 5000 acres and upwards, out of the total freehold area of 12,410,000 acres, or an average of about 12,000 acres per owner. Of the remainder, 1675 persons possess 2,144,627 acres, in areas of between 1,000 and 5,000 acres, or an average of 1,280 acres, the balance being in the hands of 41,518 persons, whose holdings average about 78 acres each. The disproportion of these figures has not failed to receive attention in the colony, and in 1891 an Act (which was slightly amended in 1892) was passed for the ostensible purpose of either disinte-

* These figures do not include land sold direct by the Maoris to Europeans for which no Crown grants have been issued, and of which there is no official record. The number and area of such holdings is believed, however, to be small.

grating the large estates, or compelling their owner to utilise them to a much greater extent than formerly, by the imposition of a land and income tax combined with a graduated land tax. This most drastic masure provides in the case of the ordinary land tax that any person or company owning land, or leasing Crown land other than for pastoral purposes, shall pay a tax on its actual value—after deducting the value of existing improvements up to £3000, and any amount owing which is secured by a registered mortgage—mortgagees being also liable to the tax. In addition to the exemptions for improvements an allowance of £500 is made when the balance, after making deductions, as stated, does not exceed £1500; and above that figure a smaller exemption is made, but it ceases when the balance amounts to £2500. The amount of the tax is fixed by an Act passed every year, that for the current year being 1d in the £.

In addition to this ordinary tax, an additional graduated tax is imposed on land valued at over £5000—after deducting the value of all improvements, but not excluding mortgages—which increases in corresponding ratio to the value of the land in the following proportion:—Between £5000 and £10,000, one-eighth of a penny in the £; for every £10,000 between £10,000 and £70,000, and for every £20,000, between £70,000 and £210,000, one-eighth of a penny extra; and for all land valued at over £210,000, a fixed tax of 1⅜d in the £. A further addition of 20 per cent on the taxation stated is imposed "in the case of any person who has been absent from or resident out of the colony for a period of three years, or over that period, prior to the passing of the annual act imposing the tax."

The total taxable value on which the tax of 1d was to be levied for 1893 was fixed at £55,105,920, which was estimated to bring in a clear revenue of £219,608; while the additional graduated land tax was to be levied on £26,743,370, estimated to bring in £72,307. The further amonnt to be received from absentees was not expected to be large. About one-half the landowners—45,192—have land of an unimproved value of less than £100, and 23,709 hold improved land of a less value than £100. Some interesting facts may be elicited from the following table which show the values of land in different areas held outside boroughs and town districts, between the years 1883 and 1892, the valuations prior to 1892 being obtained from a Property Tax which was formerly imposed:—

Areas.	Year.	No of free holders.	Values.
Acres. 5 and under 100	1883	14,766	£ 5,166,976
	1886	17,075	6,034,289
	1889	18,805	6,479,104
	1892	19,339	6,349,455
100 and under 1000	1883	14,267	17,896,558
	1886	15,471	18,140,749
	1889	16,743	17,359,864
	1892	17,538	20,533,069
1000 and under 10,000	1883	1484	13,967,591
	1886	1645	14,027,965
	1889	1634	13,228,940
	1892	1766	14,949,253
10,000 and under 50,000	1883	224	10,777,444
	1886	230	10,318,546
	1889	223	10,315,246
	1892	232	11,744,683
50,000 and upwards	1883	23	5,542,243
	1886	29	5,137,140
	1889	27	5,192,049
	1892	23	5,712,915
Totals ...	1883	30,764	53,350,812
	1886	34,450	53,658,689
	1889	37,432	52,575,375
	1892	28,935	59,289,375

It will have been gathered that the present land policy of the colony is mainly designed to prevent the building up, and if possible to bring about the subdivision, of large estates, and to make the land available for men with small means, yet in such a manner that they must either remain upon it and make the best use of their holdings, or give them up; while the popular favour also tends towards non-alienation, and perpetual leasing from the Crown. The chief difficulty in carrying out this policy lies, in the want of land suitable for settlement. It appears that of the total area of the colony (66 millions of acres), 13½ millions were held in fee simple, in August, 1892; 1,700,000 were held under lease, with the right to purchase; and 6,589,000 had been reserved for public purposes; while it was estimated that the following areas only were available for settlement in the future—

	acres
Suitable for close settlement,	2,000,000
Pastoral lands,	5,000,000
Suitable for mixed agriculture and pasture,	13,000,000
	20,000,000

In addition, there were between 10 and 11 millions of acres in the hands of the Maoris, and the Midland Railway Company,—whose line connects the east and west coasts of the South Island—hold 4,000,000 acres, received by way of subsidy for the construction of the work, on the land grant principle, part of which is adapted for settlement. In the case of the native lands, the State is gradually securing the freehold by purchase, and this land as it passes into the hands of the Government, will also be thrown open for settlement. In this matter, the Government has experienced some difficulty, owing to various causes, and the locking up of such a large area in the heart of the North Island, much of it valuable land, has been a serious bar to progress. The need of sufficient arable country for settlement is becoming a somewhat pressing question, and as in the case of South Australia, the difficulty is not so much as to the method of placing the people on the soil, as the lack of land on which to place them. The Surveyor-General says with respect to the matter *—"The want of lands suitable for agriculture is a very real one, and is every day forcibly impressed on the officers of the department. It has recently been emphasised very strongly."

It will not be surprising, in view of these circumstances, that Parliament has recently had under consideration the expediency of acquiring land now in private possession for purposes of settlement. The original scheme of the Government was that the State should have the power to resume land compulsorily where it was deemed necessary, at a certain rate of payment, and this proposal was actually carried through the House of Representatives, in 1891, but was thrown out by the Legislative Council. Eventually in,

* Annual report for 1892.

1891, the Lands for Settlement Act was passed, by which the Governor has power to purchase lands privately from individuals, at a price to be agreed upon,' which shall be paid "wholly or partly either by money borrowed, or, with the consent of the seller, by debentures issued under this Act." Power is given to borrow for this purpose £50,000 a year, on debentures bearing interest at a rate not exceeding 5 per cent per annum, and having currency for any period up to 40 years, which shall be a charge on the Consolidated Fund; and if the whole sum authorised for one year is not spent, the balance may accrue and be made use of subsequently. Land acquired in this manner is to be disposed of in areas not exceeding 320 acres, under the system of lease-in-perpetuity, and subject to special regulations which may be prepared. Already steps have been taken to acquire properties in the manner provided, and where there is a demand for land which is not easily satisfied, further action will be taken in the same direction. The Minister has stated, however, that though he "intended to give the Act a fair trial, if he found he could not get land for settlement, in districts where it was much required, then it would be his duty to endeavour to get the Act amended so as to enable the Crown to take land if necessary for settlement, and pay for its fair value, such value to be fixed by arbitration."

It will have been seen that the present policy of the colony, though a bold one, and one which proceeds far beyond what have hitherto been deemed safe lines, is prompted by an apparently genuine desire to place the people upon the soil, and to attract an agrarian population. Whether in its zeal to restrict alienation and contract the operations of persons with means, Parliament is adopting a wise course, is a matter too wide to be discussed here, nor is it desirable to introduce the subject. Much may be and has already been said and written on the question on both sides, and the results of the experiments now being made can only be awaited with the intense interest which their importance deserves. They are certainly being watched with the keenest attention on the continent of Australia. New Zealand, is distinctly in advance of the provinces of the mainland in the matter of its land system, but whether this advance has been properly directed is a question the answer to which for the present remains hidden in the womb of futurity.

CHAPTER X.

CONCLUSION.

FEW more interesting subjects for analysis and comparison are to be found in the governing systems of the Australasian colonies than the question of their dealings with land. There is some obscurity as to the very earliest methods, but the complete suzerainty of the Crown seems to have been assumed from the outset, over all lands situated within the continent of Australia and the Island of Tasmania, whether explored or otherwise, and no rights of occupation were permitted except under authority from the representative of Royalty,—the Governor for the time being. This attitude was doubtless necessitated by the exigencies and circumstances of the time though it was also probably deemed requisite to prevent the formation of settlements in proximity to British colonies, of persons of an antagonistic alien race, or of those of the same nationality who might desire to assume possession of and colonise areas beyond the control of constituted authority.

That it was not believed, however, that the right of the British Crown to the lands of the entire continent was established beyond contention may be assumed from certain steps which were deemed necessary during the early years of the history both of Australia and New Zealand. In the year 1824, rumours were rife of the intended annexation by the French of parts of the mainland, and to prevent any such action military settlements were established and other steps taken to confirm the sovereignty of the King at King George's Sound in Western Australia, and Western Port in Victoria. A few years later it was shown that these fears were well grounded in the case of New Zealand, and steps were taken to assert beyond dispute the Queen's sovereignty over the whole of the Islands. The Nanto-Bordelaise Company, a French corporation, was formed to colonise certain lands said to have been acquired by the captain of a French whaler from the Maoris at Banks Peninsula, in the South Island, and in 1840 a party of immigrants from Bordeaux, in charge of the French man-of-war L'Aube, arrived to take possession. But timely notice of the intended action had been received by Governor Gipps in Sydney, and by his direction the Lieut-Governor (Captain Hobson) sent Police Magistrates in H. M. brig "Britomarte" to exercise their functions where necessary in the South Islands, and to open courts at every spot then visited by whalers and others. This was done, and when the French vessels arrived they found the British flags flying, the courts open, and the sovereignty of the Queen visibly and incontestibly asserted.

It is not very clear what were the fundamental principles which controlled the first methods of land occupation. Apparently, the theory obtained that the use of Crown Lands should be secured only under a tenure which would permit the State to exercise more or less direct control over and impose services upon the holders in return: to this end a method was adopted under which the fee simple could not be obtained, and the land was held by virtue of grants which entailed upon the grantees service to the Crown and the payment of perpetual quit-rents. Thus in one case the cultivation of the land held might be made a condition of occupation, in others the possession and utilisation within the community of specified sums of money or its equivalent, and in others again the employment and maintenance of certain numbers of convicts. But, as already shown, no settled system appears to have been instituted to govern the issue of grants until 1824, when, though the payment of quit-rents was retained, it was made possible to purchase the right to grants, at a fixed sum per acre, which might, however, be commuted by the employment of convicts.

It will be seen that the idea had thus far been adhered to, in a rough and ready manner, of granting the use of the land on a tenure of free socage, or occupation in return for certain determinate services. After 1831, what may be described as the allodial period began. Henceforth all lands were not granted subject to the control of the State but were obtained in fee simple by purchase or held under lease. This method, in various forms, has since prevailed throughout the colonies, though of late years an alternative privilege has been granted in two of the provinces—New Zealand, and South Australia,—to purchase outright or lease from the Crown in perpetuity. In effect, it may be said, the latter provides for a return to the early system of free grants upon certain conditions. Instead of the employment of convicts, the service to the State is to be comprised in the residence upon or the cultivation or improvement of the land, and the payment of annual rents.

Even this system has again undergone modification in New Zealand, where a most important innovation has been made by the adoption, in place of perpetual leases, of leases-in-perpetuity. Under the former system, which still obtains in South Australia, leases were granted for a specified number of years, with the right of renewal in perpetuity, *subject to periodical re-appraisements of rent*. The leases-in-perpetuity assure to the lessee or his heirs or assigns the use of the land for 999 years, *at a fixed quit-rent equal to four per cent upon its capital value at the time of leasing*. To what extent this method will be adopted in the other provinces it is difficult to say, but there are indications that it may be expected to operate gradually throughout Australia. Already the granting of leases for long periods of small areas is finding favour with some of the legislatures, and as the advantage both to the State and to the public from such a course becomes manifest, it may be reasonably supposed that it will commend itself more and more to popular approval, with the ultimate result that the system of perpetual leases—or the more desirable method perhaps, of leases in perpetuity—will be generally adopted. Without a doubt if the original system of free grants, upon a proper basis and under a pure system of administration, had been adhered to, Australia would have been in a more forward position to-day.

Some remarkable facts are to be ascertained by an examination of the results attained under the systems which have been in force during the last 65 years. Prior to 1828, in New South Wales, which had a population of 36,000 about 1600,000 acres had been alienated. In 1892, with a population of 3,984,000 persons throughout Australasia, the area alienated, or in process of alienation amounted to 124,172,000 acres, or about $32\frac{1}{2}$ acres per head of the population. The total disposition of the public estate of the Australasian provinces up to the end of 1892 is given as follows *:—

* Coghlan's "Seven Colonies of Australasia," 1893.

CONCLUSION.

Colony.	Area.	Area alienated or in process of alienation.	Area leased.	Area neither alienated. nor leased.	Proportion of Area of Colony.		
					Alienated.	Leased.	Neither alienated nor leased.
	Acres.	Acres.	Acres.	Acres.	Per cent.	Per cent.	Per cent.
New South Wales	198,848,000	45,731,964	132,425,623	20,690,413	23.0	66.6	10.4
Victoria	56,245,760	22,467,388	21,140,413	12,638,059	39.9	37.6	22.5
Queensland	427,838,100	12,521,729	280,535,893	134,780,478	2.9	65.6	31.5
South Australia	578,361,600	12,802,180	195,766,729	369,792,691	2.2	33.9	63.9
Western Australia	678,400,000	5,420,910	106,530,892	566,448,198	0.3	15.7	83.5
Tasmania	16,778,000	4,729,498	636,966	11,411,536	28.2	3.8	68.0
New Zealand	66,861,440	20,498,567	14,290,096	32,072,777	30.6	21.4	48.0
Australasia	2,023,332,900	124,172,136	751,326,612	1,147,834,152	6.2	37.1	56.7

These are very remarkable figures. There is no country in the world with a similar population in which such immense areas are held by private individuals. The total private holdings represent an extent of country something like three-fifths as large again as Great Britain, which supports a population approximately ten times as numerous; and almost as great a territory as either Spain, France, or Germany, which have populations of $17\frac{1}{2}$, 38, and 49 millions respectively; while it is within $2\frac{1}{2}$ million acres of the combined areas of Italy, Holland, Portugal, Greece, and Switzerland, which between them sustain a population of over 43 millions of people.

Unfortunately the figures are not available to show how this land is at present held in four of the colonies, but some highly instructive data may be derived from the statistics bearing on the subject with respect to New South Wales, New Zealand, and South Australia. The subjoined table illustrates the present disposition of the private estate in those colonies—

Holdings.	New South Wales.		New Zealand.		South Australia.		Totals.	
Acres.	No. of Hldgs	Area of Holdings Acres.	No. of Hldgs	Area of Holdings Acres.	No. of Hldgs	Area of Holdings Acres.	No. of Hldgs	Area of Holdings Acres.
1 to 50	17,077	337,375	20,015	307,183	5,335	70,221	42,427	714,779
51 to 250	—	—	—	—	4,338	614,546	4,338	614,546
51 to 300	18,961	2,779,385	—	—	—	—	18,961	2,779,385
51 to 320	—	—	16,380	2,477,333	—	—	16,380	2,477,333
251 to 1000	—	—	—	—	7,749	4,209,736	7,749	4,209,736
301 to 1000	10,528	5,710,306	—	—	—	—	10,528	5,710,306
321 to 1000	—	—	5,123	2,776,207	—	—	5,123	2,776,207
1000 to 10000	4,307	11,370,329	1,922	5,193,984	2,692	6,789,933	8,921	23,354,246
10000 upwards	677	21,884,299	337	8,642,822	241	4,546,252	1,255	35,073,373
	51,550	42,081,694	43,777	19,397,529	20,355	16,230,688	115,682	77,709,911

These figures deal with about two-thirds of the alienated area of Australasia, and may therefore be accepted as fairly representing the circumstances in all the provinces. They show that while slightly over one-third of the total number of holdings in the Colonies dealt with is comprised within

714,779 acres,—which gives an average to each holding of 16 acres,—63,079 persons occupy 18½ million acres or an average of about 2600 acres; and 1255 persons own 35 million acres, or slightly over 20,000 acres to each holding. Narrowing it down still further, it may be stated that of a total number of holdings of 115,000, 105,500 persons possess only just over 19 million acres, or an average of about 160 acres. These may be defined roughly as the yeoman class. Then there are the 8900 proprietors of between 1000 and 10,000 acres, who occupy the position of a kind of middle landed class; and lastly we have the large landed proprietors. Approximately these, 1950 in number, own about 35 million acres, or an area slightly less than that of England and Wales together. These might be analysed still further were all the figures available. It is sufficient to say that in New Zealand 117 persons own 3,340,000 acres, in areas of between 20,000 and 50,000 acres, while 31 others possess 2,600,000 acres in areas of upwards of 50,000 acres; and that in South Australia 44 persons hold between them 1,190,000 acres in areas between 20,000 and 40,000 acres, while 14 others possess 794,000 acres, in areas of over 40,000 acres.

Such results can hardly be regarded otherwise than as appalling. That, the operations of the land systems of these three provinces for 65 years in one colony, and a little over 50 years in two others, should have resulted in 1250 persons securing almost one-half the total alienated area, while 105,000 others between them possess only just about one-fourth of the total extent alienated, is a striking commentary on the methods adopted. The unquestionable verdict must be that the systems have failed to produce true settlement. They have resulted largely in the building up of great freehold estates; the consequent locking up of capital in land which leased under a secure tenure would, probably, have shown vastly increased productive power; and the alienation from the Crown of huge areas of the most valuable country, which in the next generation or two would have supported a population of some millions of people. Is it to be wondered at, then, that two of the three colonies referred to should have seen the necessity for a change? This they have partly brought about by adopting a system of leasing lands in perpetuity, in moderate areas which, as results have shown, is calculated to stay at least the reckless squandering of their public estate, and keep within moderate limits the terrible waste of land which has been going on. It has yet to be seen, however, whether the stable door has not been closed too late, when the horse has gone. Already, as shown in the case of several of the provinces, the area of land adapted for settlement is greatly circumscribed, and it is to be feared that within another ten or twenty years it will be found that country suitable for cultivation will be available only in very small quantities, and at such greatly increased prices as to make it prohibitive for persons of moderate means to acquire the freehold in suitable areas for their requirements.

It night be rash at this early stage to hazard an opinion as to the probable success or otherwise of the system of leases-in-perpetuity, recently instituted in New Zealand. But this method possesses some of the essential elements of success in the way of preventing for the future the aggregation of unduly large properties. Amongst the most noticeable of these are stipulations that no person shall hold more than 2000 acres of land from the Crown, or acquire more than that area of Crown Lands together with other property; that no transfer of any lease shall be made except with the consent of the Land Board, and after the fulfilment of certain conditions; and that residence shall be compulsory for 10 years, either on the part of the original lessee or his transferee. Otherwise these leases—colloquially termed "eternal leases"—may be looked upon as practically equivalent to freeholds. The chief argument raised locally against the system is that the leases prevent the acquisition by the State of the "unearned increment" of value, which was undoubtedly secured by the former method of periodical appraisements of rent, under the system of perpetual leases. The views of the adherents of the present system on the other side, may be summed up in the following remarks on the subject by the Minister of Lands in a recent speech:—
"A considerable amount of objection had been raised to the leases-in-perpetuity, or the 999 years' leases, on the ground that the Crown, was giving away to the settler what is known as the unearned increment. Strange to say that objection was taken to a great extent by people who were quite prepared to sell for cash. It must be obvious that if they parted with the land for cash they would at once part with the unearned increment. It was true they also did this under the lease-in-perpetuity system. But the difference between the two systems was this, that while the Crown could not control the disposal of cash lands from one person to another, after purchase from the Crown, and thus prevent the aggregation of large estates, they could, under the leases-in-perpetuity system, control the transfer of leases, as they must be transferred through the Land Department, and the Department had power to prevent the leases being transferred to persons who already owned large estates.

Thus the Government had legislated in the direction of insuring that the lands should only be transferred or disposed of to people who would make good use of them, and not to those who would use them for speculative purposes." At the same time, it may be pointed out, the area of 2000 acres of Crown Lands which may be held by any one person is adequate for the purposes of successful farming, and the complaint cannot well be raised that there is a prohibition against a man taking up a reasonable extent of country. Without a doubt the New Zealand system of leases-in-perpetuity is one of the most interesting political experiments now being tried in Australasia, and land reformers everywhere must await with some impatience the results.

As previously indicated in the references to various Colonies, one of the most extraordinary effects of Australasian settlement has been the concentration of population within the towns, and especially within the capitals. Every census return shows, with the single exception of Perth in Western Australia, a regular and in some cases marked increase in the metropolitan population, as compared with the total population of the Colonies. The extent of this evil is shown by the following table, which states the populations in each Colony, at the last census, and of the capital Cities respectively, and the percentage of the latter to the total populations, for the three decades ended in 1891.—

Year.	New South Wales.			Victoria.			Queensland.		
	Total Population.	Sydney.		Total Population.	Melbourne.		Total Population.	Brisbane.	
		Population.	Per cent of total.		Population.	Per cent of total.		Population.	Per cent of total.
1871	503,981	137,776	27.34	731,528	206,780	28.27	120,104	15,029	12.51
1881	751,468	224,939	29.93	862,346	282,947	32.81	213,525	31,109	14.57
1891	1,132,234	383,386	33.86	1,140,405	490,896	43.05	393,718	93,657	23.79

Year.	South Australia.			Western Australia.			Tasmania.			New Zealand.		
	Total population.	Adelaide.		Total Population.	Perth.		Total Population.	Hobart.		Total Population.	Wellington.*	
		Population.	Per cent of total.		Population.	Per cent of total.		Population.	Per cent of total.		Population.	Per cent of total.
1871	185,626	42,744	23.03	25,353	5,244	29.68	101,785	19,092	18.76	256,393	7,908	3.08
1881	279,865	103,864	37.11	29,708	5,822	19.60	115,705	21,118	18.25	489,933	30,563	4.20
1891	320,431	132,252	41.59	49,782	8,447	16.97	146,667	33,450	22.81	626,658	33,224	5.30

* In New Zealand there are three other towns as large or nearly as large as Wellington.

It is needless to dilate upon these figures. They tell their own story, which is a most remarkable one. They show that while the total population of Australasia has increased from 1,924,779 in 1871, to 3,809,895 in 1891, or almost doubled itself, the population of the capital cities has increased from 434,573, to 1,166,312, or nearly trebled itself; and that while the total population of the capitals comprised only about 22 per cent of the whole population in 1871, it had increased to about 30 per cent in 1891. It is easy to trace this state of things to its ultimate inevitable conclusion, unless a change is made. In 40 years, at the same rate of progress, the total population of the Colonies will be 15 millions, of whom nearly one-half will be concentrated in the capital cities, and a considerable proportion of the remainder in the smaller towns. But a very small proportion of the people will be actually engaged in production from the soil.

What, then, is the moral to be drawn from these facts? That unless Australia is to become an aggregation of town communities, living upon each other, and with a very sparse rural or productive population, decentralisation must take place, and some radical alteration must be made in the methods of land alienation and occupation. The question as to how this can best be achieved is too large to be discussed at length here; but it may be safely asserted that so long as it remains pofitable, and people are encouraged, to speculate in land, by having the opportunity afforded of purchasing large areas from the Crown at a low rate and selling it at a higher one, so long will they prefer to sit down and wait for their certain profits than to cultivate or improve the soil. The only cure seems to be some such method as that adopted in New Zealand, which, while limiting the area that may be held, compels cultivation or other proper use of the soil; and yet, by enabling persons to obtain the use of land without the necessity for first investing much of their capital in its purchase, attracts them to it as a means of gaining a livelihood.

It may be of interest to consider here the position of the population of the Colonies in relation to the land, and to compare the results of the operations of existing systems during the last decade. The figures, seem to indicate that the people are gradually giving up primary production, except pastoral pursuits, in favour of other industries. Excluding South Australia (the figures for 1891 not being available), it appears that in 1881 the total primary producers in Australasia,—which term includes all engaged in agricultural and pastoral pursuits, mining, and similar occupations—

was 416,139, out of a total population of 2,742,000 or about 11 per cent. In 1891 the total number of primary producers was only 451,065 out of a total population of nearly 3,900,000 or about 10 per cent—a very considerable reduction both actually and relatively on the proportion for 1881. It should be explained, however, that in the matter of the occupations of primary producers, there was some difference in the methods adopted for the years 1881 and 1891 which may make a slight alteration in the totals.

It may be pointed out also that the pastoral industry employs very few people in primary production, as compared with the numbers engaged in secondary or distributive occupations, such as, wharf labourers and others. For this reason, perhaps, the advance of the urban population as compared with that of the country, may be partly attributed to the increased importance of the pastoral industry during recent years. Assuming, however, that the aim of land legislation is mainly to settle on the soil a stable and taxable population, engaged in diverse occupations, so that the foundations of Society may be broad, and the liability to damage from misfortune to one class of product minimised, the absorption of the public estate by one industry is a thing to be prevented. At present in Australia, the fall of $1d$ per lb. in the price of wool is said to mean a difference in the wealth of the community in one year of at least a million of money. This affects not only the persons directly interested in the pastoral industry, but almost the entire population. It is a question of economics which is worthy of full consideration therefore, whether it is desirable that one industry should outbalance all other interests. As matters now stand, although there may be an excellent year for cereals, and other produce, they can have little influence on account of their minor proportions in the way of restoring the equilibrium if the wool clip and the prices for wool are small. The balance can only be retained by a large relative increase in the agricultural population, which in its turn can only be achieved by well considered land legislation. There are really no conflicting interests between the two industries; there is room for both, and without the preponderance or undue influence for good or evil of one or other in the community.

The following table shows the position in 1881 and 1891 of the various colonies in the matter of population, with respect to primary producers, cultivation, and live stock:—

COLONY.	Population. 1881 No.	Population. 1891 No.	Primary Producers. 1881 No.	Primary Producers. 1891 No.	Land under cultivation. 1881 acres.	Land under cultivation. 1891 acres.	Sheep. 1881 No.	Sheep. 1891 No.
New South Wales.	751,468	1,165,300	130,501	136,375	645,068	1,179,621	36,591,946	61,831,416
Victoria . . .	862,346	1,157,804	119,990	129,950	1,821,719	2,687,575	10,267,265	12,948,148
Queensland . .	213,525	410,345	49,213	62,561	128,075	258,004	8,292,883	20,289,633
South Australia .	279,865	325,766	—	² —	2,613,903	2,533,291	6,810,856	7,646,239
Western Australia.	29,708	53,285	5,206	8,385	53,353	131,900	1,267,912	2,514,913
Tasmania. . .	115,705	152,619	74,272	22,748	374,374	516,930	1,847,479	1,664,913
New Zealand. .	489,933	634,058	97,157	90,546	1,319,460	1,565,231	12,985,085¹	18,227,186
	2,742,550	3,899,177	416,139	451,065	6,955,952	8,874,552	78,063,426	125,111,653

1 Inclusive of land under artificial grasses in the case of New South Wales, Victoria, South Australia and Tasmania. This land amounted in 1891 to 174,982 acres in Victoria, 333,238 acres in New South Wales, 17,519 acres in South Australia, 208,596 acres in Tasmania.
2 Figures not available.   3 For 1890.   4 For 1880.

CONCLUSION.

It is here made manifest beyond doubt, that the existing systems in the Colonies, as a whole have not resulted in bringing about genuine settlement. It is not possible to show the exact quantity of land alienated during the decade dealt with in the table, but it would probably be found on examination to be not far short of 40 million acres. Putting it down at 30 million acres, however,—it was over 20 millions in New South Wales and Victoria alone—it will be seen that while the population of all the Colonies has increased rapidly, the public estate has been passing at a terrific rate into private hands, cultivation has been practically at a stand-still, and the number of persons engaged in winning from the soil shows an increase quite disproportionate, to the increase of the total population. It is true that the pastoral industry has shown a most gratifying advance. But it may be fairly assumed that a similar or even perhaps better result would have been attained, if the lands devoted to pastoral pursuits had been held under lease upon a secure tenure (with compensation for improvements), without the necessity of expending capital in obtaining freeholds. It is evident that the great bulk of the land alienated during the period under review has not passed into cultivation. It must either be lying useless, or have been devoted to pastoral purposes. In any case the result is the same. As a means of placing on the land a large rural population, the present systems have failed miserably.

The time has come for the people of Australia, if they desire that the remaining portion of their territory adapted for close settlement shall not pass entirely into a small number of great private holdings, to bestir themselves and face the position. Their magnificent inheritance has been sadly torn about, until at the present but little of it suitable for tillage, remains unalienated and this only in shreds and patches. Those who have acquired it are not to blame. They have exercised their rights as citizens, and legally obtained that which was thrown open to public competition; no one consequently can have cause of complaint against them. As a rule also they are making good use, in one way, of the land they hold. But this is not an adequate reason for the continuance of the policy of tossing into the open, what remains of the public estate to be scrambled for. Rather should the public lands be jealously guarded, and the use of them granted only upon strict conditions as to their proper utilisation, and in such a manner that they cannot go to further swell already large freeholds. When this principle has been recognised in the land legislation of the Colonies, and not till then, the people of Australasia may hope to lay securely the foundations of that prosperity which should now be theirs, if Nature had, amongst her other gifts to them in the past, added greater wisdom.

APPENDIX.

SINCE the chapter on New Zealand was completed, and the manuscript forwarded, the author has been favoured by the Minister for Lands of that Colony with a memorandum, giving official opinions and the latest data, with respect to certain specific questions which were asked. This is of so much interest as to make it worthy of a place in these pages, and it is printed in the form of an appendix. The Minister (Hon. John Mackenzie) states:—

"With respect to the first inquiry, namely, as to the effects and popularity of the Perpetual Lease system, it must be borne in mind that the Land Act of 1892 which came into operation on the 1st of November of that year, substitutes a Lease-in-perpetuity tenure for that of the Perpetual Lease, or in other words, the introduction of 999 year leases, based on a 4 per cent rental, without periodical revaluations, in place of thirty year leases on a 5 per cent rental with recurring valuations, which had hitherto been the law.

The Land Act 1892 also provides for the occupation of lands, with right of purchase. The licence in the case of rural land is for a period of 25 years, the yearly rental is an amount equal to 5 per cent of the cash price of the land, payable half-yearly. The licencee, after not less than 10 (ten) years, has the option at any time during the residue of the term of his licence, to purchase for cash the freehold of the land comprised in his licence, or to exchange such licence] for a lease-in-perpetuity under the Act of 1892, without power of purchase, or to continue in occupation under his licence until the expiration of the term.

The following table gives the results of the different systems during the past three years.

System	1891		1892		1893	
	No.	Area.	No.	Area.	No.	Area.
		Acres.		Acres.		Acres.
Cash.	661	100,222	581	40,930	627	36,852
Deferred Payments	315	35,081	246	40,649	198	21,474
Perpetual Lease. .	854	290,248	1036	287,664	549	125,192
Occupation Lease with right of purchase	—	—	—	—	161	54,271
Lease in Perpetuity	—	—	—	—	964	212,701
Pastoral.	195	1,682,761	206	1,004,416	119	1,104,226
Totals	2025	2,108,312	2069	1,373,659	2618	1,554,716

The cash purchasers have varied but little during the past three years, the deferred payment selectors still show the same decline in number, which has marked that system of selection for some years past; bnt this is partly due to the fact that the system itself has disappeared from the statute-book, excepting in the case of lands selected under the 114th section of the Act of 1892 which provides that settlers already holding lands under any tenure may select adjacent lands on the same tenure up to 640 acres, inclusive of the lands they hold at the time.

The new system of lease in perpetuity shows the greatest increase of any system, which is chiefly due to the fact that in the special settlement associations the selectors have chosen this tenure.

As showing the progress of settlement during the past three years, under the Deferred Payment system and the three systems of Lease the following table gives the result.

	1891.		1892.		1893.	
	No.	area.	No.	area.	No.	area.
Deferred Payments and Leasing Systems.	1169	acres 325,329	1282	acres 328,313	1872	acres 413,638

The village settlement system has been in operation over a period of six years, and works satisfactorily. This perhaps is best shown by the financial and other results. The following are a few of the figures taken from the last annual report:—

Number of Village Homestead Special Settlements in the Colony—85.
Number of Settlers 900.
Area of land held on March 31st 1893. . 22,677 acres.
Average Area to each settler . . . . 25 ,,
Area Cultivated . . . . 11,084 ,,
Amount advanced by the Government for dwelling-houses, bush falling, grassing, etc. from the commencement of the system } £24,625.
Equivalent to an advance of £1 1s 8d per acre.
Annual Rent including Interest on advances . £2570.
Equivalent to a rental of 2s 3d per acre.

Total amount received for Rent and Interest from the commencement of the system to 31st. March 1893 £10,523.
Arrears of Rent and Interest on same date . £ 2,346.
Value of improvements now on the land . £61,699.

This valuation is below rather than above the actual value. If the sum advanced by the Government was deducted from this value, there remains the sum of £37,072, which represents the value of the improvements made by the settlers themselves, over and above those done with the amounts advanced by the Government."

With respect to the Land Tax upon Settlement and Revenue, the Minister States:—

"This tax has had very little effect on settlement up to the present, the fact being that out of 90,000 owners of land in New Zealand only about 13,000 pay land tax, and of these a considerable number pay on mortgages only. The great bulk of the settlers do not feel the present land tax.

It is possible that the graduated land tax may in time compel owners of large estates, and especially large land companies to subdivide their properties, but this cannot be known yet.

With regard to the point as to how the tax effects revenue, if by this is meant, does it affect other heads of revenue? the answer is No, certainly not, as it is found that land owners are always prepared to make improvements on their estates, if it pays them to do so. Under the Property Tax the yield was about £354,000 a year, and under the land tax £375,000.

"Very little can be said on the subject of the proposed State Farms at present, as these farms are not yet in working order. A block of land containing 1200 acres has been secured at Waverley a distance of 179 miles from Wellington, and it is proposed to commence operations at once. The object being to provide a home for elderly men with families, where in return for food and accommodation they could assist in the general work of the farm, and make its cultivation pay expenses. The work done by the inmates would be on the co-operative principle, that is to say the men would be paid for the work they really performed and nothing more."

In reply to the question, Is it the intention of the Government to stop all future alienation of land? the Minister replies:—

"No; it is not the intention of the Government to do so."

INDEX.

Australia:—
Area, 6.
Areas alienated, 168
Climate, 4.
Crown Rights, 165.
Geography, 5, 8.
Growth of Urban Population, 174.
Live Stock, 177.
Population, 6, 174, 177.
Size of Holdings, 168.
Torrens System, 7, 135.

Authorities quoted:—
Bonwick's "Romance of the Wool Trade," 11, 94.
Coghlan's "Seven Colonies of Australasia" 1893, 167.
Coghlan's "Wealth and Progress of N.S.W.," 42, 44.
Goyder's "Rep. on Public Lands of S. Australia," 119, 121.
Hartnoll's "Public Works Statement 1892," 52.
Hayter's "Victorian Year-Book," 79.
Johnston's "Tasmanian Off. Record" 1892, 58.
Moss' "Short History of New Zealand," 141.
New Zealand Handbook 1892, 159.
Ranken's "Federal Geography of Br. Australasia," 104
Ranken's "Our Wasted Heritage," 14, 15, 23, 29.
Rusden's "History of Australia," 68, 83, 93.
Report on Bureau of Industries (N. Z.) 155.
Report of Queensland Under Secr. for Lands, 102.

Dummying, 28, 71, 102, 147.
Free Selectors, see Selectors.
Gold, Discovery of, 66.
Grazing Licenses, 16, 18, 72 *sqq.*, 107, 153.
Homesteads, 78, 94, 98, 112, 115, 127, 151.
Labour Colonies, 40, 78.
Land Sales, 11, 52, 54, 63, 88, 142.
Leases, Conditional, 36 *sqq.*, 55, 72, 93, 97, 108, 145, 148.
"Mallee" Pastoral Leases 73.

Names:—
Ballance, Hon J., 151.
Bourke, Sir Richard, 16, 62.
Brisbane, Governor, 11.
Collins, Col., 61.
Duffy, Sir C. G., 69.
Fitzroy, Sir Charles, 21.
Gipps, Sir George, 16 *sqq.*, 65.
Glenelg, Lord, 63.
Grey, Earl, 21, 22, 106, 118.
Hobson, R.N., Capt., 139.
MacArthur, Capt., 10.
Mackenzie, Hon J., 155, 179.

Mitchell, Sir Thos., 24.
Phillip, Governor, 8, 9.
Robertson, Sir John, 26, 30.
Stanley, Lord, 17 *sqq.*
Wakefield, Gibbon, 138.
Young, Sir Henry, 118.

New South Wales:—
Area of Cultivation, 45.
Area of Estates, 43.
Earliest Settlement 1788, 2, 8.
Eastern, Central, and Western Divisions, 35.
Grants to Free Settlers and Prisoners, 9, 28.
Limit of Settlement, 11.
Population, 41, 42.
Products, 46.
Responsible Government, 25.
Settled, Intermediate, and Unsettled Districts, 22, 27, 30, 395.
Wakefield System, 13, 16, 17.

New Zealand:—
Area of Estates, 159, 160.
British Resident, 4.
Climate, 137.
Early Settlers 1826, 3, 138.
Free Grants, 159.
Lands-for-Settlement Act 1891, 164.
Lieut. Governor 1840, 4, 139.
New Zealand Company 1839, 138, 139.
Perpetual Leases, 146, 149, 150, 172.
Products, 137.
Responsible Government, 1853. 142.
Statistics, 179 *sqq.*
Town, Suburban, and Rural Lands, 144, 148.

Orders in Council, 1847, 22, 26, 65, 86.
Peacocking, 28, 48.

Queensland:
Agricultural, First-class Pastoral, and Second-class Pastoral Lands, 92.
Agricultural Reserves, 87, 88.
Area of Estates, 100.
Convict Settlement, 1825, 3.
Crown Lands Act 1884, 95.
Immigration Act, 91.
Proprietors, Number of, 101.
Products, 100.
Sales of Town Lands, 87.
Separate Colony 1859, 3.
Town, Suburban, and Country Lands 87.
Rabbits, 36, 48, 73, 132.
Railways, Construction of, 112.
Selectors, 26, 30 *sqq.*, 44 *sqq.*, 54 *sqq.* 69 *sqq.*, 87 *sqq.*, 110, 121, 158.

South Australia:—
Area of Holdings, 129.
Earliest Settlement 1836, 3.
Perpetual Leases, 124, 167.
Population, 131.
Responsible Government 1856, 119.
South Australian Company 1831, 117.
Strangway's Act, 120.
"The Province" and "Northern Territory," 116.
Town, Suburban, Country, Reclaimed, Special Country Lots, and Improved Lands, 120.
"Squatters," 13, 15 *sqq.*, 30, 61, 67.

Tasmania:—
Climate, 51.
Earliest Settlement 1803, 3, 52.
Free Grants, 53.
Mining Areas, 56.
Products, 51, 58.

Separate Colony 1825, 3, 86.
Town, Agricultural, and Pastoral Lands, 54.
Transportation abolished, 13, 107.
Treaty of Waitangi, 139.
Torrens Act, 7, 135.
Upset Prices, 12, 15, 18, 19, 52, 54, 63, 64, 87, 105, 107, 118, 144.
Van Dieman's Land, see Tasmania.

Victoria :—
Area of Estates, 84.
Convict Settlement 1835, 3, 62.
Exports, of Wool, 80.
Forest, Timber, and Water Reserves, 75 *sqq*.
Pastoral, Auriferous, and Swamp Lands, 75 *sqq*.
Population, 80, 81.
Proprietors, Number of, 84.

Selectors, Number of, 82.
Separate Colony 1859, 3, 66.
Village Settlements, 78, 98, 102, 151.
Wakefield System, 13, 16, 17, 116, 140.

Western Australia :—
"A," "B," and "C" Lands, 106, 108.
Area of Estates, 113.
Convict Settlement 1850, 107.
Division of Colony, 109, 110.
Earliest Settlement 1829, 3, 104.
Population, 113.
Products, 110.
Temporary Occupation 1826, 3, 103.
Town, Suburban, and Country Lands, 106.
Western Australian Company, 1838, 105.

OPINIONS OF THE PRESS
ON THE
SOCIAL SCIENCE SERIES.

"'The Principles of State Interference' is another of Messrs. Swan Sonnenschein's Series of Handbooks on Scientific Social Subjects. It would be fitting to close our remarks on this little work with a word of commendation of the publishers of so many useful volumes by eminent writers on questions of pressing interest to a large number of the community. We have now received and read a good number of the handbooks which Messrs. Swan Sonnenschein have published in this series, and can speak in the highest terms of them. They are written by men of considerable knowledge of the subjects they have undertaken to discuss; they are concise; they give a fair estimate of the progress which recent discussion has added towards the solution of the pressing social questions of to-day, are well up to date, and are published at a price within the resources of the public to which they are likely to be of the most use."—*Westminster Review*, July, 1891.

"The excellent 'Social Science Series,' which is published at as low a price as to place it within everybody's reach."—*Review of Reviews*.

"A most useful series. . . . This impartial series welcomes both just writers and unjust."—*Manchester Guardian*.

"Concise in treatment, lucid in style and moderate in price, these books can hardly fail to do much towards spreading sound views on economic and social questions."—*Review of the Churches*.

"Convenient, well-printed, and moderately-priced volumes."—*Reynold's Newspaper*.

DOUBLE VOLUMES, Each 3s. 6d.

1. **Life of Robert Owen.** LLOYD JONES.
   " A worthy record of a life of noble activities."—*Manchester Examiner*.

2. **The Impossibility of Social Democracy:** a Second Part of "The Quintessence of Socialism". Dr. A. SCHÄFFLE.
   " Extremely valuable as a criticism of Social Democracy by the ablest living representative of State Socialism in Germany."—*Inter. Journal of Ethics*.

3. **The Condition of the Working Class in England in 1844.** FREDERICK ENGELS.
   " A translation of a work written in 1845, with a preface written in 1892."

4. **The Principles of Social Economy.** YVES GUYOT.
   " An interesting and suggestive work. It is a profound treatise on social economy, and an invaluable collection of facts."—*Spectator*.

SWAN SONNENSCHEIN & CO., LONDON.

SOCIAL SCIENCE SERIES.

SCARLET CLOTH, EACH 2s. 6d.

1. **Work and Wages.** Prof. J. E. THOROLD ROGERS.
   "Nothing that Professor Rogers writes can fail to be of interest to thoughtful people."—*Athenæum.*
2. **Civilisation: Its Cause and Cure.** EDWARD CARPENTER.
   "No passing piece of polemics, but a permanent possession."—*Scottish Review.*
3. **Quintessence of Socialism.** Dr. SCHÄFFLE.
   "Precisely the manual needed. Brief, lucid, fair and wise."—*British Weekly.*
4. **Darwinism and Politics.** D. G. RITCHIE, M.A. (Oxon.).
   New Edition, with two additional Essays on HUMAN EVOLUTION.
   "One of the most suggestive books we have met with."—*Literary World.*
5. **Religion of Socialism.** E. BELFORT BAX.
6. **Ethics of Socialism.** E. BELFORT BAX.
   "Mr. Bax is by far the ablest of the English exponents of Socialism."—*Westminster Review.*
7. **The Drink Question.** Dr. KATE MITCHELL.
   "Plenty of interesting matter for reflection.'—*Graphic.*
8. **Promotion of General Happiness.** Prof. M. MACMILLAN.
   "A reasoned account of the most advanced and most enlightened utilitarian doctrine in a clear and readable form."—*Scotsman.*
9. **England's Ideal, &c.** EDWARD CARPENTER.
   "The literary power is unmistakable, their freshness of style, their humour, and their enthusiasm."—*Pall Mall Gazette.*
10. **Socialism in England.** SIDNEY WEBB, LL.B.
    "The best general view of the subject from the modern Socialist side."—*Athenæum.*
11. **Prince Bismarck and State Socialism.** W. H. DAWSON.
    "A succinct, well-digested review of German social and economic legislation since 1870."—*Saturday Review.*
12. **Godwin's Political Justice (On Property).** Edited by H. S. SALT.
    "Shows Godwin at his best; with an interesting and informing introduction."—*Glasgow Herald.*
13. **The Story of the French Revolution.** E. BELFORT BAX.
    "A trustworthy outline."—*Scotsman.*
14. **The Co-Operative Commonwealth.** LAURENCE GRONLUND.
    "An independent exposition of the Socialism of the Marx school."—*Contemporary Review.*
15. **Essays and Addresses.** BERNARD BOSANQUET, M.A. (Oxon.).
    "Ought to be in the hands of every student of the Nineteenth Century spirit."—*Echo.*
    "No one can complain of not being able to understand what Mr. Bosanquet means."—*Pall Mall Gazette.*
16. **Charity Organisation.** C. S. LOCH, Secretary to Charity Organisation Society.
    "A perfect little manual."—*Athenæum.*
    "Deserves a wide circulation."—*Scotsman.*
17. **Thoreau's Anti-Slavery and Reform Papers.** Edited by H. S. SALT.
    "An interesting collection of essays."—*Literary World.*
18. **Self-Help a Hundred Years Ago.** G. J. HOLYOAKE.
    "Will be studied with much benefit by all who are interested in the amelioration of the condition of the poor."—*Morning Post.*
19. **The New York State Reformatory at Elmira.** ALEXANDER WINTER.
    With Preface by HAVELOCK ELLIS.
    "A valuable contribution to the literature of penology."—*Black and White.*

SOCIAL SCIENCE SERIES—(Continued).

20. **Common Sense about Women.** T. W. HIGGINSON.
"An admirable collection of papers, advocating in the most liberal spirit the emancipation of women."—*Woman's Herald.*

21. **The Unearned Increment.** W. H. DAWSON.
"A concise but comprehensive volume."—*Echo.*

22. **Our Destiny.** LAURENCE GRONLUND.
"A very vigorous little book, dealing with the influence of Socialism on morals and religion."—*Daily Chronicle.*

23. **The Working-Class Movement in America.**
Dr. EDWARD and E. MARX AVELING.
"Will give a good idea of the condition of the working classes in America, and of the various organisations which they have formed."—*Scots Leader.*

24. **Luxury.** Prof. EMILE DE LAVELEYE.
"An eloquent plea on moral and economical grounds for simplicity of life."—*Academy.*

25. **The Land and the Labourers.** Rev. C. W. STUBBS, M.A.
"This admirable book should be circulated in every village in the country."—*Manchester Guardian.*

26. **The Evolution of Property.** PAUL LAFARGUE.
"Will prove interesting and profitable to all students of economic history."—*Scotsman.*

27. **Crime and its Causes.** W. DOUGLAS MORRISON.
"Can hardly fail to suggest to all readers several new and pregnant reflections on the subject."—*Anti-Jacobin.*

28. **Principles of State Interference.** D. G. RITCHIE, M.A.
"An interesting contribution to the controversy on the functions of the State."—*Glasgow Herald.*

29. **German Socialism and F. Lassalle.** W. H. DAWSON.
"As a biographical history of German Socialistic movements during this century it may be accepted as complete."—*British Weekly.*

30. **The Purse and the Conscience.** H. M. THOMPSON, B.A. (Cantab.).
"Shows common sense and fairness in his arguments."—*Scotsman.*

31. **Origin of Property in Land.** FUSTEL DE COULANGES. Edited, with an Introductory Chapter on the English Manor, by Prof. W. J. ASHLEY, M.A.
"His views are clearly stated, and are worth reading."—*Saturday Review.*

32. **The English Republic.** W. J. LINTON. Edited by KINETON PARKES.
"Characterised by that vigorous intellectuality which has marked his long life of literary and artistic activity."—*Glasgow Herald.*

33. **The Co-Operative Movement.** BEATRICE POTTER.
"Without doubt the ablest and most philosophical analysis of the Co-Operative Movement which has yet been produced."—*Speaker.*

34. **Neighbourhood Guilds.** Dr. STANTON COIT.
"A most suggestive little book to anyone interested in the social question."—*Pall Mall Gazette.*

35. **Modern Humanists.** J. M. ROBERTSON.
"Mr. Robertson's style is excellent—nay, even brilliant—and his purely literary criticisms bear the mark of much acumen."—*Times.*

36. **Outlooks from the New Standpoint.** E. BELFORT BAX.
"Mr. Bax is a very acute and accomplished student of history and economics."—*Daily Chronicle.*

37. **Distributing Co-Operative Societies.** Dr. LUIGI PIZZAMIGLIO. Edited by F. J. SNELL.
"Dr. Pizzamiglio has gathered together and grouped a wide array of facts and statistics, and they speak for themselves."—*Speaker.*

38. **Collectivism and Socialism.** By A. NAQUET. Edited by W. HEAFORD.
"An admirable criticism by a well-known French politician of the New Socialism of Marx and Lassalle"—*Daily Chronicle.*

SOCIAL SCIENCE SERIES—(Continued).

39. **The London Programme.** SIDNEY WEBB, LL.B.
 "Brimful of excellent ideas."—*Anti-Jacobin.*
40. **The Modern State.** PAUL LEROY BEAULIEU.
 "A most interesting book; well worth a place in the library of every social inquirer."—*N. B. Economist.*
41. **The Condition of Labour.** HENRY GEORGE.
 "Written with striking ability, and sure to attract attention."—*Newcastle Chronicle*
42. **The Revolutionary Spirit preceding the French Revolution.**
 FELIX ROCQUAIN. With a Preface by Professor HUXLEY.
 "The student of the French Revolution will find in it an excellent introduction to the study of that catastrophe."—*Scotsman.*
43. **The Student's Marx.** EDWARD AVELING, D.Sc.
 "One of the most practically useful of any in the Series."—*Glasgow Herald.*
44. **A Short History of Parliament.** B. C. SKOTTOWE, M.A. (Oxon.).
 "Deals very carefully and completely with this side of constitutional history."—*Spectator.*
45. **Poverty: Its Genesis and Exodus.** J. G. GODARD.
 "He states the problems with great force and clearness."—*N. B. Economist.*
46. **The Trade Policy of Imperial Federation.** MAURICE H. HERVEY.
 "An interesting contribution to the discussion."—*Publishers' Circular.*
47. **The Dawn of Radicalism.** J. BOWLES DALY, LL.D.
 "Forms an admirable picture of an epoch more pregnant, perhaps, with political instruction than any other in the world's history."—*Daily Telegraph.*
48. **The Destitute Alien in Great Britain.** ARNOLD WHITE; MONTAGUE CRACKANTHORPE, Q.C.; W. A. M'ARTHUR, M.P.; W. H. WILKINS, &c.
 "Much valuable information concerning a burning question of the day."—*Times.*
49. **Illegitimacy and the Influence of Seasons on Conduct.**
 ALBERT LEFFINGWELL, M.D.
 "We have not often seen a work based on statistics which is more continuously interesting."—*Westminster Review.*
50. **Commercial Crises of the Nineteenth Century.** H. M. HYNDMAN.
 "One of the best and most permanently useful volumes of the Series."—*Literary Opinion.*
51. **The State and Pensions in Old Age.** J. A. SPENDER and ARTHUR ACLAND, M.P.
 "A careful and cautious examination of the question."—*Times.*
52. **The Fallacy of Saving.** JOHN M. ROBERTSON.
 "A plea for the reorganisation of our social and industrial system."—*Speaker.*
53. **The Irish Peasant.** ANON.
 "A real contribution to the Irish Problem by a close, patient and dispassionate investigator."—*Daily Chronicle.*
54. **The Effects of Machinery on Wages.** Prof. J. S. NICHOLSON, D.Sc.
 "Ably reasoned, clearly stated, impartially written."—*Literary World.*
55. **The Social Horizon.** ANON.
 "A really admirable little book, bright, clear, and unconventional."—*Daily Chronicle.*
56. **Socialism, Utopian and Scientific.** FREDERICK ENGELS.
 "The body of the book is still fresh and striking."—*Daily Chronicle.*
57. **Land Nationalisation.** A. R. WALLACE.
 "The most instructive and convincing of the popular works on the subject."—*National Reformer.*
58. **The Ethic of Usury and Interest.** Rev. W. BLISSARD.
 "The work is marked by genuine ability."—*North British Agriculturalist.*
59. **The Emancipation of Women.** ADELE CREPAZ.
 "By far the most comprehensive, luminous, and penetrating work on this question that I have yet met with."—*Extract from Mr.* GLADSTONE'S *Preface.*
60. **The Eight Hours' Question.** JOHN M. ROBERTSON
 "A very cogent and sustained argument on what is at present the unpopular side."—*Times.*
61. **Drunkenness.** GEORGE R. WILSON, M.B.
 "Well written, carefully reasoned, free from cant, and full of sound sense."—*National Observer.*
62. **The New Reformation.** RAMSDEN BALMFORTH.
 "A striking presentation of the nascent religion, how best to realize the personal and social ideal."—*Westminster Review.*
63. **The Agricultural Labourer.** T. E. KEBBEL.
 "A short summary of his position, with appendices on wages, education, allotments, etc., etc."
64. **Ferdinand Lassalle as a Social Reformer.** E. BERNSTEIN.
 "A worthy addition to the Social Science Series."—*North British Economist.*

www.ingramcontent.com/pod-product-compliance
Lightning Source LLC
Chambersburg PA
CBHW020840160426
43192CB00007B/721